# Women, Work, and Property
# in North-West India

Hastings Donnan FBA MRIA FAcSS
Mitchell Institute for Global Peace
Security and Justice
Queen's University Belfast
h.donnan@qub.ac.uk

URSULA SHARMA

# Women, Work, and Property in North-West India

TAVISTOCK PUBLICATIONS
London and New York

First published in 1980 by
Tavistock Publications Ltd
11 New Fetter Lane, London EC4P 4EE

Published in the USA by
Tavistock Publications
in association with Methuen, Inc.
733 Third Avenue, New York, NY 10017

First published in paperback in 1983

Printed in Great Britain at the
University Press, Cambridge.

*British Library Cataloguing in Publication Data*
Sharma, Ursula
    Women, work and property in North-West India.
    1. Women – India – Social conditions
    I. Title
    305.4'2'0954     HQ1742
ISBN 0-422-77120-1   (hb)
       0-422-78640-3   (pb)

This book is dedicated to Sarla,
Priyamvda ('Bhabiji'), Kamla, Vidya,
Prakasho ('Bahinji'), Khadijah, Santosh
and Saroja — my sisters and friends.

# Contents

# Preface

Every research project involves the co-operation of a number of people, even if the final published product bears only one name. I would like to mention some of the many friends and relatives who helped me at different stages of the research. My husband, Om Prakasha Sharma, took a lively interest in the project and his help was invaluable when I was collecting field data in Himachal Pradesh. Our daughters Maya and Sandhya contributed in their own ways.

Indian hospitality is justly renowned, and here I must mention my brother-in-law Shri Kashmiri Lal Sharma and his wife Sarla, whose house lies about halfway between Harbassi and Chaili. We often broke our journey at their house and we have many happy memories of the times spent with their family. They gave me much practical help and encouragement. I must also thank Shrimati Priyamvada Kahol and Shri Shiv Ram Goswami for hospitality, assistance, and understanding given generously while we were in the field. They offered us affection and we were privileged to share their family life.

Many friends and colleagues discussed parts of the manuscript of this book with me. Margaret Sampson, Jacquie Sarsby, Hilary Standing, and Anjali Purewal all gave valuable advice and comments as well as moral support while I was 'writing up'. Thanks are due to Mrs J. Heath for typing the final version so quickly and efficiently at short notice.

The project was financed by a generous grant from the Social

Science Research Council. I am grateful to them and to all those who were involved in the administration of the grant at the University of Keele.

URSULA M. SHARMA
University of Keele, 1979

*Map 1* North-West India

*Map 2* Location of Harbassi and Chaili to show their relative positior

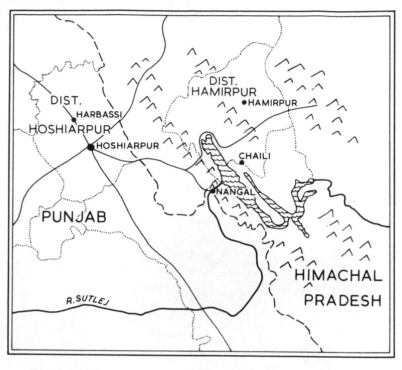

Key [⋯⋯] District boundaries [– – –] State boundaries

# 1 Introduction

I first became interested in the social role of Indian women because, being married into an Indian family, I myself had to keep some of the conventions which Indian women observe when I was in India. During my first period of fieldwork in Himachal Pradesh I gained a knowledge of rural women's life which I did not write about at the time, because my research was focussed on other areas of social life, but which provided the foundation for the present study.

Like many others, I was affected by the upsurge of feminist consciousness which led many western women to question female roles in their own society. This reactivated my interest in the question of women's position in India and I returned to do more fieldwork, this time in both Himachal Pradesh and the neighbouring state of Punjab.

The daughter-in-law role has provided an excellent vantage point for western women who have something to say about Indian society. Mrs Frieda Das and the novelist, Ruth Praver Jhabvala, are well known examples, and there is a body of ethnography written by anthropologists who, like myself, are married to Asians. Not that the daughters of the culture have been the silent subjects of research: Ramabhai Ranade, Iravati Karve, and Amrit Wilson have, in different ways, interpreted the position and problems of Indian women to outsiders. Women social scientists in India are conducting constructive research on female roles, and a considerable programme of research in this area is being funded by the Indian Council for Social Science Research (ICSSR 1977, 19-26).

This is an ethnographic book, but that is not all that it is intended to be. (There are a number of good accounts of women in North India, and if more ethnography is needed it really ought to be on south Indian women, who have been relatively little studied.) I shall try to concentrate on areas not covered by other writers, especially the economic life of rural women and certain neglected aspects of kinship and household organization, dealing summarily with aspects which have been thoroughly discussed by others.[1] My ultimate aim is to develop the discussion of Indian women at a more theoretical level.

Those who like a good straightforward ethnographic read may well groan to themselves, and this is understandable: much of the theoretical writing on women's position in society has been obscure or mystifying to the lay person with a lively interest in feminist issues, but no grounding in the jargons of academic anthropology or Althusserian Marxism. But if we want to understand not just *how* Indian women are expected to act, but *why* institutions like purdah and arranged marriage exist, then we have to start trying to fit information together in a more rigorous way. In the following section I shall try to identify some of the inadequacies in our present knowledge of gender roles in India and explain why I decided to concentrate on women's role in production.

## Women in India: the limitations of social anthropology

The efflorescence of research by British and American anthropologists on rural society in South Asia in the 1950s and 1960s yielded a wealth of ethnographic material and much sound descriptive generalization, but it seldom trod boldly enough beyond the terms of reference provided by that society's own ideologies.[2] Categories like *jati* (caste) were given substance before they had even been studied. Trapped within this frame of reference, it was difficult for anthropologists to develop any thoroughgoing and independent theory about the underlying structure of that society. There was also a general obsession with the distinctive nature of caste which precluded the asking of significant questions about many other aspects of South Asian society, in particular the social relations between the sexes.

From village studies we do obtain a fairly detailed view of the domestic roles of women and even of the way in which the norms governing women's roles as wives and daughters-in-law vary with socio-economic status. Mandelbaum notes that low-caste women may be less submissive and may appear to be less strictly integrated into the authority system of their husbands' households. They are less secluded, and in economic terms are less dependent upon their menfolk than are high-caste women (Mandelbaum 1972: 47). And we learn indirectly from the literature that many women do participate in agricultural production, either as family labourers (Mayer 1960: 137) or as paid labourers (Beteille 1976: 124) whilst high-status women do not work out of doors (Hitchcock and Minturn 1963: 227). But all this can equally be said of men, so we still have no idea of the *specific* role of women in production. Studies which have taken women's labour as their focus have generally concentrated upon the sexual division of labour in the household. Writers such as Jacobson (1970), Chatterjee (1977), Lewis (1958: 49-52) provide detailed accounts of the daily activities of women of different social groups. Most of these studies have taken the household as their focus, so that although we get a clear picture of the division of labour within the family group for different castes or social classes, we do not yet have an adequate conception of the division of labour between the sexes in the community in general.[3]

The other main theme in the discussion of women's work has been the effects of the purdah ideology on the kind of economic activities in which women can expect to engage outside the home (see Papanek 1973; Sharma, forthcoming; also Rama Mehta's sensitive account of the response of purdah customs to economic change: Mehta 1976).

**The problem of purdah; how to progress beyond the descriptive**

Women in South Asia bear a special responsibility for family honour; in so far as a woman conforms to certain standards of modest feminine conduct her family's status is maintained or even improved, whilst unwomanly conduct is a blot not just on her personal reputation but on the reputation of the whole family. The ultimate sanction for indiscreet behaviour on the part of women is the possibility that no man will wish to marry her and she will bring further disgrace upon her family by being left an old maid. (The likelihood of this actually happening is rather remote, given the low proportion of women to men in most parts of India, but people believe that it could happen and so it is effective as a sanction.) Correct feminine conduct means, among other things, being as inconspicuous in public as possible; in some communities (especially Muslim communities) it even means total purdah, i.e. public invisibility. Men also carry responsibility for family honour, of course, but less precariously than their sisters. All aspects of a woman's behaviour outside the home are a matter of concern to her kin, and this concern affects all possible activities beyond the domestic sphere.

But if the practice of purdah has effects upon women's economic roles, where lies the cause of this complex of norms? This is a question which has scarcely been tackled, let alone answered. Few writers have gone beyond one particular kind of functionalist view. Papanek, quite correctly, notes that 'female seclusion is integral to such other aspects of society as the evaluation of status, the ownership and inheritance of property, the organization of marriages, the division of labour and impulse control' (Papanek 1973: 290). But she is not prepared to allocate determinant priority to any of these factors. Jacobson, more blandly, asserts that:

'although it is true that, in general, women's status is lower than men's, it is not as low as these outward signs might indicate . . . men and women are actors in a complex social and ecological system which functions reasonably smoothly and provides benefits to both sexes . . . It is really a mistake to see women as competing with and being restricted by men; rather, male and female roles are clearly distinguished, and the sexes are seen as complementary to each other.' (Jacobson 1977: 60)

The demonstrations of deference which are demanded of women in the home, especially the de-emphasis of the husband's attachment to his wife, are seen as promoting harmony and role congruence in the domestic group. Hitchcock and Minturn write that these restrictions 'are to avoid jealousy and conflict and to ensure that the extended family takes precedence over the nuclear family' (Minturn and Hitchcock 1963: 241). Jacobson, in similar vein, notes that veiling from male affines is:

'an aid to harmony in the joint family, since it emphasizes the subordinate relationship of the woman to those in authority in the family and de-emphasizes her tie to her husband. Veiling and seclusion in her conjugal home constantly remind a woman of her position as a *bahu* (daughter-in-law) who must quietly subjugate her individual wishes to those of the group.' (Jacobson 1977: 70)

What, one wonders, are the tensions within the extended family group which would threaten to disrupt it were these institutions not called into play to control women's behaviour? Why is the persistence of the joint family so valued, when few joint households avoid partition for even one generation?

The function of purdah as status indicator has also been dealt with extensively. As Papanek points out, 'the purdah system is related to status, the division of labour, interpersonal dependency and social distance, and the maintenance of moral standards specified by society' (Papanek 1973: 292). Jacobson notes that 'well-to-do village Hindu men take pride in their ability to afford farm hands and water bearers, thus freeing their wives from the need to leave the courtyard to visit the fields or wells. The women value their status as well-cared-for ladies of relative leisure' (Jacobson 1977: 63). But this is only to say that those who have greatest wealth and rank can afford the closest conformity to whatever ideals society values as having worth and dignity. Poor women also cannot afford to observe menstrual seclusion and other forms of ritual taboo which preserve the purity of the household, nor can they afford fine clothes or jewellery. The lives of the poor are so structured that the moral riches of their society are as far out of their reach as the material riches.

A more important limitation of this essentially functionalist approach is that it leaves us with the purdah ideology as a cultural 'given', *related* to other institutions, but not *accounted for*. The only kind of explanation open once this kind of approach is adopted is a historical one; if no-one knows *why* purdah developed, then we can only discuss *how* it developed. Even here, there is little to be said save that in pre-Muslim India the restrictions upon women's participation in public affairs were probably less stringent than they later became, but that the onus for their development cannot be laid entirely at the door of Islam; the coming of Islam only gave strength to tendencies already present in Hindu practice and ideology concerning women (Thomas 1964).

Most of the ethnographic accounts of purdah in India treat it as primarily an Islamic phenomenon, or else have considered it in relation to particular caste communities. With few exceptions (such as Jacobson's commendable treatment of the relationship between Hindu and Muslim purdah, Jacobson 1970) there has not been much discussion of the way in which purdah practices of different castes and communities in India are integrated. Are we justified in applying the term 'purdah' to such a broad genus of practices as I have done here?

I would argue that there is some sense in doing so, or that if we do not, then we need to invent some other term that will fulfil this semantic function. It is logical to consider together all those norms and practices which limit women's behaviour and appearance in public places, whatever we choose to call them. Few women even among Indian Muslims observe strict seclusion, but most (in North India, at least) must observe a type of circumspection and constraint outside the strictly domestic sphere which is considered as being directly related to female sexual modesty and which is not demanded of men (although some men will be subject to other kinds of restricting rule, e.g. relating to caste purity and pollution). I shall discuss these norms more fully as they apply in Harbassi and Chaili in Chapter 3. Seclusion is only the application of these expectations taken to its logical normative conclusion, one extreme of a spectrum which includes many shades, rather than a special case. One might argue that if we use the term purdah in this way, then women in practically all societies observe purdah in some degree, western women simply standing at the weaker end of the spectrum. If my broader usage of the term reveals this, I would regard this as a recommendation rather than as a disadvantage, for then the strict seclusion observed by some Muslim women loses its exotic and remote peculiarity.

Having said this, it is important to remember that the purdah complex manifests itself variously in different communities, and quite different ideological justifications may be called upon. Among Hindus in North India, there is a general feeling that women's appearance outside the home is permissible provided that it is associated with some acceptable and definite feminine purpose or activity (see below, pp.43, 86, 97). But in practice such appearances are already constrained by the norms of etiquette between the sexes which require that a married woman avoid any senior male affine, or at any rate veil herself before him. When the notions 'senior' and 'affine' are used in a classificatory sense, this category may include up to half the adult population of the village in the case of a young bride. Consequently this has a considerable effect upon the freedom with which she can go about her daily business outside the home and communicate freely with other villagers. Among Muslims in North

India, cousin marriage is permitted and indeed approved. Hence a woman's affines are usually also her consanguines, and the force of these avoidance rules weakens if it does not altogether disappear. On the other hand, the observance of seclusion is seen by many Muslims as an indication of Islamic orthodoxy and therefore it has a religious value which it does not have for Hindus, among whom it confers mainly secular prestige. For Hindus other cultural criteria signify as indicators of status, for instance caste purity. But in either case, purdah norms have essentially the same effect of limiting women's activities outside the domestic sphere to a greater or lesser degree.

### Women's role in production and ideology

But this is still to speak in terms of the effects of purdah norms and prescriptions, when we need to ask what produces this ideology. Feminist studies in the West gathered momentum when they turned from the scrutiny of gender role ideology to the interaction between this ideology and women's position in the capitalist mode of production (Rowbotham 1973; Mitchell 1971: 173). This relationship has been discussed from a number of different points of view. One line of exploration has been to study the development of the housewife role as an historical product of changes in the economic function of the household, and the physical and conceptual separation of domestic work from other kinds of work (Oakley 1976). From another point of view, women constitute a 'labour reserve': being defined first and foremost as domestic workers, women may be drawn into the industrial workforce or excluded from it according to the needs of capitalist production and the state (see Bland *et al.* 1979: 61). The definition of women as primarily domestic workers enabled their work outside the home to be undervalued (as 'pin money' or secondary income) and hence underpaid. Their domestic work is nevertheless essential to the smooth running of the capitalist economy, even though they are not paid for this work at all. The domestic labour of women as housewives and mothers contributes both to the renewal of the labour power of the workers and also to the production of a new generation of workers.

In this fruitful phase of feminist research, starting in the late sixties, the ideological culture of gender roles and the demands of capitalist production and property relations were seen as interacting with each other. Feminist sociologists and historians did not deny the role of ideology in controlling the behaviour and expectations of individual men and women, especially through the pressure of familial roles,[4] but they did deny that the complex of norms which defines women's role in western capitalist societies as primarily domestic and maternal cân be seen as some kind of independent, ahistorical variable.

Feminist anthropologists have also realized that women's social position in non-capitalist societies (and in societies which are still undergoing transformation into capitalist societies) cannot be explained solely by appeal to the force of norms and values. Among feminists engaged in comparative research, Engels' *Origin of the Family, Private Property and the State* has been particularly influential, since Engels was concerned with the *original* subordination of women which quite evidently pre-dated the development of industrial capitalism. The ethnography upon which Engels based his speculation, and indeed the very speculative nature of his reconstruction of what may have happened in prehistory, have generally been discredited, but the central question which he posed is still regarded as a valid one. Engels rejected the idea that women's subordination could be treated simply as given by nature. But equally he dismissed the idea that it could be explained by reference to legal rules and social custom; these codes are not, so to speak, plucked out of the air but are themselves closely related to prevailing economic and political conditions. He located the *original* subordination of women – the 'world historic defeat of the female sex' – at the point when the domestication of animals created a new kind of property, herds of cattle, which could be accumulated and transmitted. This led to the overthrow of mother-right (or matrilineal inheritance, as anthropologists would call it today) which had hitherto constituted an adequate principle for the assignation of children to lineage groups and for the transmission of the 'insignificant' forms of possession already in existence. Mother-right was replaced by father-right (patrilineal inheritance) as men gained control over the new forms of wealth, and women were consequently dispossessed and devalued. This transformation laid the foundations for the subordination of women in all subsequent modes of production in which quite different forms of private property were to become important. The ultimate restoration of the female sex to its rightful status could only take place with the total abolition of all private property, i.e. with socialism. But meanwhile, writing about industrial

Europe, Engels urges that 'the first premise for the emancipation of women is the re-introduction of the entire female sex into public industry' (Engels 1972: 137). If private property enabled them to be enslaved, full participation in wage labour would enable them to begin to set themselves free.

Feminist writers have taken seriously Engels' concern to locate the basis of women's subordination in the structure of material production, and much empirical research activity has been directed to this problem, yet there has been considerable confusion about which aspects of material production need to be studied in order to yield general explanations of women's status or position in a given society. Should we attend to the kinds and amount of productive labour which women perform? Or is it more important to examine their capacity to control resources and regulate consumption (Brown 1970)? Or should we study their property rights and the kinds of property they can inherit or hold, relating this to other aspects of their situation (Maher 1974)? Some Marxist anthropologists have realized that in some kinds of society the distinction between production and reproduction has a different significance from that which it has in industrial society (especially in formations where the production of food is based on the domestic unit and there is little extra-domestic exchange). In such cases, it is important to develop models of reproduction and to discover how women (as agents of reproduction) become the objects of control by men (see Aaby 1977).

I have described this diversity of approach as 'confusion' but perhaps the situation is only confused where anthropologists try to compare women's position in societies which are at quite different stages of development. If we try to make indiscriminate comparisons we may well conclude that it is only in respect of their common role of domestic labourers that anything of universal validity can be said about women's position (see Bujra 1978: 40).

Production is only a general category of activity. The specific aspects of production which underpin the relationship between the sexes can only be identified within a particular mode of production. We cannot predict that, say, property rights, or women's role in the labour process, or any other particular aspect of production will provide some kind of universal 'key' to women's position in all societies. In the case of North-West India I shall argue that it is the distribution of property rights (especially rights in land) which we ought to look at first of all if we wish to understand the position of rural women.

The situation of women in the labour market has also to be considered however, as village men and women come to constitute a rural extension of the urban proletariat in developing areas. These are the aspects of production which are the most significant since, as we shall see, they are the ones which define women's position as the dependants of men. If we can relate the ideologies of purdah and familial roles to the organization of production, then the analysis of women's roles in India may be able to progress beyond its present descriptive phase.

**Organizing field research; questions and vocabulary**

I am still empiricist enough, though, to think that these general questions will not resolve themselves without appeal to ethnographic data. But how are we to collect and organize the information needed for this task?

One of the problems facing feminist anthropologists has been the lack of an adequate terminology for describing women's roles in ethnographic terms which permit cross-cultural comparison but which are not so bland as to be meaningless or circular. We can compare women's 'position' or 'status' in peasant societies but what (if anything) do these terms mean? If we talk, for instance, of women's 'status' then we are only talking about women's prestige in a given society and there is no way in which we can measure women's status which is not specific to the society we are considering, given that prestige depends upon a value assigned by the society itself. In any case, anthropologists such as Friedl (Friedl 1967) and Rogers (Rogers 1975) have shown that the low ideological status assigned to women in many peasant societies may obscure the real domestic power which such women may yield. Domestic power, Rogers argues, is not to be despised in a society where the domestic sphere is a far more important arena of power than it is in capitalist societies. And domestic power may 'overflow' into the public sphere without this overflow being acknowledged. (Thus Das observes that in India the important role of women in arranging marriages may have public consequences which have not been realized by sociologists hitherto (Das 1976: 132.)

Writers such as Rogers and Friedl have gone further than discussing sex roles in terms of some undefined attribute termed 'status', for what they are really talking about is power. Friedl specifies that the domestic influence exerted by Greek peasant women is derived from their ability to control property, which they bring to a marriage in the form of dowry (Friedl 1967: 106). Rogers recognizes a wider range of sources of domestic power (access to the supernatural, control of information dissemination processes, etc.) besides economic power. She notes that whilst material dependency should decrease the control which a woman (or for that matter any other member of the domestic group) can hope to exercise on the affairs of the family, there can be circumstances in which it can be counteracted by other kinds of dependency. Thus in the French village which she studied, wives of men who went outside the village to work in local factories still depended upon their husbands financially, but the husbands depended upon their wives for information about what was going on in the village which they left each day for work – information without which a man cannot hope to maintain his political position in the local community (Rogers 1975: 750).

For 'status' or 'position', then, read 'the kinds of social power which women, *as women*, are able to exert'. This seems to me to be a useful basis for description, provided only that we recognize the difficulties which attend the study of power in the field. One danger is that to which, in my view, both Rogers and Friedl sometimes succumb, of accepting the actors' definition of the kinds of power that are important. So whilst I would agree that the domestic power of peasant women has been overlooked, I do not think that either the 'myth of male dominance' in peasant society or women's lack of extra-domestic power are unimportant either. Secondly, identifying the exercise of domestic power is very difficult (the sadistic reader can watch me wrestle with this problem in Chapter 4). If, as Rogers suggests in an actual case from her work in a French village, a woman suggests that she has been able to persuade her husband to buy her a motor cycle in spite of his initial reluctance, are we to take this suggestion at face value? (Rogers 1975: 741). How do we know that it was her pressure that caused him to relent? Domestic decision-making processes are as difficult to study in the field as any political process, with the additional problem of their thoroughly private nature.

At the level of description then, we need to locate the kinds of power which village women may exercise, and also those from which they are excluded. These are the terms in which we can describe the 'position' of Indian women. But if we wish to locate the material base of this position, what kind of ethnographic facts must we turn to, what kind of data do we need to deploy in order to open up this discussion? Where do we commence the account of women's role in production?

When I began this study I was much influenced by Sanday's theory that female power in the public domain is related to women's contribution to subsistence (Sanday 1974). This accounts for my original decision to carry out a comparative study of a Punjab village and a Himachal village. I expected to find a marked difference between women in Punjab, an area where their contribution to agricultural subsistence is relatively low, and in Himachal Pradesh, where their contribution is high. I was also influenced by a common assumption made by feminists in the West, i.e. that women will remain silent and powerless so long as their roles are purely domestic. I expected that heavy participation in agricultural production on the part of Himachali women would be reflected in differences in their outlook and public status from those of Punjabi women. As will be clear from the material I present in this book, this is only partially the case. Once embarked upon my fieldwork, I realized that Sanday's theory was not very relevant to the case of India, though it may well be applicable in some tribal societies, for the reason (which ought to have been obvious to me) that neither Punjab nor Himachal Pradesh has a subsistence economy. There are still families practising what amounts to subsistence farming, but in Punjab this form of production exists alongside capitalist farming, and in both areas rural households derive additional income from wage labour in industry and government service, especially that of men.

## Women, work, and property

I found that as a field guide, using the work which rural women do as my starting point was still a useful priority. But work does not carry with it control of resources. As Veena Das has observed, 'the participation of women in the subsistence economy is not sufficient for either ensuring their control over the products of their labour, or for a high social evaluation of their participation, since this is dependent upon the already existing structural arrangements for the ownership and management of property' (Das 1976: 142). Exactly the same can be said of women's participation in other forms of production in rural India. Clearly, it is necessary to look at the specific nature of the relationship which women bear to property, especially their effective exclusion from the inheritance of land, which is largely the basis of their dependence upon men in the villages, and which may also be the basis for their symbolic devaluation.

What are the forms of property which it is most relevant to consider here? Clearly, we are not concerned with possessions as such, but with control of those resources which generate new wealth, either directly or indirectly. (I 'possess' numerous items which are either pleasing or useful – a hairbrush, a non-pedigree pet cat, an electric coffee grinder, and a cheap portable radio – but they do not contribute to the creation of new wealth, they do not enable me to appropriate the labour of others, nor can they easily be converted into other forms of wealth which might have these characteristics.) Land is without doubt the most important category of wealth-generating property in an agrarian society. But land cannot be cultivated without certain tools and equipment, and so we must also consider cattle and farm machinery. Nor must we forget forms of property which can be converted into land or agricultural equipment, e.g. gold jewellery, accumulated cash savings.

Land cannot be farmed without the consumption of labour power and most of the farmers in the areas I studied still use methods which are labour-intensive. Therefore where individuals or groups hold rights in the labour power of others, these rights may also be treated as a category of property. We might include here the rights which landowning families traditionally held in the specialist labour of client artisans and in the labour of untouchable dependent families, although these rights have largely lapsed in the parts of India which I studied. More relevant are the rights which the senior members of the rural household have in the labour of its junior and female members, which are difficult to study because they are usually acknowledged only implicitly. The rights which men have in the reproductive powers of women will be important where children are also a resource, i.e. their productive labour can be controlled or appropriated in some way; this is the case in most of the households studied.

However, all these forms of 'invisible' property take their form from the specific nature of landed property in the Indian village and cannot be understood without reference to it. Land is usually vested in males, and in most villages is concentrated in the hands of the males of particular families or castes. Rights in the labour power or earnings of others are closely related to the form and distribution of land rights. Therefore I shall concentrate on the latter, paying particular attention to the manner in which women are largely excluded from the possession and control of land.

Some relevant ideas concerning the relationship between property, production, and women's roles in peasant societies have recently been developed by Goody (Goody 1976). He builds on the distinction made by Boserup and others between social structures based on hoe agriculture (which usually involve shifting cultivation and are more common in Africa than in Eurasia) and those based on plough agriculture, of which India is an obvious example.

Goody's reasoning is as follows: plough cultivation makes the production of a surplus possible and facilitates a complex division of labour. Land becomes a scarce and valuable resource, the basis of class stratification. Class is associated with status distinctions and different styles of life:

> 'An important means of maintaining one's style of life, and that of one's progeny, is by marriage with persons of the same or higher qualification. We should therefore expect a greater emphasis upon the direct vertical transmission of property in societies with advanced rather than simple exploitation of agriculture resources. This system of vertical transmission (i.e. from parents to children) tends to make provision for women as well as men. The position of women in the world has to be maintained by means of property, either in dowry or inheritance – otherwise the honour of the family suffers a setback in the eyes of itself and others. This also means that women are likely to become the residual heirs in the restricted sibling groups that monogamy permits, the property going to female descendants before collateral males, even when these are members of the same agnatic clan.' (Goody 1976: 20)

The family's need to ensure that women marry status equals leads to the proliferation of institutions which limit women's social and sexual freedom – chaperonage, sexual segregation, and even purdah. Plough cultivation and diverging devolution (inheritance by children of both sexes) are also associated with 'male' farming systems in which men play the dominant role in agricultural production; women are valued as producers of heirs rather than as producers of food.

Although I shall disagree with some of Goody's premises and find that some of the concepts he uses are crudely applied ('complex polity' and 'advanced agriculture' and 'mode of production' are used with little precision), I think that his general argument should be borne in mind. It has the virtue of providing new ways of linking gender roles with production, and suggests an ordered structure of causation, so that one can make connections between purdah, work, property, and marriage without begging the question of how they are connected.

Property is important, but we must not forget to distinguish between different kinds of property. Land (which, as we shall see, women seldom own or control) is a form of property which is capable of generating new wealth. Other kinds of property (jewelry, domestic goods, etc.) are more likely to be controlled by women and can be considered as forms of wealth, but they cannot generate new wealth. We may also need to identify the senses in which a woman's own labour power becomes a form of familial property which can only be alienated with the consent of the family group.

This investigation of women's role in the process of production therefore has to include more than just a description of the kinds of work which women do. It must include an account of familial authority relations according to which this work is organized, and of the property relations which this authority structure realizes and maintains.

## Women and economic development

Finally, there is one other area of debate relevant to our consideration of women's role in production. This is the debate as to whether economic development actually benefits women (relative to men, that is). Writers such as Boserup (Boserup 1970) and Bossen (Bossen 1975) have pointed out that economic development may be accompanied by the actual closure of traditional opportunities for women to gain wealth or control resources, without the substitution of new ones. This observation is a useful counter to the bland optimism characteristic of many public pronouncements about development. But no useful theoretical account of why this should be so has been offered so far. Obviously, one factor may be the exportation of western models of gender roles along with the know-how and the hardware as part of the aid package. But whether such cultural diffusion is a contingent or a necessary effect of the aid relationship is unclear. Partly, the problem is difficult to resolve because it has been formulated in terms of the effects of 'development' rather than as, say, the effects of capitalist expansion or the effects of aid programmes or industrialization. The term 'development' does not convey anything very specific about the changes in the organization of production, which are surely what we ought to look at first if we wish to account for women's relative disadvantage.

In the Indian context it has been noticed that women's use of economic opportunities has not increased relative to that of men in spite of legislation designed to improve women's status in the economic sphere (Mazumdar 1975a: 262). Their participation in the labour force has not increased in relation to that of men, if this is understood as an indication of opportunity. On the other hand, we have to remember that in an area such as Punjab, the withdrawal of women from outdoor agricultural labour has for long been an indicator of any general rise in prosperity and economic confidence of the peasant proprietor. The women of the landowning classes had largely withdrawn from most kinds of outdoor agricultural work well before the coming of the 'Green Revolution'. Punjab is the richest state in India and also has the lowest participation of women in its rural labour force. So should we interpret the withdrawal of women from agricultural production in Punjab cheerfully as a signal of greater prosperity, or gloomily as a sign that women's opportunities lag behind those of men in a period of rapid economic expansion? Himachal Pradesh, on the other hand, is an area where economic development has been sluggish and has relied heavily on government stimulus; the hill peasant has few means of acquiring capital to invest in land, and the nature of the land is such that only very heavy investment would render it more productive than it is already under traditional methods of cultivation. It is difficult to establish whether any radical change in women's participation in agricultural production in the lower foothills has taken place in modern times, but it is likely that it has increased due to the migration of large numbers of rural men in search of paid work outside the area.

There are numerous reasons, therefore, why the comparison of these two areas should be fruitful. In both regions women's role in production has changed, but in quite different ways. Yet the broad cultural definitions of female roles and qualities are similar in both areas. We should expect this comparison to contribute to the clarification of the general relationship between the ideological definition of women's roles and their position in the process of production.

## Notes

1 For instance, I have not dealt with woman's ritual roles nor the way in which femaleness is symbolized in ritual and religion, for which see Hershman (1977), Wadley (1977), and King (1975).

2 See Meillasoux's criticism of this tendency from a Marxist standpoint (Meillasoux 1973).

3 One notable exception to this is the study of women in a Bangladesh village by Jenneke Arens and Jos van Beurden which does make some attempt to theorize about women's labour in general (Arens and van Beurden 1977).

4 Though it can still be argued that the family has retained a privileged position in feminist analyses of women's position in capitalist societies. See Kuhn 1978.

# 2 Harbassi and Chaili

As soon as I had decided to study the questions posed in the previous chapter I was faced with the problem of how to study them. What was the unit of Indian rural society appropriate for such an investigation – the village? The caste group? A structured sample of individuals or households? In India the group which has constituted the basis for most anthropological research has been the village – a named and geographically self-evident unit, an obvious site for participant observation, a method which by its nature must focus on the micro-community. Some anthropologists have treated the village as the microcosm of the wider society; the villages are 'blocks' from which Indian society is built, so that we can comprehend Indian society if only we study enough of them (Dube 1955: 6, Berreman 1963: 1). Others have proposed that whilst the village is not really the microcosm of the wider society, it can be treated as such for the purposes of field research. Some processes or institutions occur on a scale wider than the single village but are accessible to the anthropologist through data collected in a single village, provided that village is fairly representative of the region as a whole (see Mayer 1960: 9-10).

Whichever kind of assumption is made, the effect is the same: we learn about rural society in India through a succession of studies of individual villages and are likely to end up by assigning the village a greater structural importance than it really has.

One objection to these assumptions is that put forward most

cogently by Dumont (Dumont 1970: 154); the village cannot be treated as the basic unit of Indian society, because any search for a 'basic unit' in a substantial or empirical sense is fruitless. A second objection, which is more important from the point of view of the theme of this study, is a feminist objection. I suggest that the concentration on the village as the unit for study arises from a specifically male perspective on Indian society, by which I mean a tendency to view Indian society very much from the point of view of the male villager. Let me explain this assertion.

In North-West India, the adult women of a village enter it at marriage and their daughters will leave it when they marry to live elsewhere, since to marry within one's own village is regarded as improper. The distinction between one's *peke* (the village where one was born and brought up and where one's parents live) and *saure* (the village where one is married and where one's parents-in-law live) is fundamental to women's social experience. A woman conceives her social world as divided between relations arising from her membership in her *peke* and those arising from membership in her *saure*. At the conceptual level, the main opposition is not between the inside and the outside of any particular village but between the two villages which a woman belongs to and in which she has different kinds of membership. But for men, who do not move to another village on marriage but normally remain members of the same political and social community from birth to death, this opposition is not central to their social experience. The significant opposition for a male villager is that between co-members of his own village and the outside world in general. From the point of view of the male villager, the continuity of the village as a social unit is provided by the succession of men to positions, titles, property, roles, and offices. He has been familiar with this system of positions and relations since he was a tiny child. From his point of view, the village as a social reality means a set of enduring relations among men (women contribute to the perpetuation of this entity by providing children, but only in so far as these children are male). This view results from the efficacy of certain social arrangements – virilocal marriage, village exogamy,[1] and male authority in the community and household. It is realized in a set of practices which distinguish between those village women classed as sisters and those classed as sisters-in-law, and extend kin terms to almost all male villagers, thus creating the fiction that the entire village is a kind of family group, related through its males (see Sharma 1978a: 230).

Women concur with this view, which constitutes the dominant ideology, but this is not the only way in which they structure their social experience. For them, the social ramifications of the village beyond its boundaries through the family ties of its members are as striking as the unity (real or imagined) of its male members. The more 'female' view of the village is that of a location where a number of extensive kinship networks overlap or converge. Women are less inclined to view the tract of countryside in which their village is located as having their own village as its 'natural' centre; they are more inclined to regard it as a region scattered with their own kin, and relatives of their kin. Compare the two following statements:

(Santosh (H1)): 'My husband always loved his own village. Even when he was working in the city he used to look forward to coming here in his holidays. He loved every street, every house. He said that no other village would ever be such a happy place for him. It was the place of his grandfather and his great grandfather.'

(Tivan Kaur (H10)): 'If you want to study his district, you should come with me. There is hardly a village in this region where I do not have an aunt, a cousin, or a sister married. If only I had enough money for the bus fares I could take you all over the place, just visiting my relatives alone.'

The first statement described a specifically male experience of the locality, the second a specifically female experience. These conceptualizations do not negate one another; they simply arise from different kinds of life experience. There is no *a priori* reason why the anthropologist should adopt one without taking into account the other. In so far as they have tended to study the village as a bounded entity opposed to an external society, anthropologists have actually favoured the male villager's view. The consequence of this, not surprisingly, is that women's activities are often relegated to the 'background'; they belong to the domestic sphere and are therefore 'private', whilst it is the publicly acknowledged relationships among males that are brought 'up-stage' as having real social and political significance.

Some anthropologists have realized the limitations of the village study, though not necessarily for the kind of reason I have put forward here. Pettigrew, in her study of factions in Punjab, explicitly rejects the idea of the village as a relevant unit of study but takes 'family and faction' as her field. I would concur with her view that villages in Punjab are not self-contained wholes in any important sense, and probably never were (Pettigrew 1975: 23). How much more cogent these objections must be in the case of Himachal Pradesh, where most of the population do not live in the kind of compact nucleated village we find in the Punjab plains. Here the settlements are typically small collections of scattered houses. These groups of families may develop a sense of collective identity (see Parry 1979: 32) but they do not constitute the same kind of bounded unit as the village of the plains.

So how did I resolve the problem of defining a universe for my field study of women and production?

In the end I decided to gather data along two different dimensions. From what I knew already of Indian rural society, the household would be an important unit for study in a project concerning the role of women in production. Having established myself and my family in Harbassi in September 1977, I sought to locate families of different social types (large landlords, owner cultivators, landless labourers and tenants, and to conduct intensive studies of this limited sample. Although I did not expect caste in itself to be a very important factor, I also tried to get a fair 'spread' of different castes. In particular, I wanted to include households from high castes (Brahmans, Rajputs, Jats, etc.) and from the scheduled castes. (The scheduled castes are those 'scheduled' under the Indian constitution as being particularly disadvantaged and eligible for protective positive discrimination. Most of them, such as Chamars and sweepers, are regarded as very polluting by other castes – the so-called 'untouchables' – and nowadays fill the ranks of the tenant-labourer class.) Some of the families I contacted lived in Harbassi itself, others in hamlets nearby.

When I write of a 'sample', I do not mean that I was able to take a representative stratified sample of the population of Harbassi. To do this, I would have had to have access to information on the total proportions of each kind of household in the entire region, which was not available. I selected a number of households from the network of friends and acquaintances which I built up, doing my best to ensure that the main types of agricultural household were represented. I did the same when I moved to Chaili in April 1978, although I feel that the Chaili sample is less balanced than the Harbassi sample (see p.24). A list of the families studied, with a summary of information, can be found in *Table 1*.

The households listed in the sample were not the only ones which I was able to observe, but they were the ones on which I have the most detailed and systematically collected data. In the discussions that follow, I have tried to confine my examples to case material from the sample so that the reader can build up a profile of household types, rather than having to deal with a wide scatter of unrelated examples. Some of the households in the sample will be referred to many times in this book. To make it easier for you to identify the individuals whose statements have been quoted or whose cases have been cited, I have assigned code numbers for each household, H1-H17 for the Harbassi families, C1-C11 for the Chaili families. The actual names given in the text are all pseudonyms, as are the names of the villages themselves.

If this sample is not representative in the strictly statistical sense, I think I can claim that it is systematic.[2] Each household located was made the subject of a fairly detailed study through observation and interviewing. I used a checklist of topics on which I needed information from each household, and made sure that over time all these points were covered. It was seldom necessary to conduct formal interviews, although my informants were quite aware that I was studying them and many of our conversations were tape-recorded. These household studies yielded valuable information on women's role in the domestic economy, family decision-making processes, women's situation in the kinship system, their role in arranging marriages, etc.

To answer other kinds of questions I found it more appropriate to follow the method more conventional among anthropologists, i.e. taking a particular locality as the unit of study, but in each case the unit was larger than a single village. Both Harbassi and Chaili are large settlements (large, that is, compared with other villages in their respective areas). Both had a *bazar* (shopping area), both were on bus routes, and both constituted social and commercial centres for a group of smaller villages. I used each village as a base for the participant observation of a group of settlements – a central village and its satellite hamlets. This produced useful material on the political roles of women in the locality, the restriction on women's use of public space, changes in land tenure and methods of agriculture, etc. The two dimensions of the study – the 'household' dimension and the 'locality' dimension yielded different kinds of information and were complementary to each other.

Harbassi and Chaili therefore represent centres for the study of women and their economic roles, and the accounts which follow are descriptions of social relations in two localities rather than of the villages considered as social groups.

## The field research

When I went to Harbassi in the autumn of 1977 I was already known to one family there, although I had not visited the village before. I had come to know this family when they were resident in a city in the state of Hariana. Now, after the death of the head of the household, they had returned to Harbassi where they held land. My relationship with this family was already a very affectionate one, and my daughters and I stayed in their house during the period of my field-work in Harbassi. They were kind enough to introduce me to many other farmers, professional people, and tenants in Harbassi and its environs, and their interest in my work enabled me to make good use of my time there.

Doing fieldwork in Himachal Pradesh was less of a novelty for me as I had conducted research there ten years previously, and my husband's family still live there. Doing research in an area where one has already conducted fieldwork has its advantages and disadvantages. On the positive side, one has a storage of knowledge about local culture and language. On the other hand, it is difficult to attack a second piece of research with the freshness and naivety of the first, and one risks assuming that the impressions which one received during the previous research do not need to be verified. I decided to live in Chaili because it was near enough to Ghanyari, where I carried out my first fieldwork, to exhibit the same basic features of culture and economic organization. Yet I did not know anyone there personally and so I would be able to gather data starting from scratch, as it were. My husband had joined me by the time I moved to Chaili in spring 1978 and we rented rooms from an old school friend of his who lived in Chaili, and who proved to be most kind and helpful.

No two field experiences are alike, of course. In Chaili I was accompanied by my husband, and this was a great advantage since his presence gave me access to male views and activities which were hard for me to study in Harbassi, on account of the rather rigid segregation of men's and women's lives in rural India. He came across several old acquaintances during the period of our stay, who turned out to be living in hamlets near Chaili, as well as some distant relatives. A number of women married into Ghanyari, the village I had studied previously, had originally come from Chaili or villages nearby, and we managed to make contact with their families. These acquaintances enabled us to establish a social network in the area rapidly, an imperative given the short time available for the research.

Yet in Chaili we were unable to avoid a dilemma that most fieldworkers in Indian villages face; the social distance between the highest and the lowest castes is so great that one can establish relations of intimacy either with people at the upper end of the hierarchy, or with people in the lower echelons, but not with both. Interdictions on members of different castes eating and drinking together were more effective in Chaili than in Harbassi and did not make it easy to obtain balanced information. I think that in time I would have been able to find more informants among the lower castes – with time one can establish one's right to take liberties with local conventions – but we did not have long, and I feel dissatisfied with the research in Chaili from this point of view. The economic gap between the richest and the poorest in Chaili was not so wide as it was in Harbassi, but the ritual gap was far wider.

In Punjab I found that practice with respect to matters of ritual purity is much more a business for the individual to sort out for himself or herself. There is less tendency for the local caste group to feel called upon to pass judgement on a member's habits. Individuals in the same family may vary greatly in their practice, and may even act in what seems a contradictory manner. For instance, the friend with whom I stayed was an orthodox Brahman and was very particular that no-one should enter her kitchen without washing their hands; low caste people were not allowed in at all. Yet both she and her sons would sometimes accept cups of tea from their tenants, who were of scheduled caste, and she urged me not to hesitate to call at her tenant's houses if I ever felt the need of refreshment when I visited other villages. Caste is not unimportant in Punjab by any means, but there is less tendency to live in one's neighbour's pocket, morally speaking. Since my neighbours in Harbassi did not expect to be able to control each other's behaviour in ritual matters, they showed very little interest in my own practice. I was free to associate with members of different castes and I think that the work that I did in Harbassi is more balanced in this respect.

**Harbassi**

District Hoshiarpur is one of the northernmost districts of the State of Punjab, along the borders of Himachal Pradesh. Harbassi is a large village – or perhaps I should say, a small town – situated about fifteen kilometres from the city of Hoshiarpur, on a main road. The district is very flat for the most part, although the white peaks of the Dhaula Dhar, the nearest Himalayan range, form a backdrop to the lush green of the countryside on sharp winter days. From the lower foothills run a number of broad water courses (*cho*). These are dry for most of the winter but are liable to flash flooding in the monsoon. Rainwater from the nearby hills carries sand and grit which is deposited alongside the water courses as the pace of the current slows down on reaching the plains. This is highly detrimental to the quality of the land, the usual kind of soil in the district being a rich alluvial type. The damaging action of *chos* has been recognized as a problem by successive governments of Punjab. As early as 1900 the British passed the Punjab Land Preservation Act, giving the government the authority to appropriate land near *chos* in order to carry out operations to restrict their action. Some of the larger *chos* near to Harbassi have been contained by the planting of coarse grass and the erection of firm artificial banks, but the action of many of the smaller ones remains unrestricted. As well as damage to land, there is a yearly toll of life and property when houses and their inhabitants are swept away at the height of the monsoon season. Reclaiming land that has been ruined by the action of a *cho* is a tedious and lengthy business and can only be attempted by the wealthier land owners.

Being near the hills, this area has a rainfall adequate for the cultivation of two crops yearly on most kinds of land, fluctuating around an annual total of 90 cm. During the winter months the temperature can fall as low as 12° centigrade. Villagers use heavy cotton quilts at night and our nylon sleeping bags proved totally inadequate. From March the temperature rises to a stifling, arid crescendo in June, relieved somewhat by the breaking of the monsoon in early July. Summer temperatures can rise to 35° centigrade in June, so we were thankful that by this time we had removed ourselves to Chaili where the summer climate is a little kinder.

District Hoshiarpur has always been a prosperous area by Indian standards, (though less rich than the central districts of Punjab, such as Jullundur and Ludhiana). It is favoured by its reliable rainfall, its good soil and the high water table, which means that even before the days of the tube-well, the better off peasants and landlords could irrigate their fields by means of the Persian well, operated by animal power. From one point of view the 'Green Revolution' of the late sixties and seventies can be seen as just the culmination of a process of improvement that has been in train for many decades, perhaps for the whole of the past century (see Stokes 1978: 8). The clearance of jungle areas was almost complete by the end of the nineteenth century, but there followed an intensification of cultivation and a general improvement in farm technology and irrigation. From the turn of the century, if not before, there was a general rise in the standard of living, although this did not affect all classes equally. With the introduction of High Yield Varieties of wheat in 1966 and the possibilities which this opened up, there was a rapid increase of investment in agriculture and mechanization, first among the larger landowners, who by now have transformed themselves into a class of capitalist farmers, and later among the wealthier peasants. New cash crops are being grown and crops that were grown only for home or local consumption before are now produced for far wider markets. Most farmers in Harbassi rely on wheat and maize as their main crops (being grown in the winter and monsoon respectively) but some farmers specialize in vegetable production for the urban market, and a few in dairying and poultry. The road between Harbassi and Hoshiarpur is busy in the early mornings with tractors drawing trailer loads of potatoes, cauliflowers, or aubergines (according to the season) to the main market in Hoshiarpur, whence the goods will be sent to Delhi or other major centres of distribution.

These changes in farming methods have been accompanied by changes in social relationships among those engaged in agricultural production.[3] As in many parts of India, the relationship between the old landlord class and their erstwhile tenants and dependants has lost its personal character. In the nineteenth century many tenancies were occupancy tenancies and might persist from one generation to another. It is likely that there was a good deal of continuity in tenancies at will. There was also the form of economic organization known variously as the *sepidar* or *jajmāni* system. In this system, labourers of different kinds worked for landowners, providing either specialized craft services and/or general agriculture labour. A labouring family was attached by personal and often hereditary ties to a landowning family and work was paid for in grain at customary rates. In the case of scheduled caste labourers the bond of personal dependence was particularly strong since they were least likely to have other sources of income to mitigate their subjection. The land-owner to whom these services were rendered was not necessarily a faceless rentier; more often he was a substantial owner cultivator, personally and actively involved in agriculture. It was from this class and from the rentier landlord class (which was not totally absent) that the modern capitalist farmers have emerged.

Looking at the matter from one point of view, you could say that agrarian relations have lost their paternalist element; from another, you could say that the tenants and labourers have exchanged their position of semi-servitude for a position of powerless independence. If anything, this is more true of Punjab than of other parts of India, especially where large landlords have terminated tenancies of land and have taken to farming all their land on a capitalist basis. Where this has happened, those tenants who have not land of their own must (unless they have enough education to seek employment in the towns) sell their labour as farm servants, generally to their former landlords. In the case of one Harbassi family's estate, I was able to observe this process before my own eyes. This family owned land in a hamlet near Harbassi which was inhabited by a group of Chamars (a scheduled caste) who had all been their tenants originally. About nine years ago, the landlords informed the tenants that they no longer wished to lease the land out to them for cultivation in the winter, but would farm the wheat crop themselves, hiring labour where necessary. They had bought a tractor for the purpose with the help of a government loan and proceeded to apply advanced methods of farm technology to the winter crop. The monsoon crop of maize was still cultivated by the tenants themselves, the landlords making a yearly allocation of plots for share-cropping after the wheat had been harvested. But they were selective as to whom they permitted to farm their land. Whereas once there had been a tacit assumption that all the families in the village might be allowed to farm parcels of land, the landlords now deliberately excluded those whom they did not regard as efficient farmers. As the landlords provided the seeds and the tractor power, and claimed over half of the crop,[4] the Chamar tenants could hardly be said to be more than paid agents of the landlord so far as this crop was concerned. A few of the former tenants had acquired small plots of land themselves, some of which had formerly belonged to the landlords but which had been confiscated under new Land Ceiling Legislation. But they did not have the capital to invest in large-scale machinery or irrigation, so the fruits of the 'Green Revolution' were not accessible for them. For some of the former tenants, agriculture was now really only a sideline, and their main source of income was paid work in the towns – as teachers, labourers, clerks, according to the education they had managed to obtain. For yet others, who could not obtain land either to rent or buy, there was no alternative to working as day labourers for local landlords. This kind of labouring (*dihāre*) has neither prestige nor security, since the day labourer enters into no kind of contract with his employer. If he is sick or unable to find work he simply goes without money. *Dihāre* work is the dead end of rural employment opportunities and parents always hope that their sons will not have the misfortune to have to rely on it for a living. To be a day labourer is to be a nobody.

To this extent, those observers who have seen the 'Green Revolution' as benefitting the large landowner first and foremost and as creating a landless proletariat out of the old tenant class are substantially correct (see Frankel 1971: 38). However there are two points which must also be remembered. Firstly, although the profitability of the application of advanced farming methods to cultivation is much less for the peasant farmer with a holding of under fifteen acres than it is for the large landowners, the benefits are still enough to increase the value of his land and his general standard of living. Secondly, the proletarianization of the farmer tenant class has gone on alongside an increase in employment opportunities in the towns due to the industrial development of Punjab. This means those who are qualified have other options than to sell their labour at the miserable wages available to agricultural labourers.[5]

It must be said that the standard of living of even the poorest villager in Punjab is far higher than that of the rural poor elsewhere in India, certainly far higher than in Himachal Pradesh. Even among the scheduled caste labourers, most houses now have their own pumps for domestic water, few are without electricity and mud dwellings are being replaced by modest but sound brick houses. Among ex-tenants whom I knew well there was a sense of bitterness against the landowners who had turned them from land their ancestors had farmed, but also a feeling that they enjoyed comforts which their grandparents had never enjoyed and could not have dreamed of.

One of the consequences of this general prosperity which I shall deal with in detail later has been a general withdrawal of women from direct participation in agriculture among certain classes of the rural population. There is no doubt that in the nineteenth century all village women save those of highest caste (chiefly the Brahmans, Rajputs, and Khatris, a commercial caste) did perform some agricultural work, but nowadays the wives of the larger peasant farmers perform practically no agricultural work which requires them actually to go out into the fields. Even in some small peasant families the women perform only limited types of farm work. This general withdrawal is directly related in most cases to greater prosperity. If the women of the household do not have to labour in the fields this adds to the family's prestige, but obviously this has not always been a luxury that many families can afford, and the women of landless and tenant families cannot afford it yet.

Harbassi is a settlement with a population of about 6,500. Local people class it as a *qasbah*, rather than a village (*pind*). A *qasbah* is a settlement which may contain many agriculturalists but which also has a sizeable *bazar* and market. It has some commercial life and is more than just a community of farmers and their dependants. Harbassi used to be more important politically and commercially than it is now. It was the head of an administrative division of the Mugal empire and its members still look back to its illustrious past. It attained some fame as the home of a number of well-known Hindu nationalists during the struggle for independence from the British. In modern times it has been overshadowed by Hoshiarpur, and wealthy Harbassi people tend to go to Hoshiarpur for major shopping expeditions rather than to shop in the local *bazar*. But Harbassi still has a modest wholesale market for grain and vegetables and its *bazar* seems busy enough. It has a degree college, a police station, a petrol filling station, and a tractor repair workshop, all of which do brisk business. Therefore it remains a focus for the commercial, political, and social life of the surrounding villages.

In 1947, India achieved independence, but only at the cost of partition into two new states, the Republic of India and Pakistan. The old province of Punjab, where conflict between Hindus and Muslims had been most bloody and severe, was divided between India and Pakistan. Some of the chief landlords in Harbassi had been Muslim Rajpurts, but they all migrated in 1947, to be replaced by Hindu and Sikh refugees, and the old mosque will soon be in ruins.

Many dwellings formerly occupied by Muslim households also lie in ruins and others are empty because their former inhabitants have migrated to Canada, Britain, or other parts of the world, and this gives the outer part of the village a rather desolate air. This contrasts with the newer quarters built along the main road by the retired civil servants, professional men, shopkeepers, and large farmers who constitute the local élite. The various industries that formerly existed in Harbassi, mainly sugar refinery and weaving, have long since disappeared but there is now new employment for artisans as mechanics and in other occupations which service the modern mechanized form of agriculture.

## Chaili

Chaili is situated in the District Hamirpur division of Himachal Pradesh. It lies at a height of approximately 1,050 metres above sea level in the Sivalik range, a band of foothills which lie between the fertile plains of Punjab and Hariana, and the snowy heights of the Dhaula Dhar range. The countryside in which Chaili is situated could hardly be more different from that of Harbassi. The settlement lies on a patch of high ground in an irregular plateau dissected by many stony watercourses. These watercourses (*khad*) sometimes run in steep ravines, sometimes in shallower valleys and flood with swift shallow torrents in the monsoon. Here the waters gather which will be dispersed in the sandy *chos* of District Hoshiarpur when they reach the plains. Several small ravines run down from the ridge on which the village is built into deep wooded valleys on either side. From the top of the village one has a panoramic view of the hills all around: to the north-east the Simla hills, tawny yellow or lush green according to the season; to the north-west the Dhaula Dhar whose peaks are always tipped with white even in high summer; to the south, the scrubby foothills flanking Punjab.

Chaili is a large settlement for this area, having a population of about 1,000. It was originally settled by a group of Rajput farmers who owned most of the surrounding land. Their land was cultivated by low-caste tenants living in the village (mainly Chamars) and by tenants of other castes living in the hamlets nearby (Brahmans, Kumhars, etc.). Unlike many hill villages, Chaili has representatives of a number of artisan castes – Julahas (weavers), Suniara (goldsmith), carpenters, and potters – although not all of these continue to ply their traditional crafts. Compared with many hill villages, Chaili has almost a bustling aspect with its modest *bazar*, bus stand, bank, and post office. But its busyness must be of recent origin for I was told that a generation ago there were no shops and certainly no buses. Many of the Brahman and Khatri shopkeepers are fairly recent immigrants to the village from other villages and small towns in Himachal Pradesh. Chaili has achieved its local importance because of its situation on a new road which runs to Chakmoh, a pilgrimage centre which has grown in popularity during the past decades. The shrine there is dedicated to Baba Balak Nath, a local saint whose cult is spreading rapidly in all parts of Himachal and Punjab. Family parties and coachloads of pilgrims come there on important festivals and many alight for a few minutes to take tea or mineral water in the *bazar* at Chaili. Until the new road was built about fifteen years ago (it has still not been surfaced) and the new bus routes opened, Chaili must have been little more than an obscure agricultural community.

It is a beautiful place. I chose the name Chaili as a pseudonyn for this village to suggest to the reader the forests of pine (*chil*) which surround it on all sides. Yet it is also poor and underdeveloped. There is, and has for long been, a shortage of cultivable land in this area. According to the Census of 1961, the acreage of cultivable land *per capita* of the population in District Hamirpur was only 0.4-0.8 acres (compared with 1.6-2.0. in District Hoshiarpur). Not surprisingly, the average size of agricultural holding per cultivating household is also small, being less than 4.0 acres in most parts of District Hamirpur (compared with 8-12 acres in District Hoshiarpur). The soil if stony and difficult to cultivate, even though the rains are adequate (around 124 cm. yearly, and hence more than Harbassi) and moderately reliable; otherwise, the climate is basically similar to that of Harbassi, allowing for somewhat lower summer temperature and an earlier onset of the monsoon. As in Punjab, the main winter crop is wheat and the main monsoon crop is maize. A little dry rice can be grown in the monsoon on some parts of the village land, but it is of inferior quality. Rice is a more popular food for everyday meals than it is in Punjab, but we are not really in rice-growing country here.

With the increase in population over the past fifty years, the only way to alleviate the demand for more land to cultivate has been to clear and terrace more forest land. Land classified as 'jungle' belongs to the government and cannot be appropriated without permission. As in Punjab, the government has made some forest land over to landless or near landless villagers, but this land is seldom of good quality. Members of the old tenant class have benefitted a little, but the ecological cost of extensive forest clearance is just beginning to be felt. The soil in Chaili is loose and stony and a good deal of the top soil is washed away every year by sudden heavy monsoon showers. When the force of the water is unimpeded by the roots of trees and other vegetation the effects are even more serious. Once the lip of a terrace has been torn away, the whole ledge is liable to crumble and collapse unless constant repairs are made. There is some public awareness of the serious nature of this prob-lem[6] – although nothing approaching an ecological lobby as yet – but the local demand for land is such that the government is hard pressed to keep the incursions (officially sanctioned and other-wise) on forest land to a minimum. Another motive for this control is the commercial value of pine resin which is extracted from the trees for industrial processing. In the woods around Chaili the bark of any pine with a girth of more than 40 cm. will be slashed to allow the sap to drip down into a cup, from which it is collected from time to time. The local forest guards are supposed to keep a strict control on the felling of trees for firewood and very little new clearance is permitted in this neighbourhood now that regular contracts for resin tapping have been issued.

The limited amount of land which is available in Chaili can only be cultivated if it is levelled and terraced. The terraces are often extremely narrow and it is out of the question to use heavy farm machinery on them. Irrigation is also virtually impossible since even if a source of water could be found, the problem of distribution would be enormous. Tube wells are a technical impossibility in this kind of area and there is no local river from which lift irrigation could easily be practiced. Even domestic water has to be fetched from a mile and a half away in the height of summer when the village wells dry up.

Another factor which has inhibited agricultural development in this area is the fact that it is cut off from any large-scale network of markets. Communications have improved since Independence, but still tend to break down in the monsoon when landslips often block roads, and many routes are closed due to the bad condition of the roads. In the past, if the peasant ever had a surplus, the only way he could dispose of it was by private sales to needy kin or neighbours, or to the local shopkeeper-cum-moneylender. This largely continues to be the case. The fact that roads now link the village to Hamirpur or Bilaspur makes little difference if there are no wholesalers prepared to collect produce from the cultivators, since the latter have no means of transport (bullock carts cannot be used in the hills). The farmers in Harbassi could choose whether to sell their produce in Harbassi itself or to dealers who transported it to Hoshiarpur, and the larger farmers could take it to Hoshiarpur themselves if they wished. Farmers in Chaili have no such choice. There are no urban markets of any size within reach of the village, even assuming they had any surplus to sell, which most of them do not. The farmers of Chaili depend upon the market economy as consumers but are poorly connected with it as producers. Chaili has what might be termed a 'balance of payments' problem, or would have did not many of its members bring in cash from employment outside the village.

Some of the better-off peasants told me that they were interested in growing cash crops but that they were prevented from experimenting by practical considerations. Citrus fruits and almonds could be grown in this area and possibly grapes and pears, but farmers would have to be assured of a market, especially for perishable products. Guarding fruit crops from wild animals (not to mention small children and other human passers-by) is also a problem. Those farmers who have a few fruit trees find that the fruit is hardly given a chance to ripen on the tree. To keep such crops under constant surveillance where fields are small and scattered would be a major problem.

In general, the prospects of increasing income either through making improvements in methods of cultivation or through changing to other kinds of crop are so unfavourable in this locality that the majority of farmers feel that their best hope for a higher standard of living lies in getting paid employment for themselves or their sons. This is in strong contrast with the peasant smallholder in Punjab, who will do both if at all possible, and indeed will probably use the proceeds of urban employment to invest in improvements for his farm.

The class structure of rural society in Himachal is somewhat different from that of Punjab. In Harbassi I identified three main groups of people involved in agriculture; the large capitalist landlords (mostly high-caste), peasant smallholders largely relying on family labour, and the petty tenants-cum-landless labourers (mostly low or scheduled caste). These are not entirely discrete groups; peasant and capitalist proprietors may also rent land from others, and labourers may acquire tiny plots with which to supplement their income. Members of all groups may derive income from urban or local employment of a non-agricultural nature.

In the part of Himachal where I worked the capitalist landowner is totally absent from village society. Originally, this part of Himachal was cultivated by small groups of proprietors, mainly Rajput by caste, who would rent out some of their land to tenants of low caste who lived in a state of semi-servitude and desperate poverty. Their landlords were not much better-off: they did not own holdings large enough to live from their rents alone and could not afford to regard themselves exempt from the indignity of physical labour, unlike Rajputs elsewhere in India (and even in some parts of Himachal). It seems that these proprietors used to let out the outlying parts of their land to low-caste tenants, keeping for their own cultivation the fields nearer to the homesteads. This general structure remains in essentials, but has been blurred somewhat by at least two factors. Firstly, holdings among the former landowners and dominant castes have been fragmented due to the expansion of population without any accompanying expansion in local economic opportunities. Secondly, a certain amount of land has been transferred to members of the old tenant class, either due to recent legislation in favour of the long-standing tenant, or due to jungle land being made available to them. But the class structure of this area has been further 'scrambled' by the fact that members of all groups have taken advantage of opportunities for urban employment. There are few households whose agricultural income is not supplemented by cash earnings from outside. This district was always an area of heavy recruitment to the Indian Army, but nowadays men work in all kinds of other occupation according to their skill and education. As few opportunities arise in the actual neighbourhood of Chaili, men must generally migrate to take up such opportunities, usually leaving their wives and children behind to tend the land. All these factors mean that it is extremely difficult to identify classes as distinct groups of people since the same individual will occupy several class positions in respected of his diverse occupations. Thus Mohan Singh (C1) owned about six acres of land, sometimes rented land from others when it suited him, had formerly worked full time for the electricity board, and now owned a modest saw mill in the village. This 'scrambling' can also be seen in Punjab, but there the division between the capitalist farmers and the rest is further accentuated by their much superior standard of consumption. Not even the wealthiest peasant in Chaili can hope to own a motor scooter and a refrigerator, items which households like that of Dalip (H2) or Romesh (H4) of Harbassi took for granted. In 1978, I could see marked changes since my stay in this area twelve years earlier. The mud houses with thatched roofs which were common in 1966, especially in the untouchable quarters, have largely been replaced by more solid stone dwellings with slate roofs. All but the most depressed of landless labourers are better-off than their parents were. But people are also aware that if they are more prosperous now, this prosperity depends mainly on the demand for labour in the cities, especially the cities of Punjab. If this demand dries up, and the migrants are thrown back to rely upon the produce of their land (assuming they have any), many families will be destitute. Their main hope lies in the expansion of Himachal's own cities. There have never been many urban centres of any size (apart from Simla) in this part of India, but with the construction of the Beas Link and other projects connected with irrigation and hydro-electric power, there is a demand for technical staff, skilled and unskilled labour from Himachal itself. The government's extensive programmes for developing the road network also provides employment for many labourers. Agricultural production is not going to be a major source of new wealth in District Hamirpur in the near future and it is more and more taken for granted that any able bodied and intelligent young man will seek work outside his village, returning to the life of an agriculturalist in late middle age.

The Sivalik foothills area has had a long history of playing the role of poor relation to Punjab. For more than 150 years this region was a part of Punjab for administrative purposes. A large part of the area had been annexed to the Punjabi empire of the Sikh monarch, Ramjit Singh, in the early nineteenth century. When the British in turn annexed Ranjit Singh's empire to their own, District Hamirpur and the adjoining districts – which together constituted the old District Kangra – continued to form a sub-division of Punjab. It was only in 1966 when the Punjab was divided into the new Punjab-speaking state of Punjab and the Hindi-speaking state of Hariana that anyone had the idea of uniting District Kangra with Himachal Pradesh. The people of District Kangra were more like the other peoples of Himachal in respect of culture, language, and economic circumstances than they ever were to the people of Punjab, and this development was welcomed with optimistic enthusiasm. At last

Paharis (hill people) would be governed by Paharis. This optimism was very soon dissipated, and there followed a number of local political wrangles which led to the old District Kangra being re-formed into several smaller districts, of which District Hamirpur is one. Villagers in Chaili still feel that they are being neglected by the government and that they do not get their fair share of the resources available, although the general anti-Punjabi feeling also continues to linger.

After 1966, when District Kangra was joined to Himachal Pradesh, there was a general exit of Punjabi government staff, although a few still remain. One of these was the overseer respon-sible for the maintenance and repair of roads around Chaili. He was a Sikh from District Jullundur who had spent a good deal of his life working in Himachal. When he was first posted in Chaili, he said, he had met a good deal of hostility, both as an outsider in general and as a Punjabi in particular. In fairness it should be said that a Punjabi coming to live in a village like Chaili would be likely to judge its people as unfriendly and suspicious. Punjabi good manners are of a more boisterous style than the reserve felt proper by Paharis, and a Pahari on his best behaviour might well seem cold to a plainsman. Similarly, a Punjabi doing his best to be friendly might be felt to be overbearing and boorish to a hill villager. I hope that in writing this I offend no Punjabi or Pahari readers, but there is much room for misunderstanding due to local differences in cultural style and con-ventions in interpersonal behaviour. I was very aware of this myself, having come straight to Chaili from Harbassi.

Punjabis also entertain a stereotype of the Pahari as a backward and impoverished hill-billy. In Harbassi, one old untouchable woman who had seen famine and dire poverty in her youth, warned me when she heard that I was shortly leaving for the hills, 'No, daughter, don't you go there. Half a fistful of lentils and a spoonful of rice is all you will get to eat and a mile's walk to the nearest spring for water. Take my advice and stay on here where you can get plenty to eat and a nice *bazar* for shopping.'

But it would not do to overemphasize the cultural differences between the two areas, in spite of the profound economic differences to which I have already referred. The style of dress, the basic items of diet, and above all the language are not widely dissimilar. I could not have managed to carry out two pieces of research within one year if I had had to learn a whole culture from scratch in the second village. I shall not risk involving myself in the debate as to the relationship of the dialect spoken in District Hamirpur to either Punjabi or Hindi or the Pahari of the higher hills. It is enough to point out that a Punjabi from Jullundur or Hoshiarpur could make himself understood without too much difficulty in Chaili and it would not take him long to follow the rhythm of local speech and pick up the distinctive local words. The categories of social life are, as we shall see, also much the same; the kinship terminology is basically similar, for example. This made my move to Chaili in 1978 less of a problem than it might have been had I chosen (as I had originally intended) to study a second village in a completely different part of north India.

People often asked us which village we enjoyed living in the most, and it was always difficult to answer. I enjoyed the bustling cosmopolitanism of Harbassi and the good-humoured, bouncy cultural style of the women there. I enjoyed our winter walks under the eucalyptus trees that bordered the roads through the fields, and even our bumpier forays on the back of the tractor.

At the same time, Chaili's parochial peace and quiet was refreshing, as well as the extreme natural beauty of its surroundings. In Punjab it seems to be *de rigueur* to stare at strangers, especially female strangers, whereas in Himachal curiosity is shown in a more restrained manner. Also, the more general acceptability of women moving about outside the home made my own fieldwork easier. So I felt less conspicuous as a foreigner in Chaili although, paradoxically, the people there were less familiar with outsiders and had less idea of what sort of place I might come from than my neighbours in Harbassi. I certainly learnt a great deal from my friends in both places and am grateful for the affection and practical help which they gave me. Whether I was able to give anything commensurate in return other than a good laugh, I do not know, but I suppose the entertainment value of the anthropologist is not to be under-estimated in a community where most forms of amusement are strictly homemade.

Carrying out two spells of fieldwork in one year was not straightforward. Twice in a year we had to settle in a strange place, get to know new neighbours, learn local ways of doing things, and make our objectives known to our new acquaintances. On each occasion there were all the practical tasks of removing our household paraphernalia, locating suppliers of daily necessities like milk or fuel, finding the most convenient local bank for cashing travellers' cheques, etc. It is also difficult to write about two separate places in the space of one monograph. It is not an easy matter for the anthropologist to convey in depth the character of even one location vividly to the reader while also keeping in view the theoretical problems which he or she set out to resolve. To convey the character of two, so as to make comparisons between them, is even harder. How do I know whether, for the reader who has little prior knowledge of India, the basic *sameness* of Chaili and Harbassi will not override any attempt of mine to convey the differences.[7] And to the reader who is familiar with India or to the ethnographic literature, how do I know that it is not the profound *differences* between the two villages which will impress themselves, in spite of their many similarities? I hope that in this chapter I have managed to establish something of the character of each village so that the mental bus-rides between the two which I shall ask the reader to make in the following account will not prove too confusing or exhausting.

## Notes

1  Virilocal marriage means a system of marriage where the couple normally reside in the *husband*'s household or village. Village exogamy refers to the rule that one must seek a spouse from outside one's own village.
2  This methodology could be compared with that of Bott in her study of English families (Bott 1957).
3  For an excellent account of the local consequences of economic change in Punjab, see Kessinger's historical study of a Punjab village (Kessinger 1974).
4  Share cropping is still a common form of tenancy in Punjab. The rates vary; landowners usually claim about 55 per cent of the crop harvest, but on some estates where the landowner had provided fertilizer and irrigation facilities the tenant would pay as much as 75 per cent of the total yield to the landlord.
5  The wage for unskilled farm labour fluctuates according to season and area, but during my stay never rose above Rs 9 per day for male labourers and Rs 5 for women.
6  See 'Crisis in the Himalayas', D.M. Kalapesi, *Sunday Standard*, 14 May, 1978.

# 3 Women, territory, and property

I am now going to describe two aspects of women's general social roles in North India which are very relevant if we wish to identify the part which women play in production, for they help to define women's position as dependants of men. They are (a) the relationship between women and territory (space considered as a social rather than as a geographical reality), and (b) the relationship between women and property, especially land.

Women in North India are expected to marry outside their own villages, and a bride moves to her husband's village on marriage. She belongs to her parents' village (*peke*) in a different way from her husband's village (*saure*) and different kinds of behaviour are required of her according to where she is, i.e. according to whether her role of daughter or of daughter-in-law predominates. More general norms subject all women to restraints in their use of public space to which they are not subjected in their use of private domestic space, and limit their independent movements in the conduct of everyday social life.

In relation to property, women are defined as dependent because they only have access to the most important forms of wealth-producing property via their relations with men. Women are largely disqualified from exercising direct control over the most important form of property (land) by inheritance rules which favour male heirs, and this disqualification is related to their roles as wives and sisters. A good sister does not claim the land which her brother might inherit. A good wife participates in the control which her husband exercises over any land he may own, but does not command rights in land independently of his family.

The relationships between women, property, and territory comprise a complex of norms which are elaborate, without always being elaborated. They belong to the level of the implicit in the moral life of the village but need to be spelt out here if we are to understand why women remain dependent upon men in spite of legislation and other social measures which ought to favour their independence.

## Women and territory

Villagers account for the practice of village exogamy with reference to two main set of ideas. Firstly, there is the principle that, if possible, the bridegroom should be someone whom the bride has never before had the opportunity to meet.[1] The most honourable form of marriage is that where there is no element of prior sexual attraction between the partners. There should also be the appearance of maximum trust between the two families, and hence the minimum need actually to subject the boy or girl to any kind of 'looking over' (although this almost always does take place in practice, however discreetly disguised as a casual social visit). In so far as geographical spread is also an advantage, all these considerations favour the interpretation of the rule of village exogamy to mean not just marriage *outside* the village but marriage at a *distance* from it.

Secondly, there is the notion that all boys and girls born or brought up in the same village are in some sense brothers and sisters. Marriage within one's own village would be vaguely incestuous, and certainly in bad taste, even if no known relationship can be established between the two young people concerned. The idea that people brought up together or in close proximity are like brother and sister is often extended to include boys and girls living in adjacent villages, or to children who attend the same school. In fact, a circular process of reasoning is at work which operates to exclude any possibility of young people arranging their own unions and to keep marriage-making firmly in the control of the parents and their kin: girls should not marry boys who stand in the relation of 'brother' to them; any boy whom a girl meets must be defined as being like a brother to her; a marriage with a boy whom she already knows is like marriage to a brother and, therefore, inappropriate.

Not all women marry over long distances, but most move out of their own immediate neighbourhood at marriage. All married women have two homes – *peke* (village of one's own parents and natal kin) and *saure* (village of one's husband and in-laws). A married woman's ties with her *peke* become attenuated in later life, especially if she has neither parents nor brothers still living there. But the contrast between the kinds of experience associated with *peke* and *saure* is central to a woman's knowledge of the social structure. Before marriage a girl is reared by her parents in the knowledge that some day she must leave them. At marriage she joins the household of her husband, a household of strangers where she has no automatic claims to love and respect, and will only receive them to the extent that she conforms to the norms governing the role of daughter-in-law. This involves self-effacement and deference to all her husband's contemporaries and senior kin. She must be on her best behaviour and hope to earn her in-laws' approval. As she grows older and accedes to a senior position in her *saure*, she can claim indulgences and authority to which she cannot aspire as a young bride, but her behaviour in her *saure* must always be constrained compared with her position of privileged affection in her parents' home. Anyone who travels in the same bus as a young woman making the journey between her *saure* and her *peke* can observe the lively expression of these contrasting modes of behaviour. As the woman gets into the bus she has her head covered, behaves in a very subdued manner and bids farewell to her husband's relatives respectfully by touching their feet. As the bus nears her parents' village and the familiar landmarks appear, she becomes more relaxed. If none of her husband's kinsmen are on the bus with her, she allows her veil to slip and reveal her hair without tugging it back hastily out of respect. As she alights, she seems a different person from the deferential creature who started out, greeting her kin and friends with exuberant embraces.

But there are also other constraints upon a woman's behaviour in public which are not related to the distinction between *peke* and *saure*, and which are effective wherever she finds herself. Conceived as social space, any village can be zoned according to the degree of 'publicness' assigned to different areas. Women, whether daughters or daughters-in-law of the village, enjoy least freedom in those areas which are defined as most public. The first thing that I was told in Harbassi was that women (especially high-caste women) do not go to the *bazar*. The reasons given were usually of the order of 'Men go there to drink and you never know whom you will meet', or 'There are bad characters hanging about there'. The *bazar* is perhaps at the bottom of the league in terms of how far women feel that it is safe and dignified for them to venture there. Many women of course, must visit the *bazar*; they could not manage if they did not. But they hurry about their business there and return home briskly. They do not choose the *bazar* as a meeting place for the exchange of news and gossip in the way that men do. For Chaili's more modest *bazar*, the same holds true. Most village women have to go there from time to time, but they are unwilling to be seen hanging about there and feel self-consciously aware that they are in male territory. The house in which I stayed was one of a cluster of Brahman houses at the lower end of the *bazar*, built with their backs to the main street and looking out over the fields. But when my neighbour Vidya accompanied me to visit other women, she would always insist that we took a very circuitous route to the other end of the village, via a steep and sometimes muddy path through the fields, rather than walk through the *bazar* itself.

Not all villages have a *bazar*; indeed many hamlets in both the areas in which I studied had no main public thoroughfare. They simply consisted of a group of houses clustered higgledy-piggledy around the intersection of a few rough footpaths. In such non-nucleated villages, one area of the settlement cannot really be said to be more public than another. But where roads are metalled, shops established, and bus routes developed, the domain of the public is extended.

Jungle land, i.e. waste land lying between the cultivated fields of one village and the next, is like the *bazar* in that it is also a category of space which women should avoid, but for somewhat different reasons. It is avoided not because it is public, but because it is lonely. The euphemistic statements of villagers about the need for girls to avoid 'jungly' places refer basically to the fear of sexual molestation. If a woman were molested in the jungle, there would be no-one nearby to come to her help. Or, if a man claimed that he had taken advantage of her in the jungle there would be no-one either to corroborate her denial or to attest that it was not she who had invited his attentions. Just as there are 'no-go' areas for 'respectable' women in some European cities, so the jungle is a 'no-go' area for village women. Many women have to go to the jungle in the course of their work, to cut grass, to graze cattle, to cut wood. But they do not go there unnecessarily.

In Himachal Pradesh the tracts of wild land between the villages are very extensive and are avoided by men as well as women since they are believed by many to be the haunts of ghosts and spirits. In Harbassi the formerly quite extensive areas of jungle have now been reduced to narrow strips of scrubby, rough grazing land, but the moral categorization of jungle land is the same as in Himachal. In both areas older villagers explained that girls had not been sent to school in their young days because parents had been unwilling to allow their daughters to walk to school through the jungle. Even today, the long distances that children in some villages have to travel to school present a special problem for girls. Boys may be cheerfully sent off to make their way down several miles of dusty tracks through the forest, but there is still the feeling that women who value their reputation will avoid lonely places.

For a village woman, the place where she feels most confident and relaxed is her own courtyard and house, however constraining the etiquette she must observe to senior members of the household. Soon after I came to live in Harbassi, Santosh (H1) told me that she 'hardly ever stirred beyond these four walls'. I took this to be a comment on the circumscription of her life now that her husband was dead and her children living elsewhere. Later I realized that it had been said in a spirit of pride. She did not need to stir beyond her own four walls. A good woman is one who stays at home as far as she can. Or rather, if she does go out she must be seen to have a purpose (fetching fodder, shopping for food, paying a ceremonial visit, etc.). All the women in Chaili, and all but a few landlords' wives in Harbassi, do have to go out, and many times a day at that. It is idle and purposeless 'wandering about' that is condemned in practice. One woman in Chaili asked me whether my husband did not object to me 'wandering from place to place'. She herself, a primary school teacher, travelled further each day to work than I did, but what I regarded as the purposeful pursuit of field data looked to her suspiciously like hanging about with no more legitimate business than gossip. A woman must have recognizable business to justify her free movement in public places.[2]

One's own land is regarded as a kind of extension of the home, and so women can move about in their own fields with confidence in their right to be seen there. Even some high-status women in Harbassi, who were otherwise very circumspect about being seen in public, moved about freely and openly on their own estates. One large capitalist farmer's wife, who seldom stepped into the streets of Harbassi without a shawl wrapped discreetly about her shoulders and her eyes cast modestly down, used to go by car to her estate to watch the construction of a tube well. She would have a cot pulled up in the shade of the trees that lined the road and would sit there keeping an eye on the operations. It was not so much the public gaze itself that she shunned so much as being seen in public without some specific and ostensible purpose.

These rules are observed with differing degrees of rigour. As I have said, women of poor households cannot send servants to the *bazar* and they have to go out into the fields to work. They cannot even remotely approximate to the ideal of the purdah lady who stays at home 'within her four walls' and is never seen out of doors, though most of them would claim to subscribe to it. But they observe the spirit of the rules through their very circumspect behaviour in those parts of the village which are regarded as most public. It may be difficult for male readers to appreciate that what I am talking about here in somewhat vague and intangible terms has real social consequences. Women will know what I am talking about if they have ever stepped into what in our culture is regarded as male territory unaccompanied by a male (I still feel out of place if I enter a public house without a group of friends, and avoid pubs for this reason). I would argue that the purdah ideal has consequences of this kind even for women who cannot possibly observe actual seclusion. The body language and style of interaction of village women who are obliged to cross public spaces informs us that they do not feel free to use these spaces in the casual manner permitted to men, for the exchange of information, for political discussion, to make deals, and strike bargains. As we shall see, they find alternative venues and alternative modes of tapping local information networks, but the constraint which they must exercise in their use of public space has important effects on their economic and political roles in the local community.

The wives of high-status landowners in Harbassi, I was told, observed almost total seclusion until about thirty years ago. One woman recounted that 'if we went out at all we wore heavy shawls over our saris, pulled down to cover our faces'. These women are still the most restricted in their local movements. Yet so far as Harbassi is concerned, the interesting thing is that these high-status women are paradoxically also the most travelled and cosmopolitan. The restrictions on being seen in public operate most strongly in one's own village (whether *saure* or *peke*) and are less important in other places where one's family is not known and has no reputation to safeguard. Many women of this class accompany husbands employed in the professions, the army, or administration to the towns where they work. When one is not in 'one's own place' (*apni jegeh*) one's neighbours do not have the same power to sanction. In large towns there is in any case an anonymity about public places which make women less unwilling to venture into them, still providing always that they have some business or purpose. Kaushalya (H2), who seldom ventured out in Harbassi except to her own estate, would from time to time take a little shopping trip to Hoshiarpur with her daughter. They would take the opportunity to buy clothes or households goods not easily obtainable in Harbassi, perhaps also visiting a cinema or calling on friends before taking the bus home again. Saroja (H4) is a highly educated woman, well travelled and sophisticated in outlook. She hardly ever goes out when she is in Harbassi itself, but she quite frequently travels to distant towns to lecture on religious topics to gatherings of the Hindu sect to which she belongs. She is quite used to making journeys of 100 kilometres or more, alone if necessary, and yet would regard a stroll to the local shops as out of the question.

These principles regarding the mobility of women in public places have to be respected by all women, but the rules sit more lightly on some categories of women than on others. Women classified as daughters of the village, i.e. who were born there rather than married there, are allowed somewhat more latitude. One of my closest friends in Harbassi was an elderly school teacher, Roshani (H5), who had left her husband many years before when her children were tiny and had ever since lived in the village of her birth. She would walk about quite freely, gossiping with shopkeepers and greeting the parents of children studying in her class. No-one ever criticized her for this, indeed she was highly respected. But such freedom is only allowed to mature women who return to their *peke* after marriage. An unmarried girl would have to behave much more circumspectly if she is not to ruin her chances of a good marriage. Elderly women may also be allowed more latitude, and in the case of Roshani it was her seniority as much as her status as daughter of the village which enabled her to take liberties with the rules that restricted other women.

The women to whom these rules apply most stringently are the young married women in their *saure*. The young wife must adhere with the utmost fidelity to the forms of etiquette and deference which apply to women in general if she is not to earn the censure of her in-laws. Out of deference to her elders, a young wife will not claim greater freedom than her mother-in-law. Lata, Santosh's daughter-in-law, normally lived outside Harbassi in the small town where her husband was employed as a factory manager. She told me:

> 'I get so bored when I come here (Harbassi). It is all right for a few days, but then you long to go out and meet people. But if my mother-in-law does not like to go out much, it is not for me to suggest it. In X (where she and her husband lived) we have so many friends and almost every evening we meet other families or go for a walk together.'

When, in addition to restrictions on her movement outside the home, a young wife has to observe a quite elaborate code of etiquette and avoidance out of respect to her elders within the home, it is no wonder that in the early years of marriage the *saure* is regarded as a place where one cannot feel fully at ease.

In agricultural families where circumstances will not permit all the women staying at home, there is often an informal division of labour by which tasks which involve moving outside the home are done by senior women, so that the junior women stay at home. When Bhagat Ram (C11), a Chaili farmer, was away working in the city, his wife would make any necessary trips to the *bazar* or other public places, and his young daughter-in-law would busy herself with tasks around the house and in the family's fields. In Harbassi, Mahinder Kaur (H9) had worked out a similar system. She herself would do work such as taking the food to the men working in the fields, selling surplus milk to neighbours. Her daughter-in-law seldom stepped outside the house, her main tasks being the cooking and caring for the children.

What sanctions support this restriction of women to the private sphere and what does a woman risk by violating them? Where unmarried women are concerned the sanction which helps control all aspects of their behaviour in public is the fear that they will be unacceptable as wives if they do anything which might possibly mar their reputations. A woman who remained unmarried because no man chose her would not just suffer a private tragedy but would also be a blot on the entire family's prestige or honour (*izzat*)[3], and therefore girls are always counselled to err on the side of caution if they are in doubt as to how to behave. One young village girl in Harbassi, who earned her living by doing tailoring work for people in her village, told me that a Jat family in a nearby village had summoned her to take the measurements for a suit for one of the women. But the mother had advised her against going even if it meant forgoing the money she might have earned, she should ask the women to call at her home for the fitting because 'people might talk if they saw you wandering about there where you don't know anyone'.

For married women it is still the *izzat* of the family which is at stake, but here it is the *izzat* of the husband's family. What wife will wish to risk having to live with the disapproval of her husband and parents-in-law if they believe that her lack of circumspection in public has tarnished the reputation of their household?

## Women and property

The norms regarding women's relationship to property are in some ways more difficult to study than the norms regarding women's use of territory, yet in other ways easier. They are simpler to study to the extent that the basic rules are more explicitly recognized and easier for the anthropologist to identify. On the other hand, there is not one set of rules here, but at least two – the statutory law of the modern state, and the customary law of particular localities.

Customary Hindu and Sikh practice in both Himachal and Punjab precluded women from inheriting land as daughters, except in the absence of sons. The convention was that they received their shares of the patrimony at the time of marriage in the form of dowry. Recent legislation, the Hindu Succession Act of 1956, has enabled daughters, widows, and mothers to inherit land on an equal footing with sons but in practice few women exercise this right, least of all daughters. Immoveable property is still more usually inherited by sons, divided equally among them at the death of their father, or at some time subsequent to his death.

I think that the convention that women inherit moveable property at marriage in lieu of the immoveable property which their brothers receive later is a convenient fiction which serves to obscure a real difference between men's and women's relationship to property.

Anthropologists who have regarded dowry as a form of *ante mortem* inheritance (Goody and Tambiah 1973: 17) have tended to accept this fiction uncritically. The reason for this is probably that they have paid more attention to legal codes and summaries of custom than to the processes of gift making at weddings or partition at funerals. Attention to actual practice will reveal that it is only useful to regard dowry as a form of inheritance if we use the term 'inheritance' in a very general sense indeed. In this loose sense, a birthday present to my daughter purchased out of the savings in my bank could equally be regarded as a form of *ante mortem* inheritance. What we can quite legitimately say is that the dowry gift purchases the cancellation of the daughter's automatic right to inherit when she has brothers to whom her hypothetical share can be made over.

There are two very obvious differences in the way in which moveable goods are transferred to daughters and the way in which land is transferred to sons. Firstly, daughters never receive *all* the moveable property of their parents. The goods allocated to them as dowry were usually made or bought specially for the purpose and the parents' own goods and chattels remain to be inherited by the sons and their wives. Dowries are not conceived as shares in a specific (but partible) body of property, nor could they practically be treated in this way, since sisters are married and allocated dowry over time. The value of any one sister's dowry will depend principally on the wealth and circumstances of the household during the period immediately preceding her marriage. Also, while parents will not wish to be unfair to any particular daughter, ensuring that the bride has a dowry of similar value to those received by her sisters is not the prime consideration at the time of marriage. More important questions are how much the bridegroom's family will expect and how much is it necessary to give in order to maintain the family's current level of prestige (and to improve it if possible). If there are many daughters it is quite likely that they will not receive equal portions in their dowries. One woman in Chaili grumbled that her parents had given her less than her younger sister, who had had a very grand marriage, because (she said) the younger sister had been the parents' favourite. But as she regarded herself as having got the better husband of the two, she did not make too much of her grievance. I certainly never heard of any daughter taking her parents or sisters to court on the grounds that she had not received her fair share of the family property. Brothers, on the other hand, will frequently assert their claims to equal shares of the patrimony in a court of law, and it is recognized that they are entitled to do so. So although people will say that daughters receive their share of the family property at marriage as dowry as a kind of *ante mortem* substitute for the land which they cannot inherit, in practice dowry is treated as a passport to a good match, a high-status husband, and the favour of one's in-laws.

A second consideration is the fact that property gifted as dowry is not transferred directly to the bride. A daughter does not gain control over this property in the way that a son gains control over land on the partition of his father's estate. The dowry is transferred to the bridegroom's parents and may well be redistributed by them to a wide circle of kin. Some will certainly be earmarked as belonging to the newlywed couple, but it belongs to the *couple* rather than to the bride as an individual. As one Chamar woman in Harbassi said, 'The real meaning of dowry is that if the household is divided, if the girl and her husband quarrel with his family, or if the husband gets a job somewhere else, then they have two saucepans and a bed to set up home on their own.' This aspect of dowry, as a form of security for the young couple, is possibly not one that wealthy villagers are most aware of, but this element is certainly present in all dowry giving. Parents-in-law will not deny the right of a couple to take with them household articles from the wife's dowry should they need to set up home separately, but the initial allocation of goods given as dowry will certainly be in the parents-in-law's hands. They will effectively decide what proportion of the goods will be regarded as gifts to the whole family, to be shared out among the siblings of the groom and his aunts and cousins, and which are to be regarded as the property of the couple themselves.

This lack of control on the part of a bride over her own dowry is a very important aspect of the Hindu/Sikh dowry system and one which distinguishes it from superficially similar systems. Friedl for instance, asserts that Greek women in Vasilika owe much of their domestic power to the land they bring to their husbands' households as dowry.

'The economic power of women lies in their ability to bring land into the household as part of their dowry and to maintain control of that land which cannot be alienated by their husbands without their consent or, in some cases, without the consent of their fathers' brothers or guardians. The trousseau and the household goods a woman brings with her add to the prestige of the new household but only indirectly to its ability to produce income.'

Therefore men sought wives who would bring land to their family as well as domestic goods, but if they obtained such wives they also had to accept that as husbands they would not necessarily obtain total and unmediated control over this land (Friedl 1967: 105). The property which an Indian village woman brings to her marriage as dowry is not usually 'income generating' property in the sense that land is, and it is not necessarily the case that she will enjoy personal control over it. Even her husband's control over it is likely to be subordinate to that of his parents so long as the latter are alive. A new bride's very subordinate position in the household and the submissive attitude which she must adopt, makes it out of the question for her to assert control at the very point in time at which she would have to intervene if she wished ever to maintain her right to dispose of dowry as she properly wished. The new bride must politely and timidly turn her head the other way as her husband's kin divide up the goods she has brought with her from her father's house, and etiquette demands that she make no comment whatsoever on the procedure. In North-West India then, dowry property can only enhance a woman's position in the household in so far as it engenders respect for her parents and her family. It does not provide her with any more tangible source of power in her husband's household.

The only items of property which are explicitly and directly transferred to the bride herself at the wedding are the gifts made to her by her husband's family. They will usually consist of personal ornaments, clothes for her to wear during the first months of marriage (usually as elaborate and expensive as the groom's family can afford). The jewelry with which her parents deck her at her wedding can also be considered as a personal gift and will certainly not be redistributed among her husband's kin (although the dowry may include other items of jewelry or personal adornment which are intended for redistribution).

A word should perhaps be said about jewelry as a category of property. Girls do not wear jewelry of any value before they are married; even wealthy girls usually have to make do with plastic bangles before they are wed. At marriage the bride's parents should give her a full set of ornaments, and so should her husband's family. A 'full set' is interpreted as consisting of at least the following items: necklace, ear-rings, bangles, and nose-ring. In Himachal various kinds of head ornaments used to be included although these are now regarded as rather old-fashioned. Clearly, poor families cannot afford to provide a full set of gold ornaments for their daughters, and even a full set of silver ornaments may be beyond their means, but some part of the full set will be given. In theory a woman's jewelry is her personal property, a category of *stridhana*, female wealth, yet it has been observed that women seldom have full control over this important category of property. Luschinsky writes of the women of an Uttar Pradesh village that:

> 'according to an ideal of village family life, all major types of family property are to be held in common by family members. Women of Madhopur say that the jewelry they receive at marriage is their own, but they would never dispose of it without permission and they would have no right to protest if the family head were to sell it in time of need. They are unaware of the concept of *stridhana* and if they were aware of it, they would hardly be expected to demand their rights' (Luschinsky 1963: 582).

I tried to discover whether the same applied to women in Himachal and Punjab. The following statements are representative of women's attitudes in the areas I studied:

Jivan Kaur (H10): 'A woman can gift jewelry to her daughter in her lifetime, usually at the time of her wedding. Otherwise, what she possesses at the time of her death will go automatically to her daughter-in-law, not her daughter. The woman's daughters have no rights in the mother's jewelry once they are married. A woman cannot alienate her jewelry in practice. It is here but she should not part with it except to her daughters or daughters-in-law. If poverty forced her to do so, then it would be a matter for the whole family to decide.'

Mahinder Kaur (H9): 'A woman can give her jewelry to her daughter or to her daughter-in-law. At her death it belongs to her husband's family. Usually her daughters-in-law will receive it. But it is family property.'

Durgi (C2): 'A woman's jewelry is hers to dispose of, whether it was gifted to her by her parents or by her parents-in-law. But who would she want to give it to, other than her own daughters or daughters-in-law? She will keep her own jewelry to save money in the children's marriages. Often children wonder what their mother has in store (i.e. they will secretly expect to receive something at her death). If they think she has a lot of jewelry they will be nice to her and curry favour with her. She need not consult her husband about the disposal of her jewelry.'

Taking these three statements alone, we find some disagreement about the extent to which jewelry is genuinely a woman's own to do as she likes with. Himachal women were slightly more likely to describe women's rights in their jewelry as exclusive and inalienable, although it should be added that only recently has it been the practice in villages like Chaili for peasant families to give substantial amounts of jewelry in marriage.

Women in wealthy families in Punjab are likely to acquire jewelry after marriage through investing money which they have saved bit by bit from cash given to them by their husbands. Thus Satto (H8) accompanied me to Harbassi one day with Rs 400 in her pocket, which she had saved over a period of time. This she intended to spend on jewelry which she would give to her daughters-in-law. The jewelry was hers but, as Durgi said, to whom would a woman want to give jewelry other than to her own daughters or daughters-in-law?

A woman has an immediate control over jewelry which she does not have, say, over family land which will be registered in the name of the male head of the household. But she is expected to exercise her right of disposal over this property within strict limits. It is, after all, an inflation-proof family investment, and should not be sold or gifted outside the household without consulting the other members of the family. And in times of dire need there is no question but that the jewelry of the women folk is regarded as a common resource to be drawn on for the sake of the whole family, although in popular culture it is represented as the ultimate form of economic degradation for the women to have to part with their jewels. That jewelry is regarded as a family resource can be seen from public reactions to an incident which occurred in a village near Chaili. The wife of a wealthy Rajput had died under very distressing circumstances. She had been suffering from cancer and had been operated on unsuccessfully. She survived only ten days after the operation and died in hospital. There was, her family alleged, some kind of confusion at the hospital when her husband went to collect her body for cremation, as it seems that he was given the body of another woman who had died in the hospital on the same day. On enquiry, they discovered that his wife had been cremated by the relatives of this other woman. But the aspect of this affair which aroused the most comment was the fact that the dead woman's family had never had the opportunity to remove her jewelry from her body and that hence the entire family were prevented from recovering a valuable resource to which they were collectively entitled.

Although women customarily did not inherit land, and most of them still do not in spite of modern legislation which permits them to do so, many women will speak of land as though this discrimination did not exist. A woman will talk about 'my land' or 'our land', referring to land held in the name of her father or by her husband's family. Women do not speak as though they felt excluded from ownership. But land is not regarded as though it belonged to individuals *qua* individuals anyway. In fact no major form of property is regarded in this way, and this is perhaps why it is difficult to disentangle women's specific rights in items like jewelry and other goods given in dowry from the family's more general rights in them. Ideally, any substantial or valuable item of property is a resource which may nominally be held by an individual, but from which all the other members of the household might expect to benefit were the family in difficulties. So while land is registered in the name of the male head of the household, he is regarded as holding property on behalf of the other members, male and female. In this broad sense it is as much theirs as his, but of course he has immediate control over it and it cannot be alienated or divided unless he agrees. In this respect, women are only in the same position as junior men who have not yet attained the position of head of a household. But a woman knows that she will never be in such a position; her control over property held on her behalf will always be indirect.

The exception to this general expectation is the case of the widow who inherits her husband's land while her sons are still minors, a right conferred by the Hindu Women's Property Act of 1937. Until 1956 this inheritance was strictly conditional. She could not alienate the land and in effect she merely acted as custodian of it until her sons grew up. A widow who had no children was unlikely to be able to claim the property in practice, exercising only the right to maintenance for herself from her husband's family which custom had always permitted. If she had small children it might still be difficult for her to assert her right to take over the land on their behalf unless her own kinsmen were prepared to help her put up a fight. Otherwise her husband's kinsmen were likely to put every obstacle in the way of her registering the land in her own name. A dispute which occurred in a wealthy Harbassi family illustrates the resistance to a widow's control over land. My informant's father-in-law had a brother who died childless in about 1950. When the father-in-law also died and the entire property was divided, the brother's widow claimed that half of the patrimony should go to her to enjoy during her lifetime. After that, it would revert to her nephews. But her nephews disputed her claim and a law suit dragged on for some years. The three nephews themselves were somewhat divided over the issue. The eldest was adamant that as his aunt had no children she had no right to register land in her name, since there could be no question of her acting as custodian for non-existent heirs. The two youngest brothers had been less enthusiastic over the law suit, or so they claimed, since they considered that their aunt was unlikely to sell the land. It would come to them eventually in any case, so why grudge their aunt control over it during her lifetime? The court decided in favour of the aunt, although the two youngest brothers suspected that the eldest, who had supervised the partition of the property, had managed to get some of the land that should have gone to their aunt registered in his own name.

Even nowadays a widow with children may have difficulty in claiming what she is entitled to. Hitchcock and Minturn cite the case of a Rajput widow in a Uttar Pradesh village (Hitchcock and Minturn 1963: 234). She had one daughter, and when she decided to manage her husband's estate on her own, her husband's kinsmen beat her up. The authors mention two factors which are likely to motivate such a violent reaction. Firstly, with daughters now entitled by law to inherit from a widowed mother there is a real possibility that land which might otherwise have reverted to the husband's collaterals will eventually pass to the control of outsiders (the widow's son-in-law). This could not have happened when the widow had merely enjoyed the right to maintenance from her husband's estate because although she might have enjoyed a good deal of control over how the land was managed and the produce disposed of, she would not have been able to alienate it or to will it to anyone else. Secondly, a widow who controls property she has inherited on her own will almost certainly have to violate the rules of purdah (which Rajputs on the whole take very seriously, especially in this part of India). This is a real problem. Sumi Sridharan, writing of a village in another part of uttar Pradesh, mentions the cases of several widows who had inherited land but who depended heavily on others for help in crucial matters such as selling the produce in the market (Sridharan 1975: 46), and who therefore cannot be said to enjoy the same degree of control over their property as a man.

The right to inherit land as a widow has not always been easy for a woman to assert in practice. Yet this was, and to a large extent still is, almost the only way in which she can inherit land directly. The only other possibility for female inheritance of land has been the case of the woman who has no brothers. In the absence of sons, land could go to daughters rather than to male collaterals, though this principle has not always prevented male collaterals from staking their claims. Tambiah notes that in parts of North-West India the practice of uxorilocal residence (i.e. residence of a married couple in the wife's village) was, in effect, a means of anticipating this kind of inheritance. The *gharjamai* (uxorilocal husband) is unusual in both Himachal (see Parry 1979: 169) and Punjab, although there were a few cases in the neighbourhood of Chaili of men who had come to live in their wives' villages *after* the wives had inherited land from their parents.[4] But Tambiah has identified the principle which underlies this practice, namely that 'the uxorilocal son-in-law institution is similar to the appointed daughter arrangement, in that the logic of both lies in the production of an heir (grandson) who will inherit the estate' (Goody and Tambiah 1973: 84). So whether the land of a man who died without sons is actually registered in the name of his daughter or in that of her husband, the practice is essentially similar to the practice of allowing the widow the control of her husband's estate during the minority of her sons, that is, it is a custodial form of inheritance. The inheritance of land by a woman represents an interruption of the ideal pattern of inheritance of land by males from males. Such interruptions are unavoidable given that men cannot choose when they die any more than they can choose the sex of their children, but as soon as possible the ideal of men inheriting from men is asserted again. There is certainly no question of females inheriting land from females, in the normal way of things, though I suppose it could happen in the event of an only daughter bearing female children only and being widowed while these children were still young. (Jewelry is the only kind of property in which female lines can be established.)

In the areas I studied, a daughter who inherits land generally has a choice between two alternatives. She could move to her parents' village with her husband. But this would only be practical if she had inherited a large amount of land, or substantially more than her husband stood to inherit in his own village. There were no cases of this in my field material. If this were to happen, it is unlikely that the daughter would actually manage the land, for what man would consent to settle in his wife's village, where he is a stranger, on these terms? The other alternative would be for her to rent it to tenants and enjoy the income from the land. This would be worthwhile if the amount was fairly substantial, but the problems of recovering rents from small and distant land holdings are often so great as to cancel out the benefit. (Remember that women are always married out of their parents' village, and often at quite long distances.) If neither of these alternatives is practicable, another possibility is to gift it to some male collateral, or perhaps to sell it to a male collateral making the sale look like a gift. This alternative is likely to be attractive to an only daughter. The very fact that she has no brothers deprives her of an important source of moral and material support which may be useful to her in case of marital disputes or widowhood. By gifting the land or selling it at less than its market value to an uncle's son she may expect to build up good will and obligation which may be useful to her at some future point in the absence of a real brother. This was the solution adopted by Durgi (C2). She told me, 'I received land at my father's death as I had no brothers. I gave it to the son of my father's brother. I took a little money from him, but otherwise I did it for *khushi*' (out of gladness, i.e. as a free gesture of goodwill).

Goodwill between brothers and sisters is an important principle, and a cousin will count as a brother in a situation like this. This principle of solidarity between brothers and sisters is often given as a reason why daughters seldom claim their share of the patrimony even though the Hindu Succession Act now entitles them to do so (Luschinsky 1963: 581). Most of the traditional practices described in this section are still observed in spite of very radical changes in the laws regarding property rights of women among Hindus and Sikhs. As one old lady in Harbassi put it:

'If a brother and sister are on good terms then the sister will not take her share. She will tell her brother that she does not want her share of the inheritance. After all, if he eats, then she can eat' (i.e. the sister will benefit by the brother's prosperity as he will then help her). 'If he does not eat, how will that benefit the sister? If the brother had a lot of property already and she was poor, then I suppose it might be all right for her to claim her share.'

As I shall show in a subsequent chapter, for a sister the goodwill of her brothers is important to her after her parents' death, and a woman will prefer to be in a position to be able to call on her brothers for help of any kind should she need it after her marriage. This right may be of more advantage to her than the material gain she might obtain from inheriting a share in her father's land along with them, so she may well prefer to trade the latter for the former. There is every pressure to prevent her from claiming her share, or to put it more realistically, there is little incentive for her to insist on her share, in the face of an ideology which regards her as having already received her share of her parents' property at her marriage.

We can get an idea of how this legislation has affected women's willingness to claim the shares they inherit by looking at holdings in one hamlet near Harbassi, on which I have detailed information. In this settlement there was a total of 615 acres of cultivated land divided (very unequally) among forty-three proprietors. Four of these were women, and none of them held less than sixteen acres. Among the small proprietors, most of whom had emerged only recently from the tenant-labourer category, no daughters or widows had land registered in their names. Of the four women proprietors, not one controlled the land or farmed it herself, although one widow did share some of the management work with her son. Two women who had inherited as daughters had their land managed by their brothers along with the land the brothers themselves had inherited. The fourth woman held fifty-seven acres and her husband (a factory manager in Chandigarh) owned another twelve, and their holdings were managed as one estate by a friend who acted as agent for that family and for several other absentee proprietors.

On the other hand, there are nowadays certain other pressures which encourage the equal inheritance of daughters among the larger landowners. Where land ceiling legislation threatens the integrity of a substantial estate, the sons who inherit may prefer to register equal shares of the land in their sisters' names in order to avoid risking the confiscation of extra land. Thus when Santosh's husband died, the land he left was divided among his two sons and two daughters equally, with a share reserved for Santosh herself. An eighty-acre estate divided in five equal shares could hardly attract the attention of government. However, it continued to be managed as one estate by Santosh and her two sons. One daughter was married and resident in Canada; the other was a student and took no interest in the management of the land. What would happen to the daughters' shares eventually I do not know.

The moral of all this is that if we want to understand how property rights actually work, we have to look at customary patterns of practice and the values they presuppose, as well as what is on the statute books. What actually takes place is the product of the interaction between all these different sets of rules. But what is remarkable in north Indian society is that even in communities where women's right to inherit property is acknowledged by ancient custom or religious laws, there are still countervailing pressures which prevent women from actually claiming this right. Jeffery notes that among Muslim women in Delhi most women waive their claim to the share of their fathers' property to which they are entitled by Islamic law, and for the very same reasons for which many Hindu women waive the right to inherit granted by modern legislation. It is more important to these women to consider their brothers' needs than their own, since it is the brother who will send gifts to a woman in her husband's home, and who will receive her back if she is divorced (Jeffery 1979: 56). The ideological priority given to women's relations of dependence with both brothers and husbands prevents them from becoming (or even wanting to become) independent property holders, even where there is no institutional or legal obstacle to their doing so.

Women continue to stand in quite a different relationship to property from men. It is not a relationship of total exclusion, since there are circumstances in which a woman may hold land, and it is likely that these circumstances will become more common. But frequently a woman's holding is either nominal (i.e. land is registered in her name, but it is managed by her husband or some other male relative) or conditional (she holds it until a male heir is produced or reaches maturity). As I shall show later, many women in fact exercise considerable control over land which is formally registered in the name of a male, especially where the migration of males means that women have to take over the active day-to-day management of land.

But the ideology which specifies that land is primarily a male form of property helps to define women's position in the family as primarily one of dependence. Even if she can modify that dependence to some extent, so long as land remains the main type of wealth-generating property she is still dependent in that she can gain access to it only via her relationship with men.

In this chapter I have dealt with women's position in the family and community in terms which have been largely negative, in terms of their exclusion from public space and from the control of property. Their positive role in production and in the control of family resources will be dealt with subsequently. It is important to delineate these negative principles at the outset since they provide the boundaries within which women are obliged to operate and which define in advance the economic and political opportunities which are open to them, and also indicate the ways in which these boundaries and possibilities are different from those experienced by men.

## Notes

1 This is only the case among Hindus and Sikhs. Among Muslims in North India, quite different principles operate and the ideal marriage is contracted between cousins, or at least within a known and trusted circle of kin. I have not discussed this here because there were no Muslims in the areas I studied, but excellent accounts of the principles underlying Muslim marriage, and of their consequences for women can be found in Jeffery (1979), and Das (1973).
2 See Sharma (forthcoming) for a more detailed account of the rules and assumptions which govern women's use of public space. It is important to emphasize that whilst not all women can possibly observe these norms consistently, all women are affected by them.
3 Amrit Wilson has aptly characterized the concept of *izzat* as 'honour, self-respect and sometimes plain male ego ... It is essentially male but it is women's lives and actions which affect it most. A woman can have *izzat* but it is not her own – it is her husband's or father's. Her *izzat* is a reflection of the male pride of the family as a whole' (Wilson 1978: 5).
4 I only came to know of one uxorilocal husband near Harbassi. This was the case of Rattano's husband (H17). Rattano was a Chamar girl who had left her first husband. When she met her second husband, the couple came back to live with her widowed mother in her *peke*. There was precious little land to be inherited, but the presence of the couple in the village was much resented. I think that this was mainly because the husband's presence disturbed the political relationships between families already settled in the village by introducing a new male contender from outside. Had Rattano and her husband discreetly made their home somewhere else I do not think so much comment would have been passed on the fact of her divorce.

Table 1 *Summary of information on the twenty-eight households chosen for detailed study*

*Note:* The figures in the 'estimated total cash income' column include cash income from all types of source: salary, sale of farm produce, remittances, pensions, rents, etc. Both these figures and those in the 'land' column are approximate in many cases. People were often cautious about divulging precise information about incomes or land holdings, and where I could not check information (e.g. against village land records) I had to make a rough estimation. These approximations should still be useful, since the purpose of giving this information is to enable comparisons to be made between households. Note that the economic position of a household can only be judged by taking these two columns together: some households are short of cash, but grow plenty of food on the land they own while others may have a large cash income but are obliged to buy almost all their food.

The rate of exchange during the period of the fieldwork was about Rs 18 to £1 sterling.

| code | total members of household | members of household (with approximate ages) | occupations | land | estimated total cash income of household per month | caste |
|---|---|---|---|---|---|---|
| | | | **1. HARBASSI** | | | |
| H 1 | 7 | Santosh (widow) (50) | domestic work | 80 acres | Rs 3,000 | Brahman |
| | | Jagdish (her son) (30) | manager of government owned factory: manages family land | | | |
| | | Lata (daughter-in-law) (25) | domestic work | | | |
| | | Two dependent children of Lata and Jagdish (2, 5) | | | | |

60

| | | Member | Occupation | Land | Income | Caste |
|---|---|---|---|---|---|---|
| | | Prithvi (son) (27) | junior manager in ceramics company | | | |
| | | Anita (daughter) (20) | university student | | | |
| H 2 | 5 | Dalip (brother of Santosh's late husband) (58) | manages family land (retired forestry officer) | 80 acres | Rs 2,500 | Brahman |
| | | Kaushalya (his wife) (45) | domestic work | | | |
| | | son i, son ii } | university students | | | |
| | | Veena (daughter) | domestic work (recently graduated as M.A.) | | | |
| H 3 | 5 | Rajinder (43) | manages family land | 60 acres | Rs 2,500 | Brahman |
| | | Sushila (his wife) (40) | domestic work | | | |
| | | son i, son ii, daughter } | college students | | | |

| code | total members of household | members of household (with approximate ages) | occupations | land | estimated total cash income of household per month | caste |
|---|---|---|---|---|---|---|
| H 4 | 6 | Romesh (35) | manages family land and dairy business | 50 acres | Rs 2,500 | Khatri |
| | | Saroja (his wife) (30) | domestic work | | | |
| | | three dependent children of Romesh and Saroja (4, 6, 9) | | | | |
| | | widowed mother of Romesh (60) | domestic work | | | |
| H 5 | 2 | Roshani (separated from husband) (70) | school teacher | — | Rs 250 | Khatri |
| | | grand-daughter of Roshani (16) | student | | | |
| H 6 | 6 | Charan Das (younger brother of Roshani (59) | shopkeeper and rentier | 30 acres | Rs 1,200 | Khatri |
| | | Shanta (his wife) (45) | domestic work | | | |
| | | three independent children of Charan Das and Shanta (4, 7, 8) | | | | |

| | | | | | | |
|---|---|---|---|---|---|---|
| | | widowed mother of Roshani and Charan Das (90) | | | | |
| H 7 | 4 | Major Joginder Singh (60) | manages family land: retired army officer | 50 acres (shared with Joginder Singh's brothers) | Rs 1,500 | Jat |
| | | Swaran Kaur (his wife) (55) | domestic work | | | |
| | | son (21) | student | | | |
| | | Jasbir (daughter) (22) (two older sons and one daughter are married and live separately) | school teacher | | | |
| H 8 | 6 | Satto (widow) (55) | domestic work: some agricultural supervision | 25 acres | Rs 700 | Jat |
| | | son (i) (30) | bus conductor: farms family land | | | |
| | | Gurmit (daughter-in-law) (23) | domestic work | | | |
| | | baby son of Gurmit | | | | |
| | | son (ii) (28) | bus conductor: farms family land | | | |
| | | Surjit (daughter-in-law) (19) | domestic work | | | |

| code | total members of household | members of household (with approximate ages) | occupations | land | estimated total cash income of household per month | caste |
|---|---|---|---|---|---|---|
| H 9 | 8 | Balwant Singh (60) | farms family land; runs own transport company | 10 acres | Rs 1,000 | Jat |
| | | Mahinder Kaur (his wife) (55) | domestic work; some agricultural supervision: sells milk to neighbours | | | |
| | | son (30) | drives lorry for family | | | |
| | | daughter-in-law (28) | domestic work | | | |
| | | three dependent grand-children | | | | |
| | | Jaswinder (daughter, separated from husband (23) | domestic work | | | |
| H 10 | 3 | Jagjit Singh (50) | works for electricity board; rents out family land | 10 acres | Rs 500 | Jat |
| | | Jivan Kaur (his wife) (45) | domestic work | | | |
| | | dependent son (adopted) (8) | | | | |

| | | Members | Occupation | Land | Income | Caste |
|---|---|---|---|---|---|---|
| H 11 | 6 | Kishan Chand (50) | skilled mechanic employed by Punjab government: farms family land | 8 acres | Rs 800 | Saini |
| | | his wife (48) | domestic work: agricultural work on own land | | | |
| | | son (i) (separated from his wife) (25) | army | | | |
| | | daughter (i) (18) | student (teacher training) | | | |
| | | Balvinder (daughter) (9) | | | | |
| | | son (ii) (8) | | | | |
| | | another son and daughter are married and living separately | | | | |
| H 12 | 7 | Hemraj (37) | farm servant employed by Santosh (H1): farms own land | 1 acre | Rs 125 | Chamar (scheduled caste) |
| | | Premi (his wife) (30) | domestic work | rents 1-2 acres as share-cropper in monsoon season | | |
| | | five dependent children (1, 3, 6, 7, 9) | | | | |

| code | total members of household | members of household (with approximate ages) | occupations | land | estimated total cash income of household per month | caste |
|---|---|---|---|---|---|---|
| H 13 | 6 | Lachman (brother of Hemraj) (40) | army: farms own land | 1 acre | Rs 750 | Chamar |
| | | Bhagvati (his wife) | farms own land: occasional agricultural labour; domestic work | Sometimes rents 1-2 acres as share-cropper | | |
| | | daughter (16) | " " " | | | |
| | | three other dependent children (7, 10, 12) | | | | |
| H 14 | 9 | Bishan Das (43) | factory labourer | 1 acre | Rs 600 | Chamar |
| | | Satya (his wife) (40) | farms own land: domestic work | rents 1 acre as share-cropper in monsoon season | | |
| | | son i (20) | occasional agricultural labour (about to enter army) | | | |
| | | Kanta (daughter) (17) | occasional agricultural labour; domestic work | | | |
| | | daughter ii (16) | " " " | | | |

| Household | No. | Members (age) | Occupation | Land | Income | Caste |
|---|---|---|---|---|---|---|
| | | Four other dependent children (2, 6, 10, 12) | | | | |
| | | Budho (widowed mother of Bishan Das, Lachman, and Hemraj) (70) | | | | |
| H 15 | 6 | Rolli (50) | Landless labourer and tenant farmer (now bed-ridden) | rents about 2 acres as share-cropper | Rs 120 (maximum) | Chamar |
| | | Sita (his wife) (40) | agricultural labourer; domestic work | | | |
| | | daughter (i) (19) | occasional agricultural labour; domestic work | | | |
| | | three other dependent children (10, 12, 14) | | | | |
| | | another adult son is away from home, seeking urban employment | | | | |
| H 16 | 7 | Pyaru | clerk employed in Delhi | 2 acres | Rs 600 | Chamar |
| | | Kamli (his wife) | farms family land; agricultural labour; domestic work | another 1-2 acres rented as share-cropper | | |

| code | total members of household | members of household (with approximate ages) | occupations | land | estimated total cash income of household per month | caste |
|---|---|---|---|---|---|---|
| | | Guddi (daughter) | domestic work | | | |
| | | four other dependent children (8, 10, 11, 12) | | | | |
| H 17 | 8 | Chandu (32) | farms family land; agricultural labour | 4 acres | Rs 150 (maximum) | Chamar |
| | | Rattano (his wife: remarried divorcee) (30) | farms family land; agricultural labour; domestic work | | | |
| | | four dependent children of Chandu and Rattano (1, 2, 4, 5) | | | | |
| | | brother of Rattano (25) | agricultural labourer | | | |
| | | mother of Rattano (55) | domestic work | | | |

## 2. CHAILI

| | | | | | | |
|---|---|---|---|---|---|---|
| C 1 | 3 | Shri Ram (45) | school teacher; farms family land; dispenses traditional medicine | 3 acres | Rs 800 | Goswami |
| | | Kamla (his wife) (40) | farms family land; domestic work | | | |
| | | Pushpa (daughter: married about to leave for husband's home) | | | | |
| C 2 | 5 | Durgi (widow of Shri Ram's brother (42) | farms family land; domestic work: employed by the anthropologist to do domestic work | 2½ acres | Rs 240 | Goswami |
| | | son (22) | bus conductor | | | |
| | | daughter (18) | domestic work; farms family land | | | |
| | | two other dependent children (12, 15) | | | | |
| C 3 | 6 | Jagat Ram (brother of Shri Ram) (45) | shopkeeper; farms family land | 2 acres | Rs 900 | Goswami |

| code | total members of household | members of household (with approximate ages) | occupations | land | estimated total cash income of household per month | caste |
|---|---|---|---|---|---|---|
| | | Dipo (his wife) (42) | domestic work; farms family land | | | |
| | | Bindo (daughter: married, about to leave for husband's home) (18) | domestic work | | | |
| | | three other dependent children (7, 9, 15) | | | | |
| C 4 | 7 | Ram Das (brother of Shri Ram) (55) | shopkeeper; runs own transport business, farms family land | 3 acres | Rs 1,200 | Gos-wami |
| | | Mohini (his wife) (50) | farms family land; domestic work | | | |
| | | son (27) | works in family shop | | | |
| | | daughter-in-law (25) | farms family land; domestic work | | | |
| | | two dependent grandchildren (4, 6) | | | | |

| | | Household members | Occupation | Land | Income | Caste |
|---|---|---|---|---|---|---|
| | | servant (a distant kinsman, blind from birth) | light domestic and farm work | | | |
| C 5 | 8 | Sarla (widow) (60) | farms family land | 2 acres | Rs 400 | Brahman |
| | | son (i) (37) | shopkeeper | | | |
| | | daughter-in-law (30) | domestic work: farms family land | | | |
| | | three dependent grandchildren (2, 7, 10) | | | | |
| | | son (ii) (30) | clerk in Punjab | | | |
| | | son (iii) (20) | labourer in mill in Punjab | | | |
| C 6 | 5 | Sanjiv (30) | school teacher | none | Rs 750 | Kumhar (potter) |
| | | Pushpa (his wife) (28) | school teacher; domestic work | registered in Sanjiv's name, but he may inherit some | | |
| | | three dependent children (1, 2, 5) | | | | |
| C 7 | 6 | Mohan Singh (45) | Owns and operates saw mill; farms family land (former employee of electricity board) | 7½ acres | Rs 400 | Rajput |

| code | total members of household | members of household (with approximate ages) | occupations | land | estimated total cash income of household per month | caste |
|---|---|---|---|---|---|---|
| | | his wife (40) | employee of electricity board | | | |
| | | four dependent children (9, 12, 14, 16) | | | | |
| C 8 | 7 | Karan Singh (55) | farms family land (retired soldier) | 5 acres | Rs 300 | Rajput |
| | | his wife (45) | farms family land: domestic work | | | |
| | | four dependent children (10, 12, 15, 18) | | | | |
| | | widowed mother of Karan Singh (72) | | | | |
| C 9 | 9 | Nand Ram (63) | farms family land | 4 acres | Rs 700 | Brahman |
| | | his wife (58) | farms family land: domestic work | | | |
| | | son (i) (28) | army | | | |

| | | Members | Occupation | Land | Cash income | Caste |
|---|---|---|---|---|---|---|
| | | daughter-in-law (22) | domestic work: farms | | | |
| | | two dependent grand-children (1, 3) | | | | |
| | | son (ii) (25) | navy | | | |
| | | Prito (daughter-in-law) (17) | domestic work: farms family land | | | |
| | | son (iii) (20) | road mender | | | |
| | | three other sons are married and live separately | | | | |
| C 10 | 6 | Devraj (50) | farms family land | 12 acres | occasional remittances from son (never more than Rs 100 per month): no other source of cash income | Brahman |
| | | Tara (his wife) (40) | farms family land; domestic work | | | |
| | | four dependent children (9, 12, 15, 16) | | | | |
| | | another son is married and lives separately | | | | |

| code | total members of household | members of household (with approximate ages) | occupations | land | estimated total cash income of household per month | caste |
|---|---|---|---|---|---|---|
| C 11 | 9 | Bhagat Ram (60) | clerk, employed in Delhi; farms family land | 4 acres | Rs 1,100 | Brahman |
| | | Shila (his wife) (55) | farms family land; domestic work | | | |
| | | son (30) | clerk, employed in Delhi | | | |
| | | daughter-in-law (28) | domestic work: some farm work | | | |
| | | four dependent grand-children (1, 4, 6, 7) | | | | |
| | | daughter (16) | at school: some domestic work | | | |

# 4 Women and the household economy

## The household as an economic unit: its constitution

If we want to find out what characterizes women's position in the process of production, then it is more useful to begin by studying their position in the household than anywhere else. This is not because the household constitutes the basic unit from which the economy is built up. If households ever were discrete and self-sufficient units in the areas I studied this is certainly not the case now. It would be impossible to study the household in isolation since it is a complex system of co-operation, deriving income from a variety of different activities. We need to examine the household because it is still largely through their domestic roles that women are allocated work or leisure. Through their position in the household the pattern of their work is organized and their control over its products defined. So I shall discuss the household as a unit of both production and consumption, examining the structure of economic relations among its members.

Unfortunately I shall have to clear away some definitional jungle first. What do I understand by the term household, and are the groups which I have termed households genuinely comparable? There has been a tendency in studies of the family and household in India to look at the household mainly in terms of its composition. The key problems have been, 'what categories of relatives normally live together?', and 'how are we to describe households which contain members of more than one nuclear family?' Less attention has been paid to problems such as 'what kind of things do members of one household do together?' or 'what is the structure of co-operation among its members?' Shah rightly points out that whilst modern sociologists in India are aware that the family and the household are not the same thing, 'a considerable confusion, however, still persists because of the tendency to use the words "family" and "household" as synonyms' (Shah 1973: 138). This conflation of the genealogical model and the residential group has led to a tendency to treat the household as first and foremost a kin group, albeit 'influenced' by economic factors (e.g. Mandelbaum 1972: 47 ff.) when it should be treated as *both* a kin group *and* an economic group. An inordinate amount of energy seems to have been devoted to deciding what precise term should be applied to a nuclear family household augmented by the presence of, say, the husband's widowed sister, instead of looking at the structure of co-operation and exchange within this group.

The household is indisputably a kin group in the obvious sense that it is constituted by relations of consanguinity and marriage. In only a very few households in Harbassi and Chaili were there non-kin living as members of the same domestic group. Invariably these non-kin were living-in farm servants. In Punjab, where the practice is commoner, these servants would be impoverished migrants from Uttar Pradesh or Madhya Pradesh, labouring for little more than their keep. In Himachal Pradesh one occasionally finds a destitute or disabled villager living in as a servant or general dogsbody in a more prosperous household, but even here some distant kinship link is usually traceable. One does not find the wealthy farmer maintaining a large staff of living-in servants and maids as in pre-industrial England, for example. On the other hand, the household is more than just a kin group 'influenced' by economic factors. It is a unit of consumption: its members budget together for their needs and to a large extent share common rations and lodging. A household possessing land is also usually a unit of production – its members constitute a work team in cultivating and managing the land and preparing its products for sale or consumption. And when in households where the household itself is not a unit of production, as in labouring or tenant families, members may still co-operate in production activities or work alongside each other.

But if the household is not 'just' a kin group, what are the economic dimensions which we should regard as defining it? This is a real problem, because in North-West India the group of people who hold co-parcenary rights in a piece of land or other property may not all live together. Brothers frequently farm the patrimonial land jointly whilst living separately, as in the case of Major Joginder Singh (H7), whose land is not partitioned from that of his elder brother. Or the land may be partitioned and registered in the brothers' several names but in reality farmed as one unit, with only one of the brothers staying in the village to manage it. This was the case in Romesh's household; his two brothers worked in banking in a nearby city whilst Romesh devoted himself to full time farm management (H4). In some cases the brothers who are employed outside the village leave their wives and children behind, sending remittances to them or to their parents. This is more common in Himachal and among the lower-income households in Punjab, e.g. the households of Nand Ram (C9), Bhagat Ram (C11), and Lachman (H13). Or they may take their wives and children to live near their place of work, sending money to their parents or brothers from time to time. In such cases, a group of people related through kinship live separately for most of the year but share a high degree of financial responsibility for each other and budget together for major items of expenditure (a tractor, a daughter's wedding, sinking a tube-well).

That there are several dimensions of household co-operation and joint living which do not necessarily coincide has been recognized by most authors. For instance, Gore distinguishes residence, property holding, and use of a common hearth, evidently giving primacy to coresidence, as have most other writers (Gore 1968: 6). This, however, leaves out the question of joint budgeting and sharing of general financial responsibility in so far as this relates to matters other than land. I.P. Desai tried to overcome the complexity of defining the household by adopting a dual classification of households according to 'jointness'; one classification refers to jointness of residence and the other to jointness in terms of common responsibility and co-operation. According to this schema, two brothers who lived separately would not be 'joint' at all in the first sense. But if there were a high degree of mutual financial responsibility or other kinds of regular co-operation between their families then they could be considered to show jointness according to the second sense of the term (Desai 1964: 34). Desai's contribution is helpful in that he recognizes that if we treat residential units as discrete groups then we risk ignoring the very important relations of economic co-operation which exist among close kin who do not necessarily live together. This results in the arbitrary isolation of a unit which may not be isolable if we are primarily concerned with the economic dimension of family life. So any strict definition of the household will be arbitrary to some extent; relations of economic co-operation and financial obligation overflow the physical boundaries of the family home and it is difficult to isolate the core of kin who have primary economic responsibility for each other from the vaguer set of relatives who have less definite rights and duties towards each other. In the case of Santosh (H1), for instance, her son Jagdish lived at some distance from Harbassi where the family owns land, and was employed as a factory manager. Most of the time his wife and children do not live with Santosh, but with Jagdish. Should Santosh and Jagdish be considered as one household or as two? They budget separately for their everyday needs, to be sure. On the other hand, Santosh cannot manage the land on her own. She relies on Jagdish and on his younger brother Prithvi to visit her regularly to supervise the farm, and in most months one or other of them manages to come for a few days. The land is managed on a joint basis though in fact it is registered in the separate names of Santosh and her four children in order to avoid the effects of land ceiling laws. Santosh and her sons are mutually reliant so far as farm management is concerned and for all major expenses. Therefore, on the grounds that most of their budgeting is collective, I have treated them as constituting one household; Prithvi, Jagdish, and the latter's wife and children being 'temporarily absent members'. For the purpose of this study I have treated a group of people as a household where there is substantial economic co-operation, common property, and mutual financial responsibility. Most of the time most of its members will live together (a definition of the household which made no reference to common residence would be stretching the meaning of the term well beyond its conventional meaning) but at any one time some members may live away from the common home. This may seem an arbitrary definition, but as I have suggested, some arbitrariness is inevitable and I am not making any claims for this usage other than its appropriateness for the purposes of this study. However I have tried not to be arbitrary in my application of this definition and there is consistency in the procedures by which individuals have been included or excluded from the sample summarized in *Table 1*.

One final point needs to be made. Any household is always in the process of development. It continually loses members, gains members, divides, becomes more or less complex in its composition. The households in *Table 1* are seen as though 'frozen' at the point of time when I studied them. In case the processual character of the household is lost from view in the subsequent discussion, let me point out that after I left Harbassi, Prithvi left his employment in Delhi to come back to the village to live with his mother, Santosh. His sister will probably leave to get married within the next year. Kanta, the daughter of Bishan Das (H13), will be married by the time this book is published, and Pushpa, the married daughter of Sri Ram and Kamla (C1), left the village to live with her husband permanently soon after my own departure and has since borne a daughter. If I were to revisit Harbassi and Chaili now (only a year after the field-work was carried out) probably almost every entry in *Table 1* would require some amendment.

## The household as an economic unit: multiple sources of income

In neither Himachal nor Punjab is the household a self-sufficient unit, yet self sufficiency is celebrated as a value. In both areas farmers yearn nostalgically for a bygone age, almost certainly mythical, when each household produced all that it needed to feed and clothe its members. Food which one has not produced oneself is often considered to be less nutritious than home-grown food. One woman told me that she felt depressed when her cow went dry; quite apart from the expense of buying milk each day 'milk which you have bought from someone else does not taste so sweet'. It is true that in the past many households produced items which they now buy from the *bazar*, but the modern rural household is far from being the autonomous, self-sufficient unit which is still a lively ideal, even in those families who own large amounts of land. Very few informants of any social class felt that they could manage entirely on the proceeds of the land they owned. In Himachal this was mainly due to pressure on cultivable land because of the increase in population; holdings have been partitioned to the point where individual units are no longer economical. In Punjab this is true for the smaller peasantry, but there has also been a general rise in the standard of living and of people's expectations. New needs have been created for consumer goods and other items which the household cannot produce itself and must obtain with cash. A regular cash income over and above the proceeds of agriculture was felt to be needed in all but one or two capitalist farmers' households. That is, one or more members of the household must find regular paid employment. In Punjab and in some parts of Himachal this is not altogether new. Both were important recruiting grounds for the Indian Army in British times and continue to be so today (five of the twenty eight households in the sample had members who were or had been in the armed forces). In Punjab there is more scope for urban employment and some villagers do not have to migrate far to find work. Some do not have to migrate at all, such as Kishan Chand, a skilled mechanic who is employed by the government in the sinking of tube-wells (H11), or Satto's sons who work as bus conductors with Punjab Roadways (H8). In Himachal there is little local employment for village people and poor communications preclude commuting. Men are often obliged to take work hundreds of miles from home and cannot visit their families often. In many households in District Hamirpur it is the practice for a man to spend fifteen years or so in employment outside the village while his wife and children remain in the village. As soon as his sons are adolescent they are sent out in his place (often he can help them to find work in the town where he works himself and may work alongside them for a few years). When the father retires the sons continue to send money home. In such households a man's role in farming is sporadic or marginal for much of his adult life, but he returns to agriculture in late middle age.

When I speak of households 'needing' cash income in addition to the produce of their land, I am referring to perceived needs and not to any absolute standard of need. Of course, a household such as that of Hemraj (H12) could not survive without some source of income other than the grain they produce from their own land, i.e. they would starve. But many of the larger landowners equally felt that they could not manage without some other source of income. Santosh (H1) did not feel that her household could manage on the proceeds of their farm at the moment; even though the combined land holdings of the family amounted to over eighty acres. That is, they could not maintain the standard of living which they considered appropriate with any security unless at least one of the sons had a paid job. Partly this is an effect of the process of transition to capitalist methods of farming. This family had only begun to farm their land themselves about five years ago on the death of Santosh's husband, who had been a university professor. They still had substantial repayments to make on loans taken out for the purchase of a tractor and for the sinking of tube-wells. Other households who had made the transition to this kind of farming earlier (H3 and H4) could maintain a high standard of living on their farm income alone.

The combination of agriculture with wage labour in the peasant household is, of course, very widespread in Third World countries. The particular division of labour which we find in Himachal and among the poorer Punjabi families (men enter paid employment, women farm) is common where an agriculturally undeveloped region lies within reach of an industrially advanced area (as in many parts of Southern Africa). Where the returns of peasant agricultural production are low and industrial wages are also low in relation to the urban cost of living this pattern of interdependence is necessary for the survival of the poorer families. Note that only five households in my sample relied on a single type of income. Two of these were wealthy capitalist farmers, emancipated from the need to sell their labour (H3 and H4). Another two were families that were becoming more oriented to professional work and were in the process of cutting their links with the land (H5 and C6). One was an impoverished Brahman family which existed entirely and precariously on the produce of their land (C10).

This dependence on multiple sources of income has various consequences in India. Rao and others have noted that occupational diversity favours the persistence of joint families; there are economic advantages in members of complex households staying together when some members can specialize in urban employment and others in agriculture (Rao 1968).

Secondly it has consequences for class formation. The class position of individuals can be defined, but households are harder to characterize, since their members may participate in more than one mode of production either simultaneously or serially. Sarla, for instance, is a peasant proprietor farming her own land, whilst her eldest son keeps a small shop and her other sons work as labourers in a city (C5). Hemraj (H12) owns a little land, rents land from time to time, and works as farm servant for Santosh (H1). Class exists in an objective sense but class consciousness does not develop easily where the individual identifies with a household whose members' economic positions are so diverse (this is especially true in the middle ranges of the rural hierarchy). Caste is a more accessible focus for self-identification than class (see Parry 1979: 55). The classifications which I have used to characterize households (capitalist farmers, peasants, labourers, etc.) must of necessity be very crude and are only a rough guide to such things as income and standard of living, level of education, self-identification, etc.).

The third consequence of which we need to take account here is that women are doubly dependent. As I showed in Chapter 3, they seldom possess land in their own names; now they also depend largely on men to bring cash into the household since, for reasons which I shall describe, women play little part in wage employment at the moment.

### Rural women and employment

It is usually the men of the household who are the chief wage-earners. There are two reasons for this; firstly women are less educated relative to men and therefore are less qualified for some kinds of employment, and secondly the restrictions on women's mobility and public visibility described in Chapter 3 severely limit their opportunities for employment. In Punjab, rural women of low caste can obtain seasonal agricultural labouring work, and those who are educated can work as teachers, nurses, and social workers. But in Himachal there is little seasonal agricultural work and in any case most women are too fully occupied working their own holdings or those which they rent in the absence of their menfolk to have time to work for other people. In the entire sample there were only ten women (representing eight households) who worked for wages at any time during the fieldwork. These included three teachers, seven agricultural labourers, and one part-time domestic help employed by myself. Only the teachers worked on a permanent basis. All the others simply worked when the opportunity arose.

In both areas the prejudice against women moving about freely in public militates against their seeking work outside their own villages, even when they are qualified and when work might be available in some other district. In one Jat family in Harbassi, the daughter had passed her B.Ed. with excellent marks but was currently unemployed as there was no post vacant in the local schools and her parents were unwilling that she should go to live elsewhere away from their tutelage. Married women are somewhat less restricted, especially in Himachal, and in the hills it is not unusual for a professional woman to take up work as a teacher or social worker away from home, living separately from her husband for the duration of her service. My next door neighbour in Chaili was a well-educated woman from District Bilaspur who had taken up a post as social worker in the village. She and her two daughters lodged with a farming family in the village and her husband, who worked as a school teacher in Bilaspur itself came to visit her once or twice a month. Such women, however, face a good many practical problems, from lack of decent accommodation to downright hostility in the communities where they work, so they usually try to get a posting near to their husband's place of work.

In the past there was little scope for rural women to find professional employment because they had not been educated to the same level as boys. In the generation of women born after Independence it would be unusual to find one able to say of herself, as many of my older informants could say, that she 'never went near a school in her life', but girls are still educated to a lower level than their brothers. Or perhaps a more accurate way of putting it would be to say that there are various educational strategies for girls, but few of them lead to the girls being able to obtain the kind of qualifications which will help them to get work. Nowadays the logic is not that it is wrong to educate girls or that they will get too independent, but that it just is not worth it since they are not going to be seeking employment after all (a self-fulfilling assumption). The exception are the high-status groups where education enhances a girl's position in the marriage market. The niece of Devraj (C10), for instance, had passed her B.Ed. but her father was unwilling to let her take a teaching job. His argument was that there would be none available sufficiently close to home and he was unwilling to let her move to another village. It was all right, he said, for her to stay in a hostel while she was a student, but it was quite another thing for a grown girl to be lodging in someone else's house in a strange village. His aim was to use her education to get a good husband for her. The husband's family might then decide for themselves whether they wished her to work or not.

In Punjab girls of the very highest status groups are automatically educated to a high level, but with even less expectation that they will use their qualifications to get work. Santosh (H1) had educated both her daughters to M.A. level, but could not think of any career for them which would be compatible with her ideal of girls being *gharile*, i.e. home loving. I have the impression that many of the women who become teachers, nurses, and social workers in Punjab are drawn from the upper peasantry rather than from the Brahman and Khatri 'gentry'. Among the Jats, Sainis, and respectable artisan castes, status is still a vital consideration in determining what kind of work (if any), a girl may do, but education is regarded as more than simply an ornament.

Girls of all socio-economic groups seem to enjoy their education and take it seriously even if, as in many poor families, they cannot manage very regular attendance. It is one sphere in which they can achieve and be appreciated for their personal performance, yet in a suitably enclosed and feminine environment (most secondary schools are single-sex schools and even in co-educational schools there is considerable segregation of the sexes). Goldstein reports a similar positive attitude to education amongst urban girls (Goldstein 1972: 14a). But all the odds are against a girl of poor family obtaining sufficient schooling to get any useful qualifications. In spite of government help, the cost of education is heavy for these families and they will prefer to invest in their sons, who are more likely to find work. Quite a few girls of scheduled caste in Harbassi had reached the eighth grade, often in the face of their mothers' attitude that 'all you need is to be able to write a decent letter to your husband so that he won't forget you'. Frequently the parents take the kind of view expressed by Mahinder Kaur's daughter-in-law (H9) about her small daughter: 'Let us see how clever she turns out to be. If she is bright we might let her study up to the tenth grade.' A girl who can prove herself by exceptional academic performance may be able to persuade her parents to let her go on, but a less academic girl will stand a poorer chance, even though she needs the skills of literacy and numeracy just as much.

Another factor which militates against girls from poorer families gaining useful qualifications is the domestic and farm work which they are often expected to do. Durgi's daughter (C2) had worked her way rather painfully to the sixth grade, but had difficulty in keeping up with the work since as soon as she reached home each afternoon she was expected to do a number of routine tasks, such as fetching water and washing clothes, to help her widowed mother. Major Joginder Singh's daughter Jasbir, who taught in a Harbassi school, told me that on the whole her girl pupils were more studious and more interested in schoolwork than the boys, but most were hampered by the domestic work which prevented them from spending time on assignments set as homework. Boys are also expected to help at home and run errands, of course, but to a lesser extent than girls.

Where girls of poor families are concerned there is yet another factor which deters them from seeking paid work, namely that the wages for female labourers are much lower than those of male labourers and the work available for women labourers is seasonal and sporadic (this is the case in Punjab; in the part of Himachal where I worked it was virtually non-existent). There is little incentive for poor women to regard such work as a source of regular income. Capitalist farmers in Punjab seldom employ more than one or two permanent farm servants, invariably men. Women are employed for seasonal work such as weeding wheat, harvesting, planting vegetables, lifting potatoes. Women such as Kanta and her mother Satya (H14) are therefore liable to regard money earned in this way as a bonus to be used for meeting occasional expenses, such as clothing, or to put by for weddings and the like. I remember Kanta visiting my house in Harbassi, very elated with the Rs 50 she had just earned for a couple of weeks' work in the fields and which she was about to spend on cloth for a new outfit for herself.

I should perhaps make it clear that if there is limited scope for employment open to rural women, this does not mean that finding work is easy for all rural men. There is a great deal of unemployment among the men, some of it 'hidden'. A farmer's son may spend his time working on the family land, all the while making unsuccessful attempts to find work elsewhere. But there are still important differences between the employment chances of boys and girls. For one thing, as I have already made clear, a man has the advantage of being more mobile. He can, without prejudice to his reputation, move about alone in search of work and travel long distances if necessary. A young man of poor family who cannot find work in his own locality will often go to stay with a relative in some more promising area in the hope of finding work there. Secondly, whilst personal contacts are always important in finding employment, they are particularly important for women. A young girl may have professional qualifications, but her parents will be unwilling to allow her to work in a situation where the family have no prior contacts or where there is no trusted person who can 'keep an eye on her' and vouch for her safety and welfare. So far as labouring women are concerned, large farmers tend to advertise their needs for casual labour through their own personal contacts in the local villages. Santosh's servant Hemraj lives in the village where she owns land, and acts as recruiting agent when she and her sons need workers for their fields. Naturally, those women who are related to him or who live near to him are more likely to be told when work is available. Different landowners have their own channels for advertising their labour needs, but they are almost invariably informal and personal. There is no Punjabi equivalent of the hiring fair. Men also obtain work through such personal contacts, but a man has better chances for making and profitting by such contacts. He may hear about work simply through hanging about in public places, which would be quite unacceptable for a woman. For the same kind of reasons, a woman has no means of advertising the availability of her labour. Some village girls in both Punjab and Himachal earn money by taking in tailoring work, but as they have no acceptable means of advertising their services in public they have to rely entirely on personal contacts and recommendations.

In all but the most poverty-stricken families, the decision to work or not to work is not one which is made entirely by the individual woman herself. It is a family matter since potentially it affects the prestige of the whole household in the community. If a wife is to work for pay then it can only be with the consent of her husband, and of her parents-in-law if the couple live with them. If a daughter is to work it can only be with the consent of her parents. A woman may propose that she take paid employment (and she will not be forced to go out to work if she is unwilling or unqualified) but the other members of the household must be agreeable. Jasbir (H7), for example, was very eager to train for a job even when she was still at school and it was at her insistence that she was sent to college to train as a teacher, although neither of her elder sisters had studied beyond the tenth grade. She liked the idea of nursing, she told me, but her parents and her uncles had vetoed this idea because nursing in their view was degrading work involving potentially polluting contacts ('suppose she had to do a delivery case'). They suggested school teaching instead and Jasbir readily agreed. Her parents are very proud of the fact that whilst several other Jat girls in their village have received a college education, Jasbir is the only one who has obtained a job as yet.

In peasant families in Chaili there may be more positive pressure on girls to earn money if they are fortunate enough to have the necessary qualifications. Bindo (C3) had obtained a certificate in needlework at her parents' home without any thought of using her skills to earn money. She told me that her husband had asked her to bring this certificate with her when she came to join him in Chandigarh where he worked as she might be able to obtain work teaching needlework in a school. She was not very enthralled by the idea but was willing to take work at her husband's suggestion. The education of Pushpa (C6) to B.Ed. level had been her father's idea (he was also a school teacher) but Pushpa herself had enjoyed her training. Her father had not urged her to take paid work so long as she was unmarried, but after her marriage she had found employment and was very glad that her father had insisted on her training, not because she was specially wedded to teaching work but because she was glad of the extra income she was able to earn.

The desire to take employment therefore, is not disapproved in a woman of high- or middle-status families provided that there is work available which her family regarded as suitable and provided there is money available for her training, but it is not expected of her as it would be of a boy. Girls of poor families on the other hand, are definitely expected to help contribute to the family income if they possibly can, either directly by taking seasonal labouring work or indirectly by giving extra help in the home so that some other female member of the household can take on such work when it is available.

How do women themselves regard paid work outside the home? Studies in Britain indicate that apart from the financial rewards, many women derive social satisfaction from paid employment since it enables them to avoid the isolated tedium of housework. However dull the work, some companionship and social importance derive from it. The rural Indian women among whom I worked regarded work outside the home in quite a different way since they did not usually experience the home as somewhere that they needed to get away from. The ideology of purdah teaches a woman to regard the home as the one place where she feels particularly secure and important. And as the home is the focus for interaction among kin and neighbours, even women who observe fairly strict seclusion do not experience it as a place of isolation (see above, p.43). So they derive satisfaction from paid work in proportion as they find the work intrinsically interesting or agreeable. Roshani (H5) had refused to retire when offered the opportunity; her schoolwork was her life and she would, she said, be bored to death in her 'little cage', as she called the rented rooms she inhabited now that her children were all grown up and settled elsewhere. The social worker who was my neighbour in Chaili, on the other hand, really disliked her work, regarding the village women as sly and hostile. She looked forward to the time when she would be able to retire from full-time work. Kanta (H14) enjoyed working as a hired labourer because, she said, it was no more unpleasant than the farm work which she did on her family's own plot of land and much more entertaining, since she usually worked in the company of a gang of five to ten other girls. The foreman was her uncle, so she did not have difficulty in persuading him to allow frequent breaks for tea brewed over a fire kindled between two bricks at the side of the field. Girls from poorer families derived a real pride in their earning power. Balvinder Saini's elder sister (H11), who was about to embark upon a teachers' training course, told me with great satisfaction that she would be the first girl from her caste in Harbassi to become a teacher.

Although women are not obliged to seek paid employment in the sense that many men are, and although the decision to do so is not one which a woman can make alone, once the decision has been made she will not regard paid work as in any way marginal to her role as a woman. What the female role demands is the subordination of the individual woman's personal inclinations to the needs of the whole group, whether those needs be primarily for prestige or for cash. If suitable work is available, there is no reason why she should not fulfil her role as dutiful wife or daughter by going out to work and in this respect her attitude to her work is likely to be rather different from that of many British women who see their work role as something either conflicting with or subordinate to their roles in the family (Hunt 1980: 68 ff).

The role of an Indian village woman as paid worker is only 'marginal' in the family in the sense that she is likely to be paid less than the men of her household. Her pay is certainly not regarded as 'pin money'. Even the richer families have not yet reached that standard of living where extra income brings much scope for choice in expenditure. Most households will have a list of priorities which are dealt with as income rises, no matter who is responsible for actually earning the money. Women's earnings are not really different from those of men in this respect. So whilst in the community women are *devalued*, to the extent that they are offered less money than men for the same or similar work, within the family a female earner is *valued* in the same way as a male earner in the sense that her contribution is taken seriously.

Having said this, however, I must stress again the point that cannot be reiterated too often, namely that women seldom command the kind of income that would allow them to be independent of their husbands or fathers. Furthermore, the senior members of the household have ultimate control over the labour power of the female members of the group (and to some extent that of the junior males also) even where women obtain and spend their own quite substantial incomes. A woman can only get access to training if her parents are willing and if her father or some other relative is prepared to pay the fees, and having obtained it will not be able to work outside the home without her parents' consent. In practice, unmarried girls often need the help of male relatives in getting work in the first place, as they will not have the contacts which are needed to locate and obtain work in rural areas.

In a sense, no member of the household is regarded as having the right to sell his or her labour or to enjoy the income thus earned without reference to the other members of the group, and their needs and wishes. But because of their particular moral role (as repositories of family honour) and their particular economic position (as financial dependants) women are less likely to be able to resist this control and to participate in the labour market on the same terms as men. Only in very exceptional cases will a woman's role as earner mitigate her role as dependant.

**The organization of work in the household and the sexual division of labour**

Most writers who have addressed the question of the organization of labour within the household have looked at it primarily in terms of the way in which tasks are allocated among men and women and the degree of overlap (if any) between male and female tasks. Certainly this is important, but we also need to know how routine tasks are organized, i.e. not just who *does* what but who *decides* who does what, and who is responsible for seeing that specific tasks are done. This involves looking at the whole structure of household work – how work teams are constituted, what kind of co-operation takes place between men and women in the household, and what other criteria besides that of sex are important in the domestic division of labour.

*Table 2* summarizes the way in which routine agricultural and domestic tasks are allocated between the sexes and among the age groups (for, as we shall see, age is also an important principle in the organization of household work). This table does not reflect the actual division of labour which operates in any particular household; in some households women do virtually no agricultural work, not all households include elderly people, many possess no heavy machinery. It only represents the range of tasks performed by men and women in the community in general.

Table 2   *Allocation of tasks in the household*

|  | tasks usually done by females | tasks done by males or females | tasks usually done by males |
|---|---|---|---|
| children | occasional help with cooking and washing utensils<br><br>tending smaller children | fetching water<br>minor purchases from shops<br><br>taking cattle to pasture or water | helping to handle draught animals |
| adults | cooking<br>washing clothes<br>tending small children and babies<br>raising vegetables near the house<br>milking and feeding cattle<br>sewing and knitting | fetching water<br>weeding<br>sowing<br>threshing (old method)<br>harvesting<br>operating Persian well for irrigation<br>shopping | ploughing<br>feeding threshing machine<br>operating tube well<br>digging irrigation channels<br>operating farm machinery |
| elderly people | minding small children<br>occasional cooking | light agricultural work | |

From this summary, we see that the tasks which are almost exclusively performed by women are those relating to the supervision and care of young children and to the personal care and nourishment of family members. Women may perform many additional tasks of an agricultural nature but these 'nurturant' tasks are the preserve of women. There are fewer tasks which are exclusively male. Among these are ploughing and all agricultural operations which involve power-driven machinery. There is a very strong feeling that women should not plough, although it is difficult to locate the source of this feeling. I remember one occasion when my two daughters were learning how to sow maize seed from a neighbour in Chaili during the monsoon. Our neighbour's husband was amused by their efforts until the elder girl suggested that he should teach her to plough also. At this he looked quite horrified and said that this was not possible and that a little girl should never put her hand to the plough. One woman tried to explain this feeling with reference to the idea that for a woman to plough would be 'bad for her *izzat* (honour)', others simply stated that God had decreed that women should not plough, or that the rule had been laid down by their forebears in ages past. The fact that women do not operate power-driven machinery or drive tractors does not seem to have any such normative origins. Women explained this simply by stating that they did not know how to do these tasks; if they had ever been taught to do them, no doubt they would. One can, however, speculate about some of the reasons why women have not been taught these skills. Firstly the advisory personnel (government agents, development officers, etc.) who are responsible for disseminating information about modern farming technology are exclusively male and tend to communicate with males (see Sridharan 1975: 43), the capitalist farmers who can afford to purchase such machinery are mostly male, and (as I have already noted) the permanent farm servants employed by these farmers to work on their land are always male. This channelling of knowledge about modern farming technology through exclusively male networks is common in developing countries, as Boserup and other writers have noticed (I discuss this further in the next chapter). A second 'hidden' reason is that whoever drives a tractor or operates a tube-well must collect the necessary fuel from the filling station in the *bazar* or on the main road, venues which are rather too public for women to visit frequently. In Chaili there are no farmers who can afford power-driven machinery apart from the occasional thresher, and here also such machines are operated by men.

On the whole, the division of labour in the household is flexible within limits; whatever pattern the particular household adopts there will usually be a range of tasks which can be performed by men and women alike. It is possible to identify three main patterns in Chaili and Harbassi which can be summarized as follows (in order of degree of rigidity):

1   Capitalist farmers in Harbassi: women of the household do no agricultural work at all, unless of a supervisory nature. Men do agricultural tasks which do not involve strenuous manual labour or actual contact with the soil (driving tractors, operating tube wells and other machinery, supervising labour in the fields). (E.g. H1, H2, H3, H4)

2   Wealthy peasants in Punjab (and a very few farmers in the foothill region); men do the majority of agricultural tasks and women do domestic tasks along with a little light agricultural work and tending cattle. (H7, H8)

3   Small proprietors and tenants in Punjab, most households in District Hamirpur; many tasks will be done by both men and women. Women participate in practically all agricultural work and also take prime responsibility for domestic work. (H13-17, C1-5, C6-11)

But age is as important a principle as sex. In all but a few capitalist landlords' households, children are expected to do a fair amount of domestic and agricultural work. A work team engaged in operations such as threshing or sowing will typically include a man and his wife with one or more of their children. Elderly people, as is clear from *Table 2*, withdraw from heavy work of any kind but will continue to do whatever light or sedentary tasks are within their capacity, such as cleaning grain, taking cattle to the water, etc.

The sexual division of labour is not very pronounced in early childhood; little boys and little girls are asked to do much the same kind of work until they are about nine or ten, although girls are more frequently left in charge of younger siblings than are boys. But children have to learn the skills appropriate to their sex from the parent of the same sex, and the sexual division of labour becomes more apparent as they approach adolescence and are drawn into the adult work pattern.

In some households the difference between tasks allocated to girls and to grown women reflects an actual change in the aspirations of the family. For instance, Balvinder Saini's elder sister (H11) did not do any work in the fields, although her mother did a fair amount of agricultural work. This girl was studying to become a teacher, the first of her family to pursue a course of higher education, and it was felt that it was not proper for her to do manual work out of doors. In some households the reverse is true, i.e. the young daughters do tasks which their mothers cannot do for reasons of status. Saroja, for instance (H4) scarcely ever left her own house except for social visits, but she would send her eight-year-old daughter to the shops in minor errands as it was not considered improper for the children to go to the *bazar*.

But we do not know the significance of the sexual division of labour unless we also know about the division of responsibility. That is, we need to know not only who normally does a particular task, but who gets blamed if it is not done.[1] We have seen that in households of all social classes it is women who perform such tasks as cooking, cleaning the house, washing clothes, and caring for small children. We can add that these tasks are also the *responsibility* of women. Let us examine what this means in respect of one particular task – cooking. In Himachal most men know how to cook and some can cook very well indeed. Most men have lived away from their womenfolk at some time in their lives and have learnt how to do most routine domestic chores for themselves. The same is true of many lower-class Punjabi men, especially those who have served in the army. But village men will hardly ever be seen doing this kind of work in their own homes. If the wife is sick then some female neighbour or relative will take her place at the hearth. This is partly because it would be shaming for a man to do a woman's task if there is a woman who could do it in his stead. But it is also because cooking is the responsibility of women. If the woman who normally cooks is unable to do so, then it is up to her to arrange for someone to act as her understudy and she will not appeal to the men of the household unless she has really exhausted all possibilities of a female substitute from her own household work team or from a neighbour's. An interesting situation arose on one occasion when Santosh's brother-in-law came to stay in Harbassi for a month to attend to the land he held there. He normally lived in Delhi but visited Harbassi regularly, and on this occasion his wife had not accompanied him to the village. Santosh, his younger brother's widow, felt concerned that he did not have anyone to cook for him. She felt that as a closely related woman it was her responsibility to see that he had proper meals. Yet she also felt anxious that if she invited him to share her own meals this might be construed as taking an improper interest in him. She resolved the situation by sending him hot food, carried to his house on a tray by a servant.

The care of children is less exclusively the woman's responsibility, but it is still the mother who will be criticized if her children are unruly. For instance, the children of Hemraj and Premi (H12) were reputed to be somewhat wild, and when the eldest girl (who was about nine) insisted on climbing on farm machinery when she had been bidden not to, a neighbour remarked, 'Premi's daughters are totally without fear and it is a pity that she does not discipline them better'. That is, it was assumed that it was the more immediate responsibility of Premi than of Hemraj to punish their daughter for climbing on the tractor.

If there are several grown women in one household they will form a work team for the performance of domestic tasks under the leadership of the senior active woman. The leader need not necessarily be the oldest woman; an elderly woman who has retired from active work has probably also relinquished her role as work organizer even if the fiction is maintained that she still has this authority. The women will usually work out a regular division of labour for themselves. For instance in Durgi's household (C2) Durgi herself did most of the cooking and she also milked the cattle. Her elder unmarried daughter generally washed the clothes and occasionally cooked. The younger daughter and the son (who were still at school) took it in turns to fetch water from the well. The senior active woman will usually take the initiative in allocating tasks, but daily reminders that this or that must be done are seldom necessary except in the case of young children for whom, understandably, the idea of another ten minutes in bed or another half hour's play may be more attractive than that of fetching pots of water or of sweeping the yard.

In households where the women do little or no agricultural work, the men of the family form an independent work team, similarly organized under the leadership of the senior active male. Dalip (H2), for instance, did little strenuous work on his farm after a severe illness but he would usually accompany his two sons to their fields and would give instructions as to which fields should be ploughed or irrigated, how many labourers should be hired for a certain task, and so forth. That is not to say that the sons took no initiative, but they would not undertake any major task without reference to their father. In this kind of work team the role of the senior male is more obvious (though not necessarily more important) than that of the woman who leads the domestic work team, largely because domestic work is more repetitive at a day-to-day level than agricultural work.

Its cycle of tasks is shorter and more regular and the need to make major decisions is less frequent.

What about those households in which agricultural work is done by both men and women? In such cases, the men and women of the household will form one work team so far as cultivation is concerned. The prime mover may be the senior active male or the senior active woman – or it may be impossible to decide who actually takes the main initiative (a point I shall come back to later). Where the men are employed outside the village or where there are no adult male members (as in households H13, H14, C2, C11), the senior woman must organize the day-to-day farm routine. This may even be the case when the men are not employed elsewhere. The husband of Mahinder Kaur (H9) had his own transport business and also did agricultural work, but it was Mahinder Kaur who played the more active role in actually organizing the work. She did not do much work in the fields herself but she would go daily to the shed in the fields where her husband and the farm workers gathered to eat their lunch. Her pretext was that she took them their food to eat there, but in actual fact she would use these visits to supervise what was going on, to allocate tasks, and to survey the progress of work already started. On her way home she would collect money from the households where she sold milk. Her daughter-in-law did no agricultural work at all but did most of the routine housework, being left by her mother-in-law to organize domestic matters pretty much as she liked. In Balvinder Saini's household, however, it was very much Balvinder's father who directed the farm work, even though he was absent from the farm for most of the day working as a skilled mechanic (H11). To summarize, we might say that whilst it is more usual for a senior man to lead the agricultural work team of a household than for a woman, there is a good deal of variation according to the circumstances of particular households. It is only in the more highly segregated households of the capitalist farmers that the leader will invariably be a man.

Whilst there is a good deal of social segregation of the sexes in both Himachal and Punjab, there is no real feeling that men and women ought not to work together in the fields (see Sharma 1978b: 268). If a mixed group is engaged in a common task, either as members of the same household or as hired labourers on another person's land, there is a tendency for the women to congregate and to work at a little distance from the men, but if a man and his wife are working alone or just with their children they will not space themselves in this way. The rules of etiquette which separate the sexes in most situations do not seriously inhibit communication among men and women co-operating in the same work team, and young wives learn to reap and weed deftly with their faces modestly veiled from their fathers-in-law.

There is a third area of responsibility which I have not referred to explicitly in this chapter so far, namely the responsibility for the household's dealings with other groups and agencies – what might be called extra-household business and liaison work. So far as day-to-day shopping is concerned it is more often the responsibility of the women to see that the household is stocked with provisions and everyday necessities. It is not necessarily the women who actually *do* the shopping (least of all in those households where women observe some kind of purdah) but it is their business to see that it gets done and to commission some other member of the household to go to the *bazar* and fetch any item that is needed. (See above, p.42) On the other hand, most other kinds of dealings with official or commercial agencies are a male responsibility, in accordance with the idea that the public sphere is primarily a male sphere (see Chapter 3). Dealing with litigation, matters of taxation, registration of land, meeting government agents such as the Block Development Officer (the officer responsible for disseminating information about agricultural methods), registering children in school – these are all tasks which are primarily (though not exclusively) the business of men. Some women, either on account of widowhood or because their husbands are migrant employees, are obliged to do this kind of work on occasion. For instance Durgi (C2) had visited the Block Development Officer at Chaili to request that a sample of the soil on her land be taken for testing. The mother of Prito (C9) had represented the family in court when there was a dispute over land, as her husband was working in Amritsar and could not get leave for the purpose. But such women are pitied by their neighbours for having to step outside the household into the public sphere; had either of them had a husband or grown son at home, it would have been his business to do such tasks.

We therefore have two basic patterns of organizing work performed in the household. In one type there will be two distinct work teams; a female work team performing domestic work, and a male work team doing agricultural work and extra-domestic tasks. Or there may be two overlapping work teams; a female work team doing the domestic work, and a mixed work team doing agricultural work and extra-domestic work. There are two minor variants of the latter pattern. In the first, women are rather marginal in the agricultural work team and are only drawn in to perform certain specified tasks or only at certain very busy seasons of the year. (This is the pattern in many substantial peasant households in Punjab.) In a second variant, which is more common in Himachal, it is the men who are marginal to agricultural work for the reason that they are absent from the village for much of the time and the main burden of organizing and performing farm work falls on the women.

In the latter case, the women have a very heavy load of work and responsibility. One Himachal villager remarked to me, 'Our women are slaves; they are never free from work. Men can sit in the *bazar* and smoke or drink tea, but the women always have something to do.' In fact few men spent much time in total idleness, nor did the women think of themselves as slaves, but they did think of themselves as tied to a never-ending cycle of work and activity. Domestic work alone is seen being of itself without beginning or end. The Punjabi saying '*ghar da kam kadi na mukda*', i.e. 'housework is never finished', makes just this point and can be compared to the English saying, 'A woman's work is never done.' When the responsibility for farm work is added to this, the women understandably see themselves as doubly burdened.

## The life cycle and the domestic cycle; meeting labour crises

It will be evident from what I have said about the organization of labour within the household that an individual of either sex passes through a characteristic, ordered cycle of work and responsibilities. In peasant households a girl spends her childhood learning domestic tasks and routine agricultural work under the supervision of her mother. When she marries she may spend further years working and gaining more farming experience with her mother-in-law, or perhaps with her husband's elder brother's wife. As daughter-in-law she will initially have more work than responsibility, but she will assume further responsibility for the performance of tasks in the household either when her husband sets up an independent household separate from that of his parents or brothers, or (more gradually) when her mother-in-law begins to retire from active management of household work. As she grows older herself and as her daughters grow up and her sons's wives join the household, she is in turn in a position to withdraw from the more strenuous routine work, eventually taking a place on the sidelines so far as day-to-day work is concerned. This is a typical sequence, but there is no way of predicting at what age a particular woman will experience these stages, only the order in which they are likely to occur. At precisely which point, for instance, she will be able to shuffle off some responsibility onto the younger generation will depend on the cycle of household organization which a domestic unit undergoes as its members marry, bear children, separate their property, and die. Decisions about whether to get a son married early or late, whether to partition property, or whether a particular son should leave the village to work elsewhere are not made without reference to the labour requirements of the household at the time. (See Parry 1979: 180ff for accounts of the domestic cycle which refer to the role played by household labour shortages in determining decisions about marriage, partitions of property, etc.).

The case of Prito's household illustrates these points. Prito's parents-in-law (C9) had been anxious to arrange their son Som Nath's marriage as soon as possible because another female hand was badly needed at home. All their sons were now working outside the village and all those who had already married, except one, had taken their wives with them to the various places where they worked. The elderly couple were left to work the family land with the help of only one daughter-in-law. This daughter-in-law had several tiny children and therefore could not be expected to do so much of the outdoor work. In Himachal it is usual for a girl to spend a good deal of the first year of her marriage at her parents' home, visiting her in-laws' home regularly and gradually extending the length of her visits there. In Prito's case however, her incorporation into her husband's household was hurried along for the simple reason that her labour was badly needed. Her parents were not very happy about this, partly because Prito felt very homesick, but also because they themselves were facing a similar labour crisis. Prito's brother had married three years previously but the marriage had not been very successful and his wife had taken their baby daughter and returned to her parents' home. All Prito's brothers were working away from the village save the youngest, who was still at school. The only other member of the family permanently at home apart from Prito's mother was her schoolgirl sister. The family were unwilling that this girl should do too much farm work as she had been getting very good marks at school and they were seriously thinking of letting her continue her education beyond the fifth grade. Too much domestic or farm work would have interfered with her school performance, they felt. So Prito had become invaluable to her mother as the only other adult member of the household able to help with domestic and agricultural work, and her parents would have been very happy if she could have spent more time at home after her marriage to continue with this help.

It happens, therefore, that a household is liable to experience crises from time to time when its labour requirements cannot be met, or can be met only with difficulty. This can happen for a number of reasons. It may occur for 'demographic' reasons, for instance, if the first two or three children of a marriage are daughters and have to be married off before their brothers are ready to marry and bring home wives who will replace the daughters. This happened in the household of Bhagat Ram (C11). Both his wife and his daughter-in-law enjoyed poor health and had difficulty in managing the land while he and his son were away working in Delhi. All Bhagat Ram's own daughters save one were older than his son and had long since married and gone to live in their husbands' villages. The daughter who remained at home was only fourteen years old and could not be expected to do much work as she was still at school. It seemed likely that her parents would remove her from school so that she would be free to do more work at home, though they would have liked her to take a course in tailoring when she had completed eight standards. On the other hand, Bhagat Ram himself was due to retire soon and his presence at home might solve the problem as he was a vigorous man still, well able to do the regular strenuous work with only a little help.

In the case of Pushpa (C6) the school-teacher, the crisis was of a different nature. Her husband had quarrelled with his parents and lived separately from them. Having no land of their own at the moment, agricultural work was not a problem and both Pushpa and her husband earned their living as school-teachers. They were not badly off by local standards, but their problem was that they had no-one who could regularly look after their small children. The older boy and girl were now at school but the baby boy was cared for by various relatives and neighbours in turn. Pushpa's husband's sister had been very helpful but she was likely to marry within the next year. Understandably, Pushpa looked forward to the time when all three children would be at school and the older children responsible enough to take on some of the domestic tasks.

In the capitalist farmers' households in Punjab the crises which occur are liable to be of a different nature. The household will be in a position to hire extra domestic or agricultural help when it is needed, and heavy manual work is not done by household members anyway. Crises in this kind of household will relate to the need for there to be at least one active male member of the household at home to take charge of the day to day management of the farm, since women cannot stand in for men as they can in households of lower status groups. Major Joginder Singh (H7) told me that his farm had gone through a very unproductive phase prior to his retirement from the army. His elder brother, with whom he farmed jointly, had found it difficult to do more than keep the farm 'ticking over' on account of poor health and general infirmity. Joginder Singh was relying on the income of the farm to supplement his pension from the army and had feared that this income would be inadequate, since the land had been so neglected. His own sons were all away in the army themselves or employed elsewhere, and his elder brother had no sons. When he retired he applied himself to making the land fully productive and investing in modern machinery and fertilizers, but he feared that it would take some time for the farm to recover from the bad patch it had gone through.

When labour crises occur in peasant or labourer's households it is generally the women who bear the brunt of the work burden. It is a male responsibility to earn cash; women, as we have seen, cannot be expected to contribute so much here. The women are liable to be left to deal with shortages of household labour as best they can. Frequently these crises are of long duration, especially when they are due to the absence of males in wage employment at a distance from the village.[2] Couples are generally pleased to have a large family as it is hoped that the sons will all find employment and will be able to support their parents in comfort when they are older. But if the husband himself is absent for much of the time the double burden of agricultural and domestic work is liable to fall on his wife at precisely the period when she is also bearing children, and in such cases her load is a triple burden. Meeting one need (the need for cash), can create another (the need for labour).

**Agricultural decision making**

The wife of a migrant labourer will have not only more work than a wife whose husband is at home, but also more responsibility. She will have to be prepared to make decisions regarding the management of the land, and to 'carry the can' if things go wrong. Most migrant workers do their best to be at home during critical periods of the agricultural year, especially the monsoon sowing and the wheat harvest, but this is not always possible (for instance if the husband is in the army and is posted to a distant part of India).

I have the impression that the nature of agricultural decision making differed considerably according to the kind of farming unit concerned. While I was working in Himachal I made efforts to identify the processes of agricultural decision making. Who, for instance, decides when to sow the maize, and on the basis of what kind of information? How do people make judgements about what kind of crops to sow? I found that as far as farmers in Chaili were concerned, these were the wrong kind of questions. Firstly, they did not see themselves as having much scope for choice in farming matters. That is, they did not perceive much choice as to what crops could be grown or where they could be marketed. There were very limited possibilities open due to the lack of agricultural development in this area and the lack of capital for investment; if there is no possibility of irrigation then you have little choice but to cultivate one of the few local varieties of drought-resistant wheat. Secondly, farmers in Chaili seemed to perceive agricultural decision making as more of a collective than a household matter. That is, if a farmer gets up in the morning and begins to plough a particular field, in reality it can only be because either he or someone else in the household has considered that this would be a good thing to do. But farmers see themselves as being very much guided by a kind of local *conscience collective*. For instance, when I asked farmers how they judged whether the maize should be sown or whether it would be better to wait a little at the start of the monsoon,[3] I would receive replies such as, 'I started to sow because everybody else was sowing; it was the right time for sowing'. This does not mean that the farmers did not make decisions on an individual or a household basis, only that they were not *conscious* of the decisions as individual ones. They tended to see themselves as managing their land according to a set traditional pattern, which left less scope for conscious choice and deliberation.

This contrasts strongly with the capitalist farmers of Punjab and slightly less strongly with the smaller Punjabi cultivators, who saw their own practice in a very different light. Here there was a tendency to see decision making as very much a household matter. Farmers would certainly discuss agricultural matters with each other; evenings in winter would often be spent sitting round a stove, roasting ground nuts, and talking over the progress of the wheat crop or the demand for certain types of vegetables. Conversation would usually revolve around farm management and there would be a good deal of exchange of personal experience and opinions. But farmers saw their judgements as being based on information gathered from a variety of sources. These sources would include the views of one's neighbours, but also commercial firms and their representatives, government agencies, radio or television programmes, etc. It would be up to the individual farmer to collate this information, discuss it with the men and women of his family and come to a decision that would be right for his circumstances and for the type of farm he had.

We may note that this discussion does not necessarily exclude female members of the household even when the women are minimally involved with the material aspects of agricultural production. The long deliberations which Dalip (H2) engaged in with his family over whether or not to invest in a second tube-well definitely included his wife Kaushalya. She played an active part in discussions, as I can attest from personal observation. Sandhu, in a study of the economic contribution of women in a Punjab village, notes that in forty-eight out of seventy-four farm families the women were consulted in matters such as the sale of produce, sowing, cropping patterns, hiring of labour, etc. The author seems to regard this proportion as being low, but given that only in nineteen of the families did the women perform any kind of outdoor agricultural work, we could just as well regard it as a high proportion (Sandhu 1976: 21). It is difficult to decide how much weight women's opinions carry in such consultations, but obviously we cannot assume that because women are not seen in the fields they have no control over what goes on in the fields.

The point which I am trying to make is not that capitalist farmers make decisions in a calculated and rational way while small farmers blindly follow tradition. It is rather that there are differences in the way in which they *perceive* their decision making and these differences are ones which are important for the purposes of this study.

For if decision making is not seen as resulting from interaction among individuals with different interests, opinions, and information, but as a matter of intuitive sensitivity to prevailing conditions (climatic, sociological, ecological) then it is going to be all the harder to identify the specific role which women play in agricultural management. This point will be important later when I discuss changes in the part which women play in farm work and management in the next chapter.

Summarizing the foregoing sections, we can say that it is not possible to predict precisely what degree of control over the organization of work in the household any particular woman can hope to enjoy, but that there are certain factors which are very important. We can ask about a woman's position in the household (are there other women to help her? Is she the senior woman?); what is the composition of the household (what is the proportion of men to women, and are the men employed away from the village?); what type of farming is practised (capitalist farming or peasant husbandry?). I now turn to the question of the extent to which women participate in control over household resources.

## The disposal of agricultural produce and the control of income

Besides the wages of its members, the other source of cash for rural households is the sale of agricultural produce. In Chaili only the peasants with the largest holdings (ten acres and above; such holdings are very few) can ever hope to have a surplus worth marketing. In Punjab, on the other hand, with more productive land and larger holdings, the capitalist landowner can expect to obtain a good part of his annual income from the sale of grain or other produce. Wheat and maize are sold either to government agents or to private dealers at (in theory at least) government-approved prices. Vegetables grown in the Harbassi area may be sold to dealers in the wholesale market in Harbassi itself, but some farmers prefer to take their vegetables to Hoshiarpur and trade with larger dealers. In either case a good deal of the produce ends up in the central wholesale market in Delhi. In District Hamirpur there is no such local wholesale outlet. A vicious circle operates, as there is little incentive for dealers to visit rural areas to buy up goods when the surplus product is so scanty and uncertain. But, there being no regular market for any small surplus they might have, farmers have no incentive to switch to the cash crops which could be grown in the area and tend to stick to staple grains for their own domestic consumption. If they have a little extra wheat or maize such farmers usually sell it privately to neighbours or other local people. Small quantities of grain can also be sold direct to local shopkeepers. Much the same practice is found among some small farmers in Punjab.

Where large amounts of produce are to be sold and a visit to the wholesale market is necessary, then the marketing of the produce is invariably in the hands of the men of the household. It would be considered inappropriate and unseemly for a woman to go on business to the vegetable market at Harbassi where she would be gazed upon by the male public in general. The amazement which Hardy's Bathsheba evoked when she visited the corn exchange at Casterbridge would be nothing compared with the astonishment a Santosh or a Kaushalya would evoke if she were to make a foray into the public world of large-scale commerce.

This does not mean that women do not have any control over the agricultural produce of the household at all. In peasant households the grain kept for domestic use is stored in large bins or baskets to which all members of the family have access. There is nothing to prevent any member of the household from removing grain, selling it, or giving it in exchange for other goods,[4] though it is generally considered the senior woman's responsibility to monitor the domestic grain supply, to judge how long it will last, and to control consumption if a shortage is likely. If the household produces eggs or milk in excess of its needs then the sale of these will usually be managed by the senior woman of the household, and the cash thus earned will be kept by her (such sales are usually made to close neighbours).

There was no household in the sample which did not have one or more head of cattle. For some of the poorer families in both areas, the sale of a young bullock or heifer was an important means of raising money to meet some important but non-recurring need. For instance Sita (H15) sold a female buffalo calf to pay for the installation of a handpump in her courtyard. She hoped to raise the money for the marriage of her daughter by selling a pair of bullocks which she was rearing. Sita's husband had been chronically ill and was likely to remain bedridden, so the family had little hope of being in a position to save cash to meet such demands. The sale of young cattle was all that had stood between this family and the moneylender.

Cattle may be sold at fairs held periodically in many country districts or by private treaty. In either case a good deal of travelling outside the village is needed and the transactions will therefore generally be dealt with by the men. It is women who actually tend the cattle and it is often a woman who has located a prospective purchaser for a cow or buffalo through her network of kin and contacts in other villages; but the cash accruing from the sale of cattle is controlled by men.

## The control of cash and household budgeting

From the foregoing it will be clear that while some women have a cash income of their own, the major portion of the household's cash income, whether earned through the sale of produce or through employment, will be received in the first place by its male members. But who controls the spending of this income? What role do women play in the disposal of cash?

Arrangements in this respect are very various. In households where the husband is in employment outside the village, he will usually send regular remittances to his wife to meet the household's day-to-day expenses. If his parents are alive and are living with the couple, he may send the money to his mother or his father instead of his wife. Where a wage-earning husband is living at home, there is more scope for him to maintain a close control over the budget himself. Jyoti, the schoolmaster in Harbassi (not included in the sample), gave his wife very little cash each month (not more than Rs 20) but did almost all the shopping himself, going to the market on his bicycle twice a month. Hemraj, on the other hand (H12), made over his entire wage to his wife when he received it and asked her for cash if he wished to make personal purchases. Like Jyoti, he did a great deal of the shopping but he would ask his wife what should be bought and she would give him the amount they estimated was necessary for these purchases.

*Table 3* summarizes some of the more common arrangements among the families in the sample. It is only a very crude summary since some of the categories could be broken down further. We cannot predict much about the relative financial power of women in category C, for instance, since much depends on whether the wife receives a large and regular income for her labour or a small sporadic one. The men of category B may be ceding a lot of financial control or a little to their wives, according to how great their incomes are in

Table 3 *Control of household budgets: summary of households in the sample*

|   | types of control | numbers of households |
|---|---|---|
| A | man gives fixed allowance to wife or mother from monthly earnings for household expenditure only | 15 |
| B | man gives all or almost all monthly cash earnings to wife or mother for most kinds of expenditure | 4 |
| C | man and wife each keep respective earnings and share responsibility for budgeting | 8 |
| D | man keeps all the cash and does all kinds of budgeting himself | 0* |
| E | there is no male member of household; the woman receives all cash and budgets for herself | 1 |
|   | TOTAL | 28 |

*There were no cases of this type of household in the sample, but they were not totally unknown in the areas studied.

the first place. Also, I cannot be sure that all that my informants told me about their household budgeting was true, this being a rather sensitive area of enquiry. However, taking this distribution as a crude guide, we can see that the most usual arrangement is that which is also most usual in western industrial societies, i.e. the man gives a more or less regular allowance to his wife for her to use for housekeeping expenses, keeping the rest back for his personal expenses and for saving.

But where a woman has control over cash there are a number of factors which may inhibit her from exercising that control in a free and independent way. Firstly there is the factor of illiteracy. A number of the women from peasant households in both areas had post office savings accounts and would save small sums from their cash allowances from time to time, or their husbands would make deposits in their names. But women who are illiterate often feel embarrassed at exposing that illiteracy in public places such as the post office or the bank. Even women who are quite capable of filling in deposit forms or withdrawal slips may feel self-conscious and uncomfortable in an impersonal public place. Santosh (H1) consistently refused to visit the bank in Harbassi where she had an account, unless accompanied by one of her sons. She was a highly educated woman, easily capable of making sense of form-filling and bureaucratic procedure. But even for such a sophisticated woman, the sense of having trespassed on 'male' territory was quite real enough to deter her from visiting places such as the bank or post office independently. The same feeling deters some women from independent shopping expeditions. The wives of big landowners in Harbassi do not visit the *bazar* at all; if they go shopping it will be to make some personal purchase in a large urban shopping centre such as Hoshiarpur where they are not known to the shopkeepers. The everyday requirements of the household will be bought in by a servant or by male members of the household, albeit under instructions from the woman herself. So far as women of other social groups are concerned, much depends on the individual's personal preference. Shila (C11) felt self-conscious about visiting the *bazar*; she claimed that she seldom went shopping as she had never been to school and was afraid of being cheated or made to look foolish. The fear was probably unfounded – many illiterate village women are quite capable of making rapid and accurate calculations in spite of having had no formal education – but the feeling was real enough to her. In other families, the women would go to the *bazar* to make purchases but would go about their business briskly, not making it the occasion for casual gossip as men might do. Mohini (C4) said that she never visited the *bazar* if she could help it as she did not think it was proper for women to be seen there. Her husband would fetch the important items and a child could be sent for minor errands. She was prepared, though, to visit her husband's shop and that of her husband's brother; they were, in a sense, family territory and, to her, less public than the other shops. Similarly Sarla (C5) had no compunction about going to the *bazar* to sit in her son's shop from time to time, but she would not be seen hanging about chatting in any other part of the market. Social norms do not explicitly forbid any but a few high status women in Harbassi from visiting shops to spend money as they think fit, but they do ensure that a shopping expedition will be experienced as a venture into territory which a woman does not feel to be her own.[5] Village women usually feel more confident about making shopping expeditions in the company of other members of the family or with other women whom they know. Alone, they often feel uncomfortable about moving freely from shop to shop in search of just the goods they want at precisely the price they wish to pay.

A third factor is one which has been remarked in studies of women in western societies, the sense that money given as a regular allowance by the husband from his wages is not truly 'one's own' to spend with complete freedom. The woman does not only feel that she has been entrusted with responsibility for seeing that housekeeping needs are met, but feels positively guilty at the idea of spending any small surplus left over after meeting these requirements on herself, unless such expense is approved by other members of the household. This leads to an asymmetrical situation: while a man does not question his right to spend what he chooses on personal items (such as cigarettes or tea), a woman will feel such expenditure on herself to be an indulgence. Village women in India are less likely to be ignorant of what their husbands earn than working-class women in the West; a man's salary is one of the more public aspects of his status and a rise in wages is an occasion for family celebrations. But however large a share of it she receives in the form of a monthly allowance, she will feel responsible to the rest of the household for the way in which she decides to spend it in a way that is different from the responsibility felt by men for that part of their wages which they withhold.

**Women's control over their own earnings**

Lower-class women who earn money by doing agricultural labour, odd domestic jobs for other households, or by home tailoring, do not usually surrender their earnings to any other member of the household, but spend or save their cash as they think best. When I called to collect a suit of clothes I had commissioned to be made up by Kanta (H14), her mother told me to give the money to Kanta herself and did not seem curious about how much her daughter had charged me. Kanta planned her spending without reference to any other member of the family as far as I could see, but her purchases were usually of a fairly essential nature and were as often made for another member of the household as for herself. She would, for instance, commission me to buy wool for her when I went to Hoshiarpur so that she could knit sweaters for her brothers. She also bought her own clothes out of her earnings, and occasional items for her dowry. Her mother used most of the money which she earned as a labourer on general household expenses such as paraffin, groceries, etc. Certainly neither woman spent her money on personal indulgences. Women who earn money in this way often save privately, hiding the money against a 'rainy day' in the Indian equivalent of the tea caddy or the stocking under the bed. As one informant told me, 'Every woman likes to give her husband and her children a surprise when the family runs short of money. They will be impressed that she has been saving money all the while and they will praise her'.

A professional woman will retain control of her earnings herself if she is the one who has prime responsibility for household buying and domestic budgeting. The social worker at Chaili whose husband was employed elsewhere kept her salary to pay for the household expenses which she and her children incurred while they were staying at Chaili. Her salary was more than adequate to cover these expenses so that her husband did not have to contribute anything to their day-to-day expenditure. Indeed, she was able to contribute a good deal to their joint savings. The school teacher Roshani (H5) had always had full control of her own salary as she had been separated from her husband for many years and was responsible to no-one for the way in which she disposed of her tiny income. But Jasbir (H7) was a young unmarried teacher and she did give a substantial part of her earnings to her mother who used it to help with general household expenses. The rest she was free to spend as she wished on personal items, especially clothes.

The number of professional women which a study of small rural localities is likely to include will be too small to reveal any general patterns in the way in which such women dispose of their earnings, but it is likely that much will depend on the woman's position in the household. A junior woman may be expected to hand over a large part of her wages to her parents or parents-in-law. The literature on urban women, at least, suggests that this often happens.[7] The fact that a woman can command a responsible job where independent decision making is required of her does not mean that her family regard her labour as other than a household resource whose fruits should be put at the disposal of the whole family. But a woman who is effectively head of the household, or at least its senior woman, is less likely to be expected to hand over her earnings to anyone.

If this is so, it is in contrast to the pattern in labouring families where junior women are more likely to spend their money individually with minimal reference to other members of the household and without any regular pooling of resources.

But perhaps it is a mistake to look at household budgeting from the point of view of the relative independence which women enjoy vis-à-vis their husbands or other male members of the household. It might be more useful to look at family styles of budgeting as they affect both men and women. For instance, it seemed to me that among the low-caste labouring families I knew in Harbassi, the individual earners (whether male or female, junior or senior) had greater autonomy in spending. Some money would certainly be reserved for collective expenditure and would be pooled, but individuals were less likely to have to consult others about minor purchases. But this is less a case of greater personal freedom than of there being less scope for any kind of decision making by anyone, owing to the poverty of the families. Kanta and her mother (H14), for instance, both earned money from time to time as seasonal agricultural labourers. Kanta's father worked in a factory several hundred miles away, and was away from home most of the time. Satya, Kanta's mother, received monthly remittances from him and budgeted for the household rations from this money. She also supervised most short-term expenditure on their land (the hire of a tractor for ploughing, etc.). Kanta was mistress of her own small income and did not give her mother any part of her earnings, spending them chiefly on clothes for herself and small items for her dowry. When her brother earned money as a labourer he too would spend his money independently, usually on clothing and shoes for himself. We could say that all the adult members of this household enjoyed freedom to spend their money as they chose, but in fact there is a very restricted choice. This family had practically no surplus (if we consider their total earnings) after their basic needs were satisfied. In theory, Kanta was free to spend her wages on ice-cream or tickets for the cinema, but she would have been severely criticized by her family if she had wasted her money in this way. It was her responsibility to spend her own money in such a way that she relieved other members of the household from some of the pressure to provide basic necessities. Below a certain level of affluence there is no question of 'choosing' how to spend money and for the person who has the main control of the household budget that control does not confer privilege, only responsibility.

A second common pattern is found in many more prosperous peasant households in both Harbassi and Chaili where the chief source of cash income is the wages of the senior man, especially where this chief wage earner is a migrant labourer. In these households it makes more sense to ask questions about discretion and choice since there will be more cash to spend or goods to dispose of. Here we find a style of budgeting where there is a far sharper definition of the financial responsibilities of men and women, and responsibility is less diffuse than in the poorer labouring families. Typically, the wife (or senior woman) will receive a monthly remittance from her husband (or son). She will have almost complete control over this allowance, using it for all short-term domestic expenditure on non-recurrent items, e.g. house construction and repairs, agricultural machinery, weddings, and other rituals). Kamla's household (C1) is a good instance of one where this pattern is followed, others being C7, C8, C11, H11. Kamla's husband Shri Ram is employed as a school-teacher in a village about twenty miles away and he gives her a regular portion of his salary each month. She also receives cash from the sale of milk when her buffaloes are producing milk in excess of the family's needs. She spends virtually all this money on ordinary household expenses. Shri Ram, she says, does not enquire how she spends it. He is responsible for seeing that some of his income is banked and he also sees to the cost of his own board and lodging near his place of work. Kamla does expect to participate in decisions about major items of expenditure and is indeed consulted, but in this household there is a far more distinct demarcation of the sphere of responsibility of the various members than in, say, Kanta's household.

A third pattern is found in the households of commercial capitalist farmers in Harbassi. Here also there is a demarcation of financial responsibility between men and women. The wife or senior woman is given a monthly allowance for housekeeping and the husband sees to saving and major expenses, as in peasant families. But here the area of control within which the woman operates is much narrower. Firstly, the sum given to the wife will represent a smaller proportion of the entire income of the household. Secondly her responsibility may be more restricted, limited to a rather specific set of expenses, mostly relating to fuel and food. A housewife in this kind of household may well receive far more money than the wife of a migrant labourer or rural employee but her sphere of discretion is far narrower seen in relation to that of her husband. Kaushalya (H2), for instance, has responsibility for organizing the buying of food and for paying the woman who comes twice a day to wash clothes and clean dishes. Her husband Dalip deals with virtually all the other household expenses – buying petrol for their car, paying their sons' college fees and pocket money, agricultural expenditure of all kinds, and clothing for himself and the two sons. Kaushalya bought her own clothes normally and could usually save money from her allowance to spend on the more trivial non-recurrent items, such as small ritual gifts to neighbours. When she wished to make any larger purchase she would have to apply to Dalip for cash. For instance, while I was in Harbassi she made a major shopping expedition to Delhi to buy clothes for her daughter's forthcoming engagement ceremony. Dalip gave her a very large sum from money saved in an account held in his name to cover the entire cost of the expedition. Like Kamla, she was included in discussions about major items of expenditure which Dalip made on the family's behalf (the tube-well which he had bored during my stay in Harbassi, their daughter's dowry), but her area of direct personal responsibility was narrower than that of Kamla, who controlled virtually all regular domestic expenditure.

These types are not exhaustive. For example, I have not dealt with budgeting in households where the control of finances is entirely or almost entirely in the hands of a senior woman (H8, H5, C2, C5). But it should be clear that if we want to assess women's part in the control of household resources this control has at least two separate dimensions: (a) the absolute size of the household's income (does the family have enough money for the question of choice and decision making to be important?) and (b) the demarcation of responsibilities for expenditure of different kinds (what is the range of a woman's responsibility relative to that of her husband or other members of the household?).

## Conclusion

The structure of the household economy is more elaborate than would appear at first glance. There is a complex pattern of collaboration between men and women in the household; all members of the group who are not infants are expected to contribute to the group in ways appropriate to their sex and age and capabilities, and to their status in the household. The contribution of women to this work is central; even in households where the women do no outdoor agricultural work, their domestic labour is essential. Men need women for the work they do in the household; I came to know of no household in either area where all the resident members were men, though there were a few all-female households.

Why, then, do we speak of women being dependent upon men, rather than of men being dependent on women?

Firstly, however large a role individual women play in decisions about the household resources, land is still held by men for the most part, and men are still the chief earners of cash. Most men, therefore, have a source of power in the household to which few women can ever aspire. If men share control of land and household income with the women (and, as we have seen, most of them do to some extent), this sharing takes place because the men have permitted it. Secondly, women continue to depend upon men to conduct transactions concerning the household in its relation to ourside agencies, most importantly transactions which concern the household resources – marketing goods, banking savings, registering land. Women are implicitly debarred from this kind of function by norms which restrict their mobility in public places, their contacts with unrelated men, and frequently by their lack of education relative to men. Furthermore, there is one agricultural operation which women are explicitly barred from performing – namely ploughing – and this renders every woman farmer dependent on her menfolk for carrying out this essential piece of work twice a year.

Men, of course, depend heavily on women to cater for their domestic needs – to cook, clean, wash clothes, and care for their small children. These are tasks which few men would care to perform for themselves at home. But if a man's wife is sick or absent from home he is likely to be able to find a female 'substitute' to do the essential domestic work in her place from among female relations or neighbours. A woman whose husband is away will find it harder to manage without her man, though many are obliged to do so. She cannot ask just any male relative to do highly responsible tasks such as dealing with legal business, signing documents, marketing grain. Even finding someone to plough for her may not be an easy task. If she has more than a few fields ploughing will be a major task and one which a relative, however well disposed, will be chary of taking on at a time of year when he will probably be busy with his own ploughing.

It was at ploughing time that Durgi (C2) complained most bitterly of her widowhood; no-one was prepared to plough her fields for her without being paid, and even those who would do it for pay would only do it after they had completed their own ploughing.

As we shall see, the norms of marriage exaggerate this asymmetry by permitting a man to take another wife if his first wife dies or deserts him, whilst in all but a very few castes it is unacceptable for a widow or divorced woman to marry again. The need for a household to have a stable source of cash income further exaggerates the dependence of women upon men, given that few women can get regular or well paid work themselves. A woman without a husband or a son to earn for her is in a difficult position. Where women do work for wages, their labour is regarded as belonging to the family in a more definite way than that of men. A woman cannot use her wage to become independent of men and as we have seen, their right to take work outside the home is controlled by the family. They may have considerable control over household resources, but effectively only with the agreement of the men who receive or earn the cash income. The decline in the self sufficiency of the household unit has actually increased the dependence of women upon their husbands and sons.

## Notes

1   As feminists have pointed out, we may obtain a very false picture of the relations between men and women in the household if we do not look at the distribution of responsibility. If men in England help their wives wash up this has scarcely eroded the wife's burden of responsibility for seeing that such tasks actually get done, since to wash up is still seen as 'helping the wife' (Oakley 1974: 159).

2   In Himachal Pradesh the absence of migrant males tends to favour the persistence of joint family living since this allows some rationalization of tasks among the women, although there are other considerations involved besides the question of labour shortages. See Parry (1979: 181), and Sharma (1977: 297-8).

3   The decision to sow the maize at the beginning of the monsoon is one of the most critical decisions of the agricultural year. If the farmer sows and it turns out that what he thought was the onset of the monsoon was an isolated shower, then the seed germinates but soon shrivels from lack of water in the interval before the monsoon proper begins. On the other hand, if he delays too much, valuable growing time is lost.

4   Hawkers and small shopkeepers will often accept grain in lieu of cash for goods sold, and sales between neighbours are often made in this way also.

5 It does not provide her with her main chance to meet and gossip with her neighbours as is the case in many British communities, where a trip to the shops, even if there is no item which is urgently needed, represents relief from the isolation of the home.

6 Pauline Hunt, in her account of some British working-class couples, notes that 'However a couple may handle their money it is usually more difficult for the woman to earmark part of their money for her own use. This is due to ideological and practical reasons' (Hunt 1980: 47).

7 Promila Kapur cites several cases in which professional women were expected to hand over their earnings to their parents-in-law or husbands, this often leading to great friction and dissatisfaction on the part of the wife. In many of the urban families she studied the educated wife's labour was clearly regarded as something which she was only entitled to put on the market provided that she put her earnings at the disposal of her seniors in the household (Kapur 1970: 141, 152, 326, etc.). The same expectations held sway in some Asian households in Britain (Wilson 1978: 119).

# 5   Women's work: agricultural and domestic

## Women in agricultural production; changes over time

It is a common observation that an increase in prosperity among peasant farmers in India goes together with a withdrawal of their womenfolk from outdoor agricultural labour. The fruits of irrigation, better technology, or opportunities to buy more land, are invested in status and leisure, and labourers are hired to do work which was formerly done by the women of farming households. In some communities there are ideological incentives which especially favour this tendency; for instance, among Muslims a religious value is given to keeping women in purdah.

Since the growth of modern technology and the 'green revolution' there is a third factor to be considered. Are women really *withdrawn* from agricultural work, or are they *squeezed out* of agriculture by the expansion of a technology which is controlled by and disseminated by men? Writers such as Boserup have drawn attention to the fact that with capitalist farming, the opportunities for women to participate in agriculture and to benefit by this participation have actually diminished in some parts of the developing world (Boserup 1970; Bossen 1975: 24; Mazumdar 1975b). This is a problem of which professional and articulate women in India are well aware and to which some attention has been given in the national press. In fact, during the period of my fieldwork there was quite a spate of articles in newspapers and journals on women's role in economic life.

Let us examine the factors affecting the degree to which women participate in agriculture in Punjab and Himachal Pradesh.

If we are talking about women's participation as family labourers (labourers working on their own fields) then we find 100.71 female cultivators per 100 male cultivators in Himachal Pradesh, compared with only 34.04 female cultivators per 100 male cultivators in Punjab. When it comes to participation as agricultural labourers (i.e. paid workers on another person's land) the difference is just as great. There are 49.88 females per 100 male labourers in Himachal Pradesh, compared with only 12.70 females per 100 male workers in Punjab (Gadgil 1965: 30). The contrast is striking. The fact that many commentators and observers have regarded this low rate of participation in Punjab as something recent also invites us to enquire why the women in such an agriculturally advanced area should take so little part in farming.

Kamla Nath, writing in 1965, notes that in a village in Central Punjab women:

'probably never worked in the fields in the way in which women of some other cultivating groups do. But the trend towards women not doing any work in the fields is recent. The change has occurred only during the last 15-20 years and is related to agricultural prosperity, increase in education and in urban influence. The older women in several households said that earlier they used to go to the fields to pick cotton, bring fuel and vegetables for the home and fodder for the livestock.' (Nath 1965: 813)

Many of my informants from the ranks of the rich peasantry, such as Jivan Kaur (H10) and Satto (H8), made similar observations. Jivan Kaur's brother's wife told me:

'I do not work in the fields. I only go sometimes to take my husband his food if he cannot come back to the house. My mother did more work than I have to do. That is because in the old days there was more poverty. People nowadays can afford to hire labourers, but people like us could not afford that when my mother was young.'

Statements like this from young or middle-aged women would corroborate Nath's suggestion that if there has been a shift, it has taken place during the period since Independence. Yet in the late 1920s and 1930s Darling noted the tendency in undivided Punjab for prosperous peasant wives to withdraw from labour in the fields for reasons of status. He observed that there were many factors favouring the spread of this withdrawal, though they were not all economic. Among Muslims there was the appeal of religion and the modern desire to conform more closely to what the peasant understood to be the dictates of orthodox Islam. Among the Rajputs there was the old ideal of princely living and the avoidance of manual labour from either sex (Darling 1930:350). In many cases, Darling observed, this conformity could ill be afforded, and was yet another contributory cause of indebtedness when they paid hired labourers to do work which their own families were capable of doing. But in some groups, the withdrawal of women was quite the opposite, a positive indicator of a rising standard of living, especially in the canal colonies (Darling 1928: 164). In Central Punjab the new prosperity among peasant cultivators enabled women to both enjoy and expect a more leisured style of life.

> 'Gone are the days when to buy your clothes was a mark of extravagance and pride, and as the machine cloth comes in, the spinning wheel goes out. Moreover, with the growing refinement in dress, there is much less inclination to perform the menial tasks such as collecting cow dung and making it into cakes for fuel.' (Darling 1928: 165)

Kessinger's reconstruction of life in a Jullundur village in the nineteenth century paints a different picture. Around 1848, all members of a household would contribute their labour to the farm, including the children. But women seem to have specialized in the processing of agricultural produce. 'The processing included the shelling of maize, carding and spinning of cotton, grinding of wheat, and the making of various milk products, particularly *ghi* (clarified butter, the principle cooking oil used in the village)' (Kessinger 1974: 54). There was very little need for the women to go out to collect cowdung or draw water, as these tasks would be done by village menials (*sepidars*) who also provided extra agricultural labour when it was needed. The Hoshiarpur District Gazetteer confirms this picture for the area I studied, noting that all women (save Brahmans, Khatris, and Rajputs) did some work in the fields (*Hoshiarpur District Gazetteer* 1883-4: 56, 58).

Much of the processing work which Kessinger specifies as having been the work of the women in the nineteenth century now takes place outside the household altogether. Grain is ground in power-driven mills, machine-loom cloth is usually worn, clarified butter is supplemented by vegetable *ghi* and various other kinds of cooking oil processed in factories and sold in village shops. One can look at this process, as Darling does, as a matter of families buying leisure for their women by relying more and more on bought goods. Alternatively, one can look at it in terms of women being pushed out of their traditional roles in production by the economics of mechanization and capitalist manufacturing, much as women of a lower social class are being pushed out of processes like irrigation, or threshing, which are being mechanized today.

The historical evidence therefore is difficult to sift. We might do worse than accept the general picture given to me by many informants in Harbassi. I was told that there were some women who have never done agricultural work and others who had always done such work. The former were mainly Khatris and Brahmans. As traders and professionals these groups were definitely part of the rural scene, but many had urban connections and until recently they had mostly rented their land out to tenants rather than cultivate it themselves. There had formerly been Muslim Rajput landowners in the Harbassi area whose women had never worked in the fields, but these had all migrated to Pakistan in 1947. Among the landless labourer and tenant class, the women had always worked in the fields and there was no indication that they would change this practice as long as the opportunity remained.

It was only among the women in the intermediate groups that things had changed much, my informants told me, i.e. among the larger owner-cultivators, who were largely (though not exclusively) Jats. The withdrawal of women in this class from outdoor agricultural labour has taken place over time and is probably not complete even today. There is certainly no reason to suppose that it has been solely a product of the 'Green Revolution'. It is really a product of rising living standards in this group, a rise which has been taking place over a long period and for a variety of reasons. In Darling's day members of this class had invested money earned through military service in the purchase of land, or had been rewarded for their services by the British with grants of land in the new canal colonies. Nowadays, these families have prospered either through the application of modern technology on their farms and the rise in the value of agricultural produce, or through well-paid urban employment in Indian cities, the Middle East, Europe, or America.

Even this general picture does not tell us whether there has been a real decline in the proportion of Punjabi women engaged in agricultural work because for all we know, the withdrawal of women which takes place in substantial peasant households has been compensated for by the re-entry of women into agricultural production in groups which have been downwardly mobile. For instance, in a village near Harbassi there was a settlement of Brahman cultivators. Most of their women folk worked full time in agricultural work and the holdings were very small, resulting from the fragmentation of a larger estate. It was clear there here was a family who had seen better times and whose women might not always have done so much outdoor labour.

Yet we can say with some certainty that there is not much likelihood that women will play a greater part in the near future. The increase in mechanized capitalist farming discourages the participation of women in two ways. Firstly, capitalist farming involves direct control with dealers, commercial firms and government agencies – all the world of public commerce and the market from which women of 'good family' are effectively barred.[2] In fact men as well as women in capitalist farming families withdraw from most outdoor labour in the fields, if by that we mean the actual manual work of sowing, weeding, harvesting, etc. But they continue to perform the supervisory and managerial work which it is difficult for women to do. Secondly, at the lower end of the social hierarchy, mechanization displaces both men and women of the labouring tenant class, though probably more women than men, since any permanent farm servants who are hired will be men, and women are retained only for poorly paid seasonal work. Romesh (H4) employs one permanent farm servant who drives the tractor and operates the threshing machine, and another two permanent attendants in his dairy unit. The only women he ever employs are untouchable labourers hired to sort, plant, and harvest vegetables at certain times of year. Santosh (H1) employs one permanent servant and offers fairly regular employment to two or three other men, but the only women hired are employed for weeding and reaping wheat – about ten days twice a year. The women hired are the wives of men who were formerly tenants but who were displaced when the family decided to farm the land themselves, and who would formerly have been working most of the year on their rented plots of land. The use of tractors, seed drills, threshing machines, etc. displaces labour of both sexes and one should not exaggerate the difference, but any permanent opportunities of employment which such mechanization creates are really only for men. All the factors which Boserup specifies as discouraging the participation of women in the modern agricultural sector are present in Punjab, and it is understandable that concerned observers have argued that planners should consider ways in which women might be compensated for this displacement (ICSSR 1977: 10); Bhasin and Malik 1975: 49; Mazumdar 1975a: 262).

In Himachal the situation is rather less complex, although there are fewer historical accounts available to help us judge the extent of change. It is clear that in the lower foothills the vast majority of women do all kinds of outdoor agricultural work apart from ploughing, and that in all probability they always have done. Even the wives of Brahman shopkeepers in Chaili worked in the fields, although some of them could certainly have afforded to employ hired labourers had they thought it important to do so. Devraj's cousin's wife (C10) was a B.A., I was told, yet she carried manure to the fields like everyone else. The stereotype of the hardy Pahari woman who turns her hand to all kinds of work and labours alongside her husband in the fields seems to reflect the truth (see Parmar 1975), except that nowadays her husband is as likely to be in the army or away working in the cities as in the fields.

On the other hand, not all areas of the lower foothills are so impoverished as District Hamirpur and in some districts there are women, chiefly Rajputs, who do not work in the fields. In the Gazetteer of India we find that in District Bilaspur (adjacent to District Hamirpur) women are still prevented from doing agricultural work by conformity to purdah ideals, although Brahman and Kanet women are not so handicapped from 'helping' their menfolk.

What about the past? Is this abstention on the part of some Himachali Rajput women a remnant of a once more rigorous observance of purdah, or is it a movement towards a withdrawal from agriculture such as we have seen among some groups in Punjab? Karan Singh (C8) gave the following account:

'In the old days, about one hundred years ago, we Rajputs were the military caste. Our work was ruling and fighting. Even now, if you ask a Rajput boy what he wants to do he will tell you straight away that he wants to go into the army. The Rajputs were experts in fighting. The men went into the army and the women stayed at home. They kept purdah in those days and they did not work in the fields. All the work was done by tenants. In those days tenants were glad to get work. Now they do not want to work for us any more because they can get good wages mending the roads or working in the towns. And so our wives have to do a lot of hard work.'

Yet the wife of Mohan Singh (C7) told me, when I asked whether Rajput women had always worked as hard in the fields, 'Well, there may be some Rajputs who do not, but in a poor place like this they just have to. There are Rajputs and Rajputs, that is all I can say.' Even the oldest Rajput women I questioned could not look back to a time when the women in their families had not worked in the fields. Maybe this is because the area round Chaili was never prosperous enough to sustain this kind of lifestyle, even among its most substantial cultivators.

In other parts of the hills there seems to be evidence that Rajputs did once practice a stricter form of purdah than they do now. The rules by which the aristocratic Mian Rajputs maintained their claims to status included the injunction that women should be secluded (Parry 1979: 208) but Parry also notes that many Mian Rajputs in District Kangra no longer observe this rule and it certainly seems to have been the norm for all women in the area his research was carried out to do some outdoor work (Parry 1979: 256, 179).

The even greater reliance of Pahari households on earnings brought in by migrant male members, and the consequent absence of many men for most of the year, means that it is less and less likely that women will withdraw from agriculture in the near future. It is true that in some households where migrant men are earning a good wage in secure employment the family could, if they chose, employ others without becoming insolvent. But in such families it is only the substantial cash savings derived from employment which made tolerable the social cost and inconvenience of the men's absence. For all that she grumbled about how hard she worked, I do not think that Kamla (C1) would regard any extra leisure she gained as worth the extravagance of hiring labourers to do her farm work. As it was, her husband was effectively paying for the substitution of her domestic labour in the village where he boarded during the week. (Most Himachali migrant workers complained about the cost of maintaining two establishments even when they lived very simply in what amounted to dormitory accommodation.) Kamla and Shri Ram only feel that they are doing what thrift and common sense dictate, given that in the hills there is no great social pressure for a Brahman woman to stay at home, even if she is a school-teacher's wife.

## Women, work, and status

Obviously, if we wish to explain why some women work in agriculture and others do not we must look at the traditions of particular caste and the local social ethos, as well as economic factors. Caste groups and different religious communities have their own work ethics so far as both men and women's labour is concerned. There is the Rajput ideal of aristocratic leisure for both sexes with purdah for the women, which is common to the more prosperous Rajputs over a wide area of North India (Hitchcock 1959: 12). Among Punjabi Jats, on the other hand, there has never been quite so strong a feeling that manual work diminishes their standing. Satto's sons would readily change into old clothes and work behind the plough or harrow after coming home from their jobs as bus conductors. I am not suggesting that they particularly enjoyed such hard physical labour, but they would consider paying hired labourers to do what they could do themselves a waste of hard-earned money. Some Punjabi cultivating castes have a strong tradition of women working in the fields, and even of hawking agricultural product in the villages (Darling 1930: 7, 207). Not all 'caste ethics' discriminate between men and women in respect of the acceptability of outdoor labour, but as women are the repositories of family honour it is likely that the more rigorous prescriptions will be made their case. Not all people can afford to live to the pattern which they feel is dignified and fitting for people of their caste, but these traditions do affect the ways in which people evaluate themselves and others. The practice of a particular household is the result of the interaction between the economic position of that family and pressures to conform to a self-image which they feel is appropriate.

While all groups regard land-owning as prestigious, agricultural labour (even on one's own land) brings no positive credit. In some ways it is seen as non-work, in much the same way that housework is regarded as non-work in western societies. I remember how one woman asked what her husband's occupation was, replied, 'He does not do anything, he just stays at home'. It took further questioning to reveal that she had not meant to imply that he was idle, only that he cultivated his own fields and had no outside employment. When Pahari women take over the share of work which their husbands formerly did so that the men can go outside the village to work, they undertake a burden which brings them absolutely no additional credit or prestige. Not being paid, the agricultural work of the family labourer is no more 'proper' work than washing the dishes.

Attitudes are slightly different among the new capitalist farmers in Punjab, although we should remember that the agricultural work they do on their own farms does not include the more arduous forms of physical labour. This is done by hired labourers and the land-owner will usually confine himself to the operation of machinery, driving tractors, and supervisory work. A conversation between two wealthy farmers' sons which I overheard one winter evening in Harbassi reflects changing attitudes towards farm work among men of this class. Satish argued that he was very happy in his city job as a company executive. 'What is the fun in farming? You work in the sun all day and have illiterate labourers for company.' His friend Sanjay defended his preference for farming:

'But you can earn several thousand rupees a month without too much difficulty, and you are your own master. In your job you are someone else's servant, whatever you may say. And don't tell me you live such a riotous life after hours. I come back to my own home at night, while you come back to lodgings in someone else's house.'

Sanjay could contrast the apparent independence of the farmer with the life of the employee; the term used for employment (*nokri*) translates as 'service' and has the connotation of not being one's own master.

Most peasant women however are not in a position to make this contrast and hence to derive satisfaction from their independence as farmers. There is little *nokri* available to women and as farmers, they are still dependent upon their husbands who actually own the land. So if there are social or moral satisfactions to be got from working on one's own land, these are much diminished for women.

Women in capitalist farmers' households do no outdoor agricul-tural work and play at most a minor role in management and super-vision. Some of the women whom I knew might even have enjoyed a greater involvement in their husband's farms. Kaushalya (H2), for instance, told me that if only it were acceptable for a woman of her status, she would have enjoyed starting a little market gardening concern of her own in the village where her husband held land. But for most women of the peasant and labouring groups, agricultural work meant back-breaking toil in the sun and they would find it hard to share Darling's disapproval of the purdah woman's lack of opportunity for healthy outdoor exercise. Nor would they be much moved by the feminists' concern that they are being pushed out of agricultural production. Few regard agricultural work as satisfying and would welcome the chance to earn money in non-agricultural work.

It is important not to project western attitudes when we interpret behaviour which from our own point of view might seem irrational or extravagant. I could not at first understand why Premi (H12) did so little agricultural work. She belonged to a scheduled caste with a long tradition of female labour and with little prestige to lose by working in other people's fields. Also her family could hardly afford to forgo her labour on the tiny plot of land her husband had acquired. And yet, her husband was the poorest of four brothers and her other two sisters-in-law in Harbassi worked hard both on their own land and that of the local big landlord. There was certainly no question of Hemraj hiring labour to cultivate his plot. He simply worked twice as hard himself, fitting in work on his own land with his full-time job as Santosh's farm servant. I found it difficult to make out who had made the decision that Premi should not work outdoors. She herself claimed that Hemraj and his brothers had decided at the time of her marriage that she should not be sent out into the fields and that she had simply concurred, even though she was aware of the cost to her husband. It might be that the family decided that since Hemraj was the poorest of the brothers he should compensate for his lack of cash by having a wife who lead a life of honourable domesticity. But if this was the case, I can hardly imagine that the wives of the other brothers approved, since Satya and Bhagvati were constantly being asked to do small tasks which Premi considered inappropriate for herself and for which Hemraj, busy man that he was, had no time. This exacerbated the already rather tense relations among the three sisters-in-law, which I describe more fully in another chapter.

There were one or two other poor Chamar women in Harbassi who did no agricultural work in spite of a very small household income. One of these was the wife of a schoolmaster from a labouring family who had recently managed to acquire about one acre of land. This man had been working outside the village for several years and his wife had accompanied him, leaving the land to be farmed by relatives for a small rent. When he found a post nearer home and the couple returned to Harbassi, they continued this arrangement. Both claimed that they did things this way because the wife did not like to do agricultural work, even though it seemed that they ought to make more out of their land if they terminated the tenancy agreement and farmed it themselves. But I wonder if there was not an unacknow-ledged reason, namely that on the husband's small salary they could not afford the investment in agricultural tools and equipment which they would have needed to make if they were to work the land them-selves. Being the son of poverty-stricken labourers, the husband had inherited neither land, implements, nor draught animals. In this kind of situation the marginal benefits to be gained from farming a tiny plot may well be so small that one might as well rent it out and reap whatever glory may be got from having a wife who has not stained her hands with manure. Presumably the school-teacher hoped that his wife's leisure might be taken as a sign of status rather than indigence.

## Women's perceptions of agricultural and domestic work

I found it interesting that even women who actually spent more hours in the fields than on housework still tended to identify their duty as women in terms of domestic work. 'A woman's business is to cook and clean the house, and to look after the little children. These are the main things which a woman has to do', said Sita (H15), who spent most of her time cutting grass for fodder and weeding other people's fields. Women claimed usually to like domestic work more than farm work. When asked which routine tasks they found most enjoyable, and which they found least enjoyable most women expressed preference for cooking, with sewing and knitting in second place. Tasks like collecting manure and threshing were least liked. I am still not sure how much these answers reflected actual pleasure felt in doing the tasks or how much they reflected the social value assigned to them. Making chapattis or maize bread over a hot stove when the temperature in the shade is above 100° Fahrenheit does not seem to me a very enviable task. But in preparing and serving food a woman experiences her family's dependence upon her in a very direct way; she is conscious that she controls a vital resource. And then there is the positive moral evaluation given to the preparation of food and the ritual purity of the cooking hearth in Hindu tradition, in which the women presiding over the kitchen can feel that she shares (Khare 1976: 4).

Women regarded housework as more satisfying and more related to their feminine roles than agricultural work, but they did not regard it as entailing any particular skill other than the skills of economy. For the poor families there were not enough opportunities to vary the way in which the work is done. Even in wealthy families the possibilities are limited, for in rural areas one has to buy what is available locally, and there may not be much variety. The main difference between Santosh's cuisine and Premi's is that Santosh can afford more generous portions and cooks with more *ghi* and spices, not that she prepares a greater variety of dishes. Wealthy women in Harbassi can afford to visit Hoshiarpur or even Delhi to obtain household gadgets and consumer goods – refrigerators, stainless steel dishes and cutlery, airtight plastic containers, fancy crockery, and so forth. In this class there was the incipient idea that a woman might show individual taste and skill in the way in which she arranged her home and organized its daily routine.[3]

Another task which many women found interesting and rewarding was the care of cattle. In all households save those of a few big landlords who employed servants for the purpose, the care of the cattle was the woman's task. There were only seven households in my sample in which the women were not involved in feeding and milking of cattle, four of these being families who did not possess any cows or buffaloes. This is work which women take very seriously and which sometimes affords real pleasure. Premi kept two bullocks which she was rearing to sell. She also had a cow and a buffalo to provide milk, and sometimes she would buy a young goat to rear. She was really fond of these animals and would tell me tales of the calves the cow had borne, what had happened to them and where they had been sold, the names she had given them, and how sad she had been when a calf died. Women were prepared to spend a great deal of time and patience on milch animals, administering to their needs when they calved or when they were sick. Most had a detailed technical knowledge of breeding and rearing, and what conditions make for the best milk yield or the strongest calves. Though they relied upon men to take animals to the veterinary surgeon for care or artificial insemination, and to conduct sales when necessary, they took a great interest in cattle breeding and the birth of a calf was an eagerly awaited event. If, as Sandhu calculates, the net value of a milch animal's yield is Rs 3,239.06 per lactation, then the value of women's labour in this area is considerable and can hardly be called a 'side activity' in families whose total monthly income is only a few hundred rupees. (Sandhu 1976: 20-21). But even apart from the utilitarian aspect of this work, here was an activity which clearly gave many women a real sense of achievement.[4]

The care of young children is regarded as part of housework (*ghar da kam*) and therefore the preserve of women. In British middle-class culture there is an emphasis on spending time with one's child, the idea that the moral training and cultivation of the child's potential is achieved by the parents (and particularly the mother) paying special kinds of social attention to him or her. But few Punjabi or Himachali women saw child care as something that 'takes up time' except in so far as the physical needs of children have to be satisfied. The proper training of children was seen as something for which the parents were certainly responsible, but not as some kind of specific task for which time had to be allocated, and hence which might interfere with other activities in a busy routine. Most women considered that children learn through doing. You do not have to spend time teaching your daughter to make chapattis. She just picks it up from doing it. 'First she plays with the dough beside you in the kitchen. Then she rolls out a few chapattis, then she tries to cook a few, and with experience she gets the knack of turning them at just the right time, so that they are light and soft.' Most women recalled their own experience in this way. They could not remember anyone actually taking time to *explain* how you do a particular task, or deliberately instructing them. Agricultural skills are passed on in much the same way, although in one or two occasions I did observe observe a father giving a teenage son lessons in ploughing.

Among some of the wealthy Punjabi families one finds a different attitude. Here women are beginning to see the children's education as something which requires their active supervision, and possibly participation. Saroja (H4) complained to me that the local village schools were very poor.

'The teachers just sit around and gossip all day and then set the children homework to cover what they have not been able to make them understand. That means that if the child is ever to learn any-thing, then parents have to go over it with him at night. I have to spend several hours on seeing that my children do their homework every day.'

This was no exaggeration. She really did spend the latter part of every afternoon supervising her children's studies and they were not allowed to go out to play until they had completed their work. Parents in this class felt that a child was not educated just through the fact of attending school. The quality of the schooling counted and they were sufficiently educated themselves to be critical of what their children received. They also realized that though some of their sons would become farmers, others would probably seek urban employment and that therefore a high standard of educational achievement was important to them. Here we see the beginning of a tendency which is very obvious in urban middle-class families in India. One of the wife's most important duties is to supervise the children's education, to see that they do their homework, and to help them with it if necessary. Cooking and cleaning can be delegated to servants by those who can afford them, but education cannot. In this class a wife's education is not just a status symbol. It is vital in ensur-ing that the children of the marriage receive a good enough educa-tion themselves to maintain the family's prestige and class position.[5]

The presence of small children in itself is not seen as interfering with the mother's capacity to do agricultural work unless they are many and there is no other woman in the household to help her. A mother can take her children, even small babies, to the fields with her and let them sleep in the shade of a tree or play in the dirt. Or she may leave them at home with her mother-in-law or sister-in-law, even with an older child. Much depends on the structure of the household. Even the village social worker in Chaili did not see any conflict between the demands of her children and the demands of her work, or none that amounted to more than occasional inconveniences. During the children's school term she adjusted her work to fit in with school hours. During the vacations she took the children to her office if she was doing paperwork. If she had to visit some other vil-lage she would leave her daughters on their own. The elder child was nine and quite sensible enough, she said, to be left in charge of her younger sister. Pushpa (C6) who was a school-teacher, took her two elder children to school with her, although they were not yet of school age, and they played in the classroom alongside the other children. The baby was left in the care of other relatives and some-times spent quite long spells in his maternal grandparents' home. I did not find any feeling that working mothers *ought not* to work because of the effect on the children, only that combining work and children made for certain practical inconveniences. The prime responsibility for supervising and caring for children is still the mother's, even if she does work outside the home, and to my neighbours it seemed perfectly natural that my own two daughters should accompany me on field trips, since their own practice was similar.

## The relationship between agricultural and domestic work

It should be clear from what I have said in this chapter and the preceding chapter that we cannot discuss women's work in isolation from the work which men do (although my focus has been on women's contribution to the household because this is a book about women). Some changes in women's patterns of work are a result of general changes which also affect the kind of work available to men, as when mechanization pushes women out of paid agricultural labour faster than it displaces men. Some changes come as a direct consequence of changes in male patterns of employment, as for instance when women take on more agricultural work to compensate for their husband's absence as migrant labourers. Or it may be the other way about, i.e. a change in women's work responsibilities affects men's work load in the same household, for instance, when men are obliged to take on agricultural work which women no longer do but for which they cannot afford to hire labourers. What is common to all these possible patterns of change is that the domestic component of women's work load is never transferred to men. There is no trend towards any greater involvement of men in housework and childcare, although some wealthy women in Punjab are able to shed some of their domestic tasks either by hiring maidservants or by investing in labour-saving gadgets of one kind or another.

One of the problems which confronts us when we consider the relationship between agricultural and domestic work in rural house-holds is that in many families these tasks are not discrete spheres of activity, but part of a continuum of tasks. Cleaning a cattle shed and milking a buffalo might be regarded as agricultural work since they contribute to the production of a basic food, milk. But these activities could just as well be seen as preliminaries to a domestic activity, the preparation of a meal. For the woman who does the work, the distinction is not very relevant. The work is all part of a round of activities which are done in the home or in the family's fields, all of which she does in her capacity of wife or daughter. Work place and home are only distinct and separate places for those women who are in paid employment, whether in agriculture or some other kind of work. (Only in eight of the twenty-eight households in the sample were women engaged in paid employment outside the home.) The conceptual separation of 'work' (income-producing activity) and 'housework' (processing goods for consumption and servicing the family) is emerging in the capitalist farming families, and here it coincides fairly consistently with the division of labour between men and women. Other Punjabi families model their pattern of household activities very much on the practice of the wealthy farmers and the sexual division of labour operating in such homes, so the distinction between housework and agricultural work needs to be registered even if no such distinction can be made empirically in the majority of households.

It is a distinction which is certainly made by women themselves in both areas. Women spoke about *ghar da kam* (work in the house) as distinct from *kheta da kam* (work in the fields) and, as we have seen, they generally evaluate the former as more dignified and rewarding. But this distinction is a crude one and there are some tasks which may be performed in or near the home and are regarded as part of a woman's domestic duties, but contribute directly to agricultural production. When Romesh (H4) hired women to sort and clean peas and seed potatoes for planing, it was his wife Saroja who supervised the hired women working in the courtyard, even though she claimed that she never did agricultural work herself. Premi (H12) shelled her maize on her sitting room floor, and in almost all households women tended milch and draught cattle, even if they were not responsible for actually going out to cut fodder. Swaran Kaur (H7) also performed some managerial tasks, supervising women hired to weed and harvest wheat, even though she did no manual agricultural labour herself. The social segregation of men and women in rural society means that in some ways it is easier for a woman to supervise other women, and a wealthy farmer's wife may do such work regarding it as a natural extension of her duties as housewife. We

We also have to take into account the contribution which women make to agricultural decision making which, contrary to what one might expect, does not necessarily diminish when women abstain from outdoor labour (see Chapter 4).

In almost any household where the men are involved in cultivation, the women will also contribute to agricultural production in some capacity, even if the women themselves (and indeed the men) look on this contribution as part of 'housework'. We therefore need to be cautious in our evaluation of statements about the decline in women's participation in agriculture, such as I discussed at the start of this chapter. We need to ask whether the withdrawal of women from farm work which is being described is not really the withdrawal of women from the more strenuous and publicly visible forms of outdoor labour, while the women continue to contribute to production in more discreet ways. If there is also a positive moral and social value given to women *not* doing outdoor agricultural work, it is likely that informants and interviewees will encourage researchers to underestimate the agricultural work which women do. If in addition to this, there is a tendency for family agricultural labour of both sexes to be regarded as 'non-work', then even more of the agricultural work performed by women will be 'lost' from observers' accounts. So although I would conclude from my limited material[6] that the growth of capitalist farming and the application of modern farm technology does lead to the displacement of women *in some classes* from agricultural production, I think that we have to be very cautious about the way in which we interpret data in this area. The bias compounded of the informants' values and the observer's attitudes to work is more likely to lead to the underestimation of women's contribution to agricultural production than the reverse.

### Notes

1    Darling disapproved of women's deprivation of healthy outdoor occupation, especially as it coincided with the replacement by the power mill of the handmill, or *chakki*, which had given purdah women their only opportunity to get regular physical exercise within the home. Nath's younger informants looked at it differently. To them, the replacement of the *chakki* meant the removal of a major source of quarrelling among women; the task of grinding had been so disliked that it was a constant source of discord in the household (Nath 1965: 813).

2 Women are also debarred from this world by the nature of the education they receive. Girls are not sent to college to learn agriculture or commerce, so it is difficult for them to acquire the knowledge of management and modern technology which would be necessary for them to participate in capitalist agriculture on the same terms as men.

3 Both Nath and Sandhu observe that among those prosperous Punjabi households in which women have been liberated from agricultural work, they give attention to making the home more comfortable and devote more time to personal hygiene and personal adornment (Nath 1965: 814; Sandhu 1976: 20-21).

4 Nath notes that in the village she studied, 'Women do not mind looking after the animals – indeed they are proud of it, because presence of milch animals in the house has always been considered a sign of prosperity in Punjab villages' (Nath 1965: 813).

5 See Caplan 1978: 110 for an account of urban women's educational role in the home.

6 I would point out that information presented in this chapter is drawn from my actual observation of what work men and women do, and not only on what informants claim that they do.

# 6   Sisters and wives: marriage, kinship, and female roles

It is now time to turn to women's roles in the system of kinship and marriage and to see whether a fresh look at this area of social life will tell us any more about women's economic and political position.

Anthropologists have tended to treat kinship systems in two divergent ways. At one level kinship can be treated as a cognitive system, a way of ordering the symbolic world, a structure of norms and representations which can be considered as having its own logic. Kinship in this sense is an ideological definition of the relationship between the social and the biological worlds and, as such, may for *some purposes* be treated more or less independently of the economic and political system in which it is embedded. But kinship in everyday life is also experienced as practical activity. Kinship roles specify the form and direction of co-operation, exchange, mutual aid, and ritual obligations The most rigorous obligations and the most concentrated forms of co-operation are those within the household itself, but in India – as in most other societies – this co-operation overflows the limits of the actual residential unit.

Those anthropologists whose interest in kinship has been of the first kind have noted the refraction of female roles in Hindu society. Hershman notes the contradiction between women's role as sexually active beings (whose sexuality is negatively valued and seen as threatening) and as mothers (whose fertility is positively valued, but can only be realized through sexual activity). These contradictory values are juxtaposed, though not finally resolved, through powerful symbols – the sacred cow and the mother goddess who is also a virgin (Hershman 1977: 291). Wadley notes that a model of women's role in the Hindu cognitive system would be threefold. As wives, women are 'good' but only so long as they are subordinated to male control through conformity with cultural roles. As mothers and as mother goddesses, women are both 'good' and threatening, and need to be propitiated or induced to control their own dangerous power. Women who have been translated into ghosts or demons (typically through death in childbirth) are totally malevolent and the best that can be hoped for is to mitigate the dangerous effects of their malice through appeasement (Wadley 1977: 125). Men's roles are not thus refracted. That is, specific duties are demanded of men in their capacities of husbands, fathers, sons, and brothers, but these roles draw on a very general model of manly behaviour (duly modified by considerations of juniority and seniority). A brother is different from a husband, but he is not a different kind of *man*.

Turning now to kinship as a system of concrete rights and obligations, the crucial distinction to be made here is that between women as *affines* (primarily wives, but also daughters-in-law, sisters-in-law, etc.) and women as *consanguines* (sisters, daughters, etc.). This categorization extends beyond the immediate household so that the women of an entire village, according to whether they were born there or married there. Appropriate behaviour is specified for either kind of relationship. Daughters are a category; one gives first and foremost to one's own daughter at the time of marriage but one also participates in the giving to the daughters of close kin. The making of gifts to any woman classed as a 'daughter' is a meritorious act and sometimes a person who has no living daughter will designate the daughter of some friend or relative to receive ritual gifts in lieu of a real daughter.[1] Daughters-in-law are also a category. One expects very specific services from one's own son's wife, but respectful and submissive behaviour is expected from the daughter-in-law of any kinsman. Also, one does not only receive gifts from one's own daughter-in-law's family. One often has a share in the gifts brought by the daughters-in-law of close kin, especially at marriage and other major rituals.

This categorization at the level of active social roles reproduces the refraction of female roles in the cognitive scheme, but only in an approximate and distorted way. The distinction between women considered as sexually active (wives) and women considered as sexually inactive (sisters) is present, but mothers (central to the symbolic system) do not constitute a category of persons comparable to daughters or daughters-in-law. One's mother's sister or one's own father's brother's wife can be 'like a mother' but they are not referred to as mothers. Mothers are only treated as a category when a person refers to his or her father's polygymy. One woman told me 'I have two mothers', meaning simply that her father had two wives, both of whom participated in her upbringing. In general, the relationship with the mother is considered too intense and specific to be generalized.

From the point of view of the women themselves, this refraction of female roles is reflected in the duality of *peke* (parents' home) and *saure* (in-laws' home) which I referred to earlier. A woman sees her social world as radically divided between those to whom she is related consanguineally (as sister, daughter, etc.) and those to whom she is related through her husband (as wife, daugher-in-law, etc.). For the village woman who has not travelled much, these categories may be virtually exhaustive; all the members of her social universe are subsumed under one or the other, given that all members of her *peke* village are 'like' her own kin, and all members of her *saure* village are 'like' in-laws to her. It is only those women who have lived in more impersonal communities, in cities or cantonments, who have experience of close relationships with people who cannot be assimilated to either category but who must be classed simply as neighbours or friends.

The division between affines and consanguines exists for men also, of course. A man will identify his wife's natal village and the people to whom he is related through her as his *saure*, but the opposition between one's own village and that of one's spouse is not significant in the same way for men because they are not required to move from one to the other on marriage. Men's experience differs from that of women further in that men, being more mobile and more likely to leave their own villages in search of work, are more likely to know a large number of people who are not related to them in any way and cannot be subsumed to either category.

Sisters and wives have different kinds of claim upon the resources of a household. A sister has the right to expect a decent dowry at the time of her marriage and has a right to maintenance until that time. After marriage she has no automatic right to maintenance from parents and brothers. The sister can give nothing to her brother (unless she is much his senior), yet if her marriage is unhappy or threatens to break up she may need to return home. Not being entitled to maintenance as of right, she must rely on the goodwill and tenderness of her brothers or parents. As I have indicated, I think that it is confusing to regard dowry as a form of *ante mortem* inheritance on the part of female heirs, but it does make sense to the extent that the giving of dowry is regarded as terminating the father's responsibility to maintain the woman, a responsibility which is transferred to the husband. The songs which women sing at the time of the departure of the bride, when her dowry is carried out of the house, emphasize the theme that she is now someone else's responsibility and a 'stranger'[2] in her father's household, that is she has no rights there any more (other than in the circumstance of her father dying without other heirs, in which case she might inherit his property). However, her marriage gives her rights to maintenance in her husband's household (and residual rights in his property if he dies before her) and these rights only lapse if she remarries after her husband's death or if she leaves him voluntarily.

## Dowry and the role of women

A consideration of dowry is relevant here because some writers have seen the nature and direction of marriage payments as being related to the economic contribution of women to the household.[3] If marriage payments do reflect this contribution in a direct and proportionate way, we should expect *bride-price*[4] to be given where women's contribution to the household is greatest (compensation of the father for the loss of his daughter's income or services). We should expect *dowry* to be given where a woman's contribution is limited or negligible (compensation of the husband or his family for the expense they will incur in supporting the wife as a dependant).

Clearly this explanation cannot account for the world-wide distribution of dowry and bride-price. Bride-price is the dominant form of marriage payment in African horticultural and pastoral societies, and in such societies women's contributions to production is in no way less than that of men. In most parts of India, both bride-price and dowry are found side by side, the more common pattern being the payment of bride-price among landless labourers and small peasants and dowry among the upper peasantry and landlord and urban classes. This does make sense in terms of the 'compensation' theory of dowry if we accept that it is in the poorest households that women's labour or income is likely to be most important to the household economy. The upper-class woman, confined mainly to domestic work, does not generate income in the same way and can be to this extent regarded as a financial liability for whom dowry has to be paid.[5] (A local version of this theory, cited by some informants in Punjab and Himachal, justified dowry as a compensation to the groom's parents for the expense they have incurred in educating their son so that he may earn money to support his bride). This explanation also works to some extent when we consider the shift from bride-price to dowry which has occurred in the past thirty years among some peasant cultivators where this shift has been accompanied by the withdrawal of women from agricultural labour (Epstein 1973: 199).

But in North-West India we have a situation in which there has been a massive shift from bride-price marriage to dowry marriage among all but the lowest castes, not just those who have affected the withdrawal of their women from outdoor labour. In Punjab this shift is almost total. Bride-price was uncommon even among the low-caste Chamars in Harbassi, although it is probable that some bride-price payment still takes place that is not publicly admitted, and it is certainly still paid among low castes in some parts of Punjab (Jammu 1974: 68-9). Thus structural change has also been accompanied by a quantative change, for dowries have increased enormously, quite out of proportion to the general inflation from which the Indian economy has suffered. One informant in Chaili judged that a *dāj* (dowry) nowadays seldom amounts to less than the equivalent of whatever the bride's father's annual cash income might be. In Punjab, I would estimate that in most groups the dowry will amount to more than this. This trend has been in motion for some time. It is likely that in modern times there have been two periods of particularly rapid increase; the period immediately after the First World War, and the past two decades. These were periods during which the peasant cultivators increased in prosperity, or perhaps one should say in creditworthiness, and found it easy to borrow money for marriage expenses by mortgaging their lands if necessary.[6]

None of my elderly low-caste informants in Harbassi had had bride-price paid at the time of their marriage (or none admitted that it had been paid) so perhaps we may assume that dowry has been the dominant form of marriage in Punjab for at least forty years. On the other hand, the fact that dowry has been paid does not mean that a bride-price has not also been paid, and this makes it very difficult to identify the point at which the value of the dowry came to exceed the value of the bride-price.

In Himachal the shift from bride-price to dowry is far from complete. Bride-price is commonly paid in low-caste marriages and by impoverished households of any caste, although there are also some intermediate forms which are not, as far as I know, usual in Punjab nowadays.[7] In the early years of this century, bride-price marriage was common among the impoverished Brahmans and inferior Rajputs of District Kangra and District Hamirpur, although the superior Rajputs with princely connections always paid dowry (Parry 1979: 239-46). Nowadays, Brahmans and Rajputs of all but the most indigent families pay dowry at marriage and all admitted that dowry payments were on the increase, though not yet reaching the extravagant levels found in Punjab. Yet in Himachal this shift to dowry giving has not been accompanied by any withdrawal of women from agriculture or any other diminution of their contribution to production in the household, and so the compensation theory is not very useful here. A Brahman girl like Prito (C9) is no more of a 'liability' than her mother would have been. Yet her mother had no dowry paid for her (this was an exchange marriage) and Prito had a sizeable dowry, which her father could ill afford (bed, table, two chairs, a trunk full of bedding, a box of household sundries such as a glass jug and a set of tumblers, embroidered mats and so forth, and about a dozen suits of clothing for the groom and his relatives).

Another way of looking at this shift is to see it in terms of greater conformity to the classical ideal of *kanya dān* (the most prestigious form of marriage according to Hindu tradition), the gift of a virgin in marriage against which nothing whatever is accepted in return from the wife-takers. Van der Veen notes that this is an important feature of change in marriage pracgices in Gujerat and refers to it as 'Brahmanization' (Van der Veen 1972: 27). Brahmanization is perhaps not a very happy term to apply to this process in Punjab or Himachal Pradesh although we can accept Van der Veen's point that it must be regarded as a cultural process as well as an economic process. In Punjab it was the politically powerful Jats who provided the most prestigious model of family life, whereas the Brahman was traditionally regarded as a rather effete and weakly character. In Himachal the Brahman was a more dignified and prestigious figure but it was the Rajput who provided the dominant secular ideal. In any case, as I have stated, in Himachal bride-price marriage could be found even among Brahmans until very recently, so they cannot have provided a very orthodox example in this respect. But it is certainly true that in both areas those groups who wielded the greatest political power and who carried the greatest social prestige did practice dowry marriage, so what we actually call this process of emulation is perhaps immaterial. The trend towards the abandoning of 'deviant' forms is a result of greater knowledge of how prestigious groups outside the immediate neighbourhood organize their alliances, along with a greater sense that it is quite legitimate for the common man to aspire to a similar style of marriage. In some Himalayan areas, such as that described by Berreman, even the local Rajputs regularly practised bride-price marriages, and the tendency to shift to dowry marriages represents an attempt to emulate high-caste plains people, who act as a reference group outside the locality in question (Berreman 1963: 128-9). Certainly in villages like Chaili, when men start to travel more outside the village in search of work, they develop a greater awareness of the divergence between local practice and the practice in the plains (supposed to be more orthodox). This may have a good deal to do with the shift towards dowry marriage.

If this is the case, then the tendency for dowry to increase at the expense of bride-price is part of a general and widespread tendency to cultural convergence all over North India, favouring the forms of marriage considered most prestigious and virtuous in the Sanskritic literature.

But this only accounts for the shift from bride-price to dowry, and not the tremendous inflation of dowries which is also taking place. Satya (H14) is the daughter of a poor untouchable cobbler, and her marriage must have taken place around 1955. She said that she hardly had any dowry – just a bed, table and quilt, and five cooking pans. Her younger sister-in-law, Premi (H12) was married in 1968 or thereabouts and received considerably more, though her parents were not much better off than Satya's. Premi received two beds, a table, chairs, ten or eleven cooking utensils, two quilts and other items of bedding, besides a number of suits of clothing for her husband and his family. Both women expected to spend at least Rs 3,000 on their own daughters' weddings when the time came. In some high-status groups the cost of marrying a daughter with reasonable credit and honour to the family has increased tenfold in the past fifty years.

This inflation, coupled with the anxiety which parents patently feel about the settlement of their daughters in marriage, seems to betoken a situation where a surplus of women are actively competing to attract mates from a reduced supply of eligible men. Many of my informants were under the impression that this was the case and told me that dowry marriages had become more popular than bride-price marriages because there were now too many women in the population, whereas formerly there had been too few. In fact this is not the case. The demographic imbalance in both Punjab and Himachal has long favoured women in the marriage market. The proportion of women to men has increased in modern times, but in both states there were still fewer than 960 women per 1,000 males in the population at the last census. In some social groups the position of women seeking hubands may have been 'better' in past times due to the practice of female infanticide. Indeed one wonders how there comes to be such a deficit of women in Punjab (865 women per thousand men) unless girl babies are being given less food and medical care than their brothers. Also in the past, some high-status groups regularly married their daughters to even more prestigious groups outside their immediate locality, thereby removing them from competition in the local scene. Older informants in Chaili told me that earlier there had been a preference for marrying daughters in a south-westerly direction, i.e. choosing sons-in-law from villages nearer to the plains, and taking brides from higher in the hills. The reason for this, they said, was that the higher one went into the hills, the poorer and rougher the life which small farmers led, and the more farm labour was expected of women married there. Naturally any wise mother or father would seek to marry their girls where they might expect to have a relatively easy time, but would seek a daughter-in-law who had been brought up to hard work in a more rigorous environment. In some hill areas women were even sold to strangers from the plains who were prepared to pay (Berreman 1963: 74) though I did not find any evidence of this in Chaili. These practices meant that it was very difficult for the man who lived at the top of the mountain, but at the bottom of the regional system of hypergamy, to obtain a bride. The daughters of hill peasants would have had a fair chance of getting suitable husbands easily, to the detriment of the daughters of poor Punjabis who had to compete for husbands with 'cheap' wives imported from the hills.

But the overall demographic pattern in both states is still actually in favour of the girl who is seeking a husband rather than the boy who is seeking a wife. I came across a few middle-aged bachelors in both districts, but no confirmed spinsters. So unless there is large-scale importation of wives from other parts of North India, there should be enough men to go round and some to spare. Why then do the parents of girls speak as though marrying their daughters was the hardest of tasks and decent husbands were dearer than gold?

I think that while all the interpretations I have discussed have some value, if we want to explain *both* the shift from bride-price to dowry *and* the inflation of dowries, we have to return to the 'economic compensation' theory but give it a new twist. This theory will work provided that we do not interpret it too literally. We have to see the compensation element not as relating to the actual work which the wife does or does not perform in the household, but as relating to her general financial dependence for her maintenance upon her husband and his family. As I have shown in Chapter 4, in most families women perform work (agricultural or domestic) which is essential to the running of the household, but this contribution on their part does not lessen their dependence upon men. They depend upon their husbands for their participation in rights to land, since in the normal run of things they are excluded from the inheritance of land. Secondly, they depend on men to earn cash, since few women are in a position to obtain well paid work outside the home and some kind of cash income is regarded as essential. Only the wholesale entry of women into the cash economy as sellers of produce or as wage labourers equal to men would make much difference to their situation as dependents. So we could regard dowry as a form of compensation, or inducement to the husband, on his acceptance of the responsibility for the wife's maintenance. To the extent that men's opportunities for earning cash are still far ahead of those enjoyed by women, we would expect dowries to increase until such time as this gap is narrowed.[8] If this theory is right, women's dowry rates will have little to do with women's participation in agricultural production as long as we are talking about their work as family labourers. (It might be a different matter in the unlikely event of women beginning to earn high cash wages as paid labourers.)

All the same, we must not lose sight of the function of dowry as a status symbol, which complicates any attempt to treat it as a purely economic phenomenon. In the *kanya dān* type of marriage the girl is given as a free 'gift' to her husband, decked in whatever jewellery her parents can afford and with a dowry commensurate with their means. The dowry consists of three elements: household goods and equipment to be used by the young couple, personal ornaments and clothes destined for the husband and his kin, and a trousseau of ornaments and clothes to be used by the bride herself. These gifts are made publicly at the time of the bride's departure from her parents' house after the *lāvā* ceremony, and will be displayed to the groom's kin and neighbours on arrival at his home. Even before the actual wedding, the business of ostentatious gift making has begun at the engagement, which involves ceremonial presentations to the groom's parents. Subsequently the bride's kin will make further gifts to both her and her husband on a number of important ritual occasions. A gift relationship is established in which the bride's father or brothers must continually give, and the amount of dowry indicates the kind of expectations which the husband's family may entertain. The scale of gift making and entertainment at the wedding also indicates to the public at large the bride's family's aspirations to generosity and good form. From the bride's point of view, her family's status must be asserted for her benefit, since she expects that if her parents are generous she herself will be treated well in her husband's home.

All these pressures make any restriction upon spending at the time of marriage very difficult to achieve, and it is not surprising that legislation to curb this kind of spending has proved impossible to enforce. The marriage of a daughter can bring few short-term benefits of a tangible kind, at least if the ban on receiving anything from a married daughter or her family is strictly observed. But a wedding celebrated with the correct amount of style and ostentation is an opportunity to invest in reputation and status. Dowry is a means of impressing one's neighbours as well as one's in-laws, and it is unlikely to diminish in importance while this is the case.

## Arranging marriages: the role of women

In this section and the following one I shall consider the role of women in an important area of household decision making, the arrangement of marriages. How much control do women have over the making and dissolution of marriages, both their own and those of other women in the family? How much freedom does a woman have to choose sexual partners?

Women certainly play a vital role in the arrangement of their own relatives' marriages. *Table 3* summarizes information about thirty couples in the sample. In the overwhelming majority of cases the marriage was arranged through the agency of a kinswoman of the bride to a man living in or near her husband's village or place of work, frequently a relative of her husband.

The rules which govern marriage among most groups in villages in northern India specify that (a) the bride must come from a different village from that of the groom, (b) she must be of a different clan, or *gotra*,[9] (c) there must be no known consanguineal link between the couple, and (d) the couple must be of the same caste. These are the minimal criteria of eligibility for a match.

A man's primary contact with people of his own caste is with his caste-fellows in his own village, but their children will be ineligible as spouses for his own sons and daughters. A man who is employed outside his native village may come into contact with unrelated families of his own caste, but his most significant contacts with unrelated caste-fellows will usually be made through his wife's connections or through other women married into his family (aunts, sisters-in-law, etc.). Women, therefore, play a very important part in bringing suitable girls to the attention of their husbands' kin.

The seven marriages in *Table 4* which were arranged through the agency of men took place mainly in high-status Punjabi families where the father of the bride had developed an extensive network of acquaintances through his work. Major Joginder Singh (H7) had arranged his elder daughter's marriage through a fellow officer.

Table 4   *Marriages of thirty women in Harbassi and Chaili: mode of arrangement*

| | |
|---|---|
| arranged by a female relative of the bride to one of her husband's kinsmen | 13 |
| arranged by a female relative of the bride to an unrelated neighbour or associate of her husband | 6 |
| arranged by unrelated female neighbour to one of her own kinsmen or acquaintances | 4 |
| arranged by an unrelated male friend or neighbour to one of his kinsmen or acquaintances | 2 |
| arranged by a male relative to one of his neighbours or associates | 5 |
| TOTAL | 30 |

Dalip's daughter Veena (H2) was engaged to the son of a business associate of his brother, who lived in Delhi. But even in fairly cosmopolitan households, if the family belongs to a caste whose membership is very scattered, there will be more reliance on the mediating offices of women. Shri Ram and his brothers (C1, C2, C3, C4) are of the Goswami caste, a relatively small group in Himachal. In their daily routine, none of these men is likely to come into contact with other Goswamis (apart from his own immediate kin) since the dominant population in Chaili consists of Brahmans and Rajputs. The only other Goswamis they are bound to meet are those to whom they are related as affines. So we need not be surprised that this group of brothers is married to a group of related women, all from the same village in Punjab. It was a woman of the generation senior to Shri Ram and his brothers who arranged the marriage of her brother's daughter to her husband's brother's son (Ram Das, C4). Ram Das's wife in turn arranged the marriages of her two younger sisters to two of her husband's brothers. The youngest of the four brothers, Shri Ram himself, is married to a first cousin of Ram Das's wife.

Women in a caste which has a very dispersed population are likely to have to marry at a great distance from their parents' homes. Shri Ram's wife and her cousins were born near Garhshankar in Punjab, about fifty kilometres from Chaili, and she told me that when she was informed that she was to be married in the hills, she wondered what kind of place her parents had consigned her to, subscribing to the general Punjabi view of Himachal as a very backward and up-country area. She came from a fairly well-to-do landowner's family, and was further discouraged to find that she would be expected to do all kinds of agricultural labour. In her own words she 'did not know one end of a sickle from another' as she had done no outdoor work before. Language was also a difficulty. 'Now I have forgotten Punjabi and I speak the local dialect like any Pahari woman, but when I first came to Chaili I could hardly understand what people said. I just looked at my husband and waited for him to tell me'. The daughter-in-law of Ram Das (C4) was also married into the Chaili family from a distance, as she was born in a village near to Rampur, beyond Simla, 100 kilometres away in the higher hills. She had to learn a completely different method of agriculture on her arrival in Chaili, as her parents had cultivated irrigated rice and apple orchards. Maize cultivation had been quite new to her, though she had picked up the necessary skills from her mother-in-law. In her parents' village the practice of *ghungat* (veiling from the husband's senior male relative) was unknown (*ghungat* is not practised in the higher hills) and she had to conform to this custom when she married, picking up the rules as best she could. She seemed to have adjusted happily after seven years of marriage, but one could sympathize with her wish to have her younger sister married to the son of Durgi (C2). She would obtain thereby an ally and companion in Chaili, someone with whom she could speak in her native dialect and with whom she could share memories of her parents' home. Durgi had liked the idea at first, but eventually rejected it, so she told me, on two counts. First, her son could not really be married yet to anyone, as there were two grown daughters to be considered. 'Once he is married there would be little ones, and then a dozen new expenses, so how would we manage to marry the girls?' Second, to marry a son at such a distance would be beyond the means of a poor widow. To hire a truck or bus to take the wedding party to the bride's home would cost more than Durgi could afford, and even after that there would be additional expenses every time her son visited his in-laws.

Where a woman brings her sister or niece to marry a kinsman of her husband, she usually hopes for an ally or friend in her *saure*. But it does not follow that the relationship will work out like that. Durgi constantly quarrelled with her cousin Kamla (C1) and Kamla complained that Durgi and her sister Dipo (C3) 'ganged up on her.' In Harbassi, Lachman's wife (H13) was not on good terms with her sister, whom she had brought to marry one of her husband's cousins. As Premi (H12) remarked dispassionately, 'They must have got on well before they came here or the elder sister would never have brought the younger here in the first place.'

Satto's daughter-in-law Gurmit (H8) arranged the marriage of her younger sister to her husband's younger brother. Happily, in this case the sisters had a very close relationship and Gurmit was able to do much to help Surjit during the early months of her marriage. This is a difficult time for most brides, suddenly transported to an environment where they know virtually no-one and have to be on their best behaviour. Soon after the wedding, Surjit began to suffer from spells of dizziness and fainting. Satto was sympathetic and saw to it that she had proper medical treatment, but Surjit was evidently anxious in case Satto should think that she habitually enjoyed poor health and that this had been concealed from her at the time of the marriage. In this situation, Surjit was very glad to have her sister's company and reassurance, and Gurmit would accompany her to the doctor's surgery for treatment.

Of the marriages arranged by a female relative of the bride to one of her husband's kin, the most common type is the marriage of a sister to the husband's younger brother, or of a brother's daughter to a husband's brother's son. But it is interesting that in some cases there was no regard to generation (otherwise an important principle in north Indian kinship). Age proved to be far more important. Shila's daughter (C11) arranged the marriage of her own brother to her husband's sister's daughter.

There is no prejudice against men forming alliances where their brothers or uncles have married before them – it is not essential that every marriage breaks new social ground. But none of the marriages in the sample reversed the direction of wife giving established by previous marriages. That is, women may bring in their sisters or their brothers' daughters to marry their husbands' brothers or nephews, but they do not introduce their husband's sisters to their own kinsmen. The flow of gifts established at the time of marriage (from the wife givers to the wife takers) persists into the next generation in the form of the gifts made by the mother's brother to his sister's children. It would be denying the principle of *kanya dān* to arrange alliances that reversed this flow. This was one of the reasons which was given to me for the decline of exchange marriages (marriage of a brother and a sister to a sister and a brother) which had been common in District Hamirpur and among some low-caste Punjabis in previous generations. As long as the quantity of dowry and other gifts made by the bride's parents was negligible, the contradiction between the notion of *giving* one's daughter and *receiving* a daughter from the family to whom one had given one's own was less apparent. As the flow of material gifts increased in groups who had had little to give in the past, this contradiction became obtrusive. (I do not think that this is the only reason for the decline of exchange marriage in recent times, but it was probably an important factor.)

It is clear that it is the structural role of women in the kinship system that makes them important as intermediaries in the arrangement of marriages. But what does an individual woman get out of such activity? The satisfactions are not immediately obvious. The role of matchmaker is a very responsible one. As a rule, a girl's parents are obliged to marry her into a family which they know only by repute. Yet concern for their daughter's happiness and for the honour of their own family ensures that they will not marry her off to just any boy who fulfils the criteria of caste endogamy and *gotra* exogamy. They depend heavily on the person who makes the introduction to provide reliable information about the boy and his prospects, the habits of his family and their standing in the community. The closer the relative who makes the introduction, the less likely he or she will be to try to pass the boy off as better than he really is or to give misleading information about a girl, resulting in a disappointed groom. Some women avoid the role of matchmaker, just because of the great trust and responsibility which it involves. Sushila (H3) told me 'I have never arranged any marriages myself. If the marriage works, then you do not get any credit. But if the bride and groom are not pleased with each other, then you will certainly get the blame. It is not worth the trouble.' There is a real fear on the part of parents of eligible boys or girls that they will be duped into making alliances for their children which turn out to be unsuitable. Every village has its horror stories about marriages where some vital fact about the boy or girl or their families was not revealed in time. Roshani told me:

> 'There was a girl, the daughter of a goldsmith. She used to be a pupil of mine. When the wedding ceremony was completed, the father-in-law started to demand that her family should promise a television set in addition to the dowry. The girl took off her wedding bangles and threw them down. She said, "If you are asking for a television today, tomorrow it will be a motor car. If I cannot get it then you will beat me, so you can marry your son to someone else." If her parents had known that the family were so greedy, of course they would never have arranged the marriage in the first place. In another case, the groom fell down unconscious at the wedding feast. The girl's father thought that he must be an epileptic or something like that, and was angry that no-one had told him. Anyway, they sent the wedding party back and got their girl married somewhere else. Such things do happen. Harbassi is a little place and we are bound to hear all about it.'

In cases like this, it can hardly be imagined that the social credit of the person who arranged the match will be much enhanced. On the other hand, it is clear that some women derive great satisfaction from the business of making matches. Shri Ram's aunt, whom I have already discussed, was evidently one of these. Another was Jivan

Kaur (H10) who had been responsible for introducing several couples in Harbassi who had made successful marriages. It was she who had been responsible for arranging the marriage of Satto's elder son to her own brother's daughter, Gurmit. Satto was not related to either Jivan Kaur or her husband, but the two women were very friendly and when Satto visited the *bazar* for shopping she would always call at Jivan Kaur's house on the way home, to exchange news. When the marriage of Satto's son to Gurmit prospered and the two produced a grandson for Satto, Gurmit herself proposed that her younger sister Surjit be married to Satto's other son. Jivan Kaur warmly seconded the idea and helped Gurmit conduct the necessary negotiations with her own family. Three women from the same village were now married in Harbassi, and whenever one of them returned to her *peke* she could take news of the others. The happy unions of Gurmit and Surjit to Satto's sons further cemented the bond between Satto and Jivan Kaur, and the two women had even more interests in common. Hardly a week passed without Jivan Kaur paying a visit 'to see how her brother's grandson was getting on.'

When I left Harbassi Jivan Kaur had just initiated negotiations for another marriage, this time between her sister's son and a girl who was no relation of hers but who lived nearby in Harbassi and who had been a pupil of Roshani's. (Roshani was also a friend of Jivan Kaur and had rented rooms in the same house for several years.) Jivan Kaur obviously derived a great deal of satisfaction and pleasure from making matches and it helped to reinforce and extend her own network of friends and relatives. She herself had been unable to bear children, and after years of making religious vows and keeping fasts in the hope of conceiving a baby, she had adopted the infant son of her husband's younger brother. With only one son she had but limited opportunities in front of her for extending this network through the alliances of her own children, and she had the time at her disposal to put a good deal of effort into this kind of activity.

Once a marriage has been arranged and proved successful, the persons who made the introduction receives no special recognition. The role is not formalized or ritualized and there are no very definite rewards to tempt women who, like Santosh or Sushila, are not disposed by temperament or inclination to this kind of social entrepreneurship. But a man or women who does undertake it may indulge in a virtuous glow at having discharged the duty incumbent on the relatives of any eligible young persons to see that they are married to the credit of the whole family.

Probably the role of women as matchmakers will decline as families become more mobile and men travel farther in search of employment. This has already happened in the more urbanized families where the men's business and professional networks are an important source of new contacts.[10] But the important role which women play at present is the consequence of their structural position as the connecting links between groups of agnatically related men. It is also congruent with their role as 'servicers' of the relationships between their families and other families with which they have ties. This role is not at all obvious at first sight, since it is the men who conduct all formal transactions between one family and another and act as the household's public representatives. Superficially, women appear as more or less passive symbols of their families' wealth and honour. But it is primarily the responsibility of women to visit the families of relatives or neighbours at ritual events and all important occasions, such as deaths or marriages. At an informal level, it is women who act as ambassadors for their household in the community. Santosh accounted for women's dominant role in matchmaking by saying that 'it is only the women who have the time for these things.' This idea would seem risible to her low-caste neighbours, overburdened with domestic and agricultural work, or to the women of Chaili, similarly lacking leisure. But she is correct to the extent that women of all classes are expected to *make* time for the kind of social activity which links their own family informally with others in the community.

### Arranging marriages: the procedures of matchmaking

Once an introduction is made and the two sets of kin brought together by the matchmaker, the process of arranging the wedding takes its own course. The part which the matchmaker plays in what follows depends on his or her relationship to the parties concerned. The formal negotiations for the marriage will largely be conducted by the menfolk of the households concerned, but a wide range of kin and friends – both male and female – will be consulted, and indeed will *expect* to be consulted.

As in the matter of family budgeting, the specific role which any individual plays in decisions about marriages is hard to identify because the dominant ideological conception of the way in which a wedding is arranged is that it is a collective process, in which the whole family participates. This means that it is hard to specify the power of women in this department of life. Another problem is that much negotiation takes place in terms which are implicit; in a delicate area of operation, tact requires the use of delicate codes, indirect suggestions and proposals. Consultation often does not take place in an explicit manner, and nor do negotiations in their early stages. The negotiating parties do not usually know each other already, and a false step or a careless comment might jeopardize the honour of either.

At the level of the explicit, it is generally stated that the young people themselves will not be consulted; the whole rationale of arranged marriages is that the boy and girl are too immature to make the necessary judgements themselves. The bride certainly ought (ideally) to be innocent of what is going on, in conformity with the idea that an unmarried girl has a maidenly ignorance of matrimonial affairs and too much sexual modesty to take an interest in her own marriage before the event. Yet it is quite clear from some of my informants' accounts that not all girls get married without their preferences being taken into account. Sushila (H3) told me that when she first came to Harbassi as a bride she was not too happy.

'I had told my mother not to marry me to a farmer. My parents lived in Jamshedpur in Bihar, where my father was working at that time, and I liked town life. The first boy that my parents considered for me was a farmer in a tiny village, but I said that I did not want to marry him and they did not press me. I was not really very keen on the idea of marrying in Harbassi, but my cousin who arranged the marriage told me that it was a nice place and that I would like it. It was a big village, she said, not some little out-of-the-way hamlet. My parents wanted the marriage to be done quickly so that my younger sisters could be married. So I agreed and it was all done in a month or two. I did not like Harbassi much at first, but I soon got used to it, and now I am pleased that I was married here.'

Clearly, in this case, a compromise between the girl's preferences and the needs of the family as a whole was worked out, so she must have had the opportunity to make her wishes known at some point, however indirectly.[11]

Traditionally, while it was permissible for the girl's family to see the groom, it was bad form for the groom's family to ask to see the bride. I think that the idea behind this was that it is humiliating for a girl's family to have to display her when the ideal for unmarried girls demands that they be completely sheltered from the public gaze, and the best kind of girl is the one who has no reputation at all because she has never done anything to attract anyone's attention. But naturally, every boy's mother will be interested in the manners and appearance of her future daughter-in-law. As one informant pointed out, there are informal ways of trying to find out something about the girl – by trying to get a glimpse of her in the *bazar*, by deputing a trusted friend to do the same and report back, or through other modes of matrimonial espionage.

Among the richer Punjabi families there is greater likelihood that there will be some kind of viewing of the bride, perhaps under the guise of a family visit. Santosh (H1) had married her elder daughter to her sister's husband's sister's son. The boy's parents called at Santosh's home one day under the pretext that they just 'happened' to be visiting Hoshiarpur and had thought it would be nice to pay their respects. In fact, Santosh's sister had hinted in advance that such a visit might take place. Santosh knew that they had come to have a look at her daughter, but said nothing to the girl herself. 'If my daughter was aware of the purpose of the visit, she said nothing about it. But she must have known instinctively, because she just stayed in the kitchen making tea until I called her to meet the guests. Then she just slipped away again.' When Veena, the daughter of Santosh's sister-in-law Kaushalya (H2), was about to become engaged, a much more explicit procedure was followed, and among educated urban Punjabi families it is less unusual for the boy and girl to meet each other at a stage in the proceedings when it is not too late for either party to withdraw with honour if the prospective spouse is unaccceptable. The whole family went to stay in Delhi at the house of the relative who had proposed the match in the first place. An outing was arranged for the young people, and Veena was not asked in so many words to give her opinion of the boy, but she was aware that her parents were receptive to her views, and she discreetly let it be known that he seemed a nice person and his family were pleasant people. The engagement was formalized soon after this, and the couple were given several more opportunities to meet before the wedding (though always chaperoned and in the context of family visits).

   This kind of arrangement would be totally unacceptable in any but the most sophisticated families. For the rest, the parents of a marriageable boy or girl must learn to 'read between the lines' and interpret the coded information given by others. The matter of dowry is seldom discussed explicitly, for this would smack of a commercial transaction. Yet obviously, the matching of the groom's family's expectations with the girl's family's capacity to give is crucial. In some wealthy Punjabi families, specific demands may be made by the groom's parents (for instance, that some particular item be given in the dowry) but even these are seldom put in such a way that they can be discussed explicitly, for this would be to make a bargain of what is supposed to be a gift. One anecdote was told to me – it may be apocryphal, but it is significant nonetheless – about what can happen when the cues are misread. A family of radically modern outlook arranged the marriage of their son with a girl of respectable family, but told the bride's people that they did not want to cause any unnecessary expenditure and would be sending only a very small wedding party. Feasting the groom's party is a major expense for the bride's family and a point of honour for her family as a whole, but they did not dare believe that the groom's family would really let them off with a party less than thirty or forty strong. They therefore arranged a lavish feast at a smart restaurant so that their daughter might never feel ashamed of her parents when she went to her in-laws' house – only to be embarrassed and dismayed when the groom arrived accompanied by only four kinsmen.

   Far more often the bride's family underestimate the demands of the groom's family and this may be a source of much unhappiness after the marriage, when demands may be made much more openly. It is usually the bride who will suffer if her in-laws are disappointed with what they have received from her family.

   The range of kin who are explicitly consulted about a marriage will vary according to the family's circumstances. An ideal which was influential among the low castes in Harbassi and most castes in Chaili was that the whole of the local caste brotherhood (*birādari*) should be involved. Premi told me, 'All the *birādari* people have to agree to a marriage. If the family do not consult them, this means that they are effectively outside their own caste.' I think that it is unlikely that every single member of the local caste group will be canvassed individually, although the proposed marriage will be mooted generally so that anyone having an objection may raise it in time.

Premi's statement refers to the idea that the marriage takes place with the blessing of the caste community, in conformity with its standards and customary practices. An informant in Chaili suggested that the involvement of the caste group at the time of the marriage ensures that they recognize it as valid. 'The bride's *biradari* attend the ceremony to see that it is done right, so that no-one can repudiate the marriage by saying afterwards that it was not done properly in front of everyone. And when the bride goes to her husband's house all his community attend the feast to show that they accept the bride as one of themselves.'

In wealthy and professional families, the parents will tend to restrict their consultations to those members of their local caste group and kin who are of a similar social standing to themselves. I do not suppose for one moment that Major Joginder Singh (H7) thought it necessary to obtain the consent of Satto to the marriage of his daughter. Satto's dead husband was a distant kinsman of Joginder Singh, but the latter had led the more cosmopolitan and sophisticated life of an army officer and did not regard Satto and her bus-conductor sons as his social equals, although he got on with them very well as neighbours. A great deal depends on the composition of the local caste community.

What appears to happen in most cases is for a narrower range of kin to be drawn into the negotiations, relatives whose opinion is thought to be particularly useful. Trusted friends and neighbours may also be involved. When Bishan Das (H14) arranged the marriage of his daughter Kanta, the following people were primarily involved: Bishan Das and his wife Satya; Satya's brother (through whom the introduction had been made) and his wife; Satya's mother; Bishan Das's brother Lachman (a relatively educated and articulate member of the family, who was helpful in representing the family's interest in a tactful manner); Premi (H12), the wife of Lachman and Bishan Das's youngest brother, who was considered to be a shrewd judge of character. Before the engagement ceremony took place all these relatives of the bride went to meet the groom and his family at a tea house in Harbassi so that they could have a look at the boy and give their opinion of him. No parents would expect to make such an important decision on their own.

Although there are no clear rules about who is entitled to share in decision making regarding a match, it is obvious that the role of the women of the family is all important. This is openly acknowledged to be the case on the boy's side, for it is the women of the groom's household with whom the bride will have to co-operate after marriage in the daily routine of domestic or agricultural work. Yet all the explicit negotiations are carried out by men (occasionally by senior women) and the symbolism of the wedding ritual emphasizes the transfer of the bride to her husband's family as a transaction between *men*. At the *milni* – the ritual meeting of the male kinsmen of the bride and groom – it is the bride's father who embraces the groom's father, the bride's maternal uncle or brother who carries her out of her parents' house to participate in the *lāvā* ritual when she and her husband walk round the sacred fire together. One has to look behind the public symbolism to perceive the vital part played by women in the politics of matchmaking.

## Divorce and the breakdown of marriages

What control does a woman have over her relationship with her husband after marriage? Does the economic and moral dependence of women on their families preclude them from governing their own matrimonial affairs as adults? In particular, can a woman choose not to live with a husband with whom she cannot agree? In a society where the bonds of co-operation and dependence that tie a woman to her husband are so tight, we should not expect a high rate of marriage breakdown so I was surprised to find as many as eleven cases of permanent breakdown in the two villages I studied. It is almost certain that there were other cases which were concealed from me, or which I simply never came to hear about. Besides these eleven, there were another three cases in which there had been a long period of conflict and separation which might well eventually become permanent (I have termed these 'ruptured marriages'). *Table 5* summarizes information on these cases. Nine of them occurred in the twenty-eight households included in the sample, or concerned the marriages of close kin of members of these households. There are no statistics for either Punjab or Himachal Pradesh on marriage breakdown which would help us gain an idea of the proportion of all marriages which end in permanent separation; divorce figures will only tell us about those marriages which end in the divorce courts and these are a minority of broken marriages.[12]

The ideology of the adaptable and submissive wife makes it difficult for villagers to countenance marriage breakdown as a social fact rather than an individual misfortune. There is a positive celebration of the dependence of women upon men, especially among high-status groups. One woman told me with great pride that she would never take money with her in her handbag when she and her husband travelled together since this would look like lack of trust in him. Roshani (of whom more later) had actually lived independently of any man for many years after she separated from her husband, but for a long time had maintained the polite fiction that she was supported by her brothers – a tactful gesture to the ideal of the dependent woman. The fact that dependence is a moral value as well as an economic reality makes it very difficult for a woman to acknowledge that she wishes to break away from a husband with whom she is deeply unhappy.

Table 5 *Summary of information on 11 cases of broken marriage in Harbassi and Chaili*

| outcome of separation: | | |
| --- | --- | --- |
| wife lives with parents or close kin | | 5 |
| wife settled with another man | | 4 |
| wife settled in her own independent home | | 2 |
| TOTAL | | 11 |

| mode of separation: | | |
| --- | --- | --- |
| wife left husband | | 9 |
| husband left wife | | 1 |
| wife 'transferred' to another man in husband's family | | 1 |
| TOTAL | | 11 |

| caste and area: | Harbassi | Chaili |
| --- | --- | --- |
| 'clean' caste | 6 | — |
| scheduled caste | 4 | 1 |

To balance this, there is also a strong awareness that marriage is a relationship in which trouble can be expected, if not from the husband then from his family. This realistic acceptance of the possibility of conflict underlies the sister's desire to remain on good terms with her brother. If problems should arise in her marriage, to whom else can she turn for moral or economic support? The brother-sister relationship is celebrated in a number of festivals and rituals in which sisters honour their brothers and wish for their good fortune and long life. A woman hopes and expects to remain in touch with her brothers after the death of their parents. The tacit assumption is that whilst the formal responsibility for the woman's maintenance and welfare is transferred to her husband at marriage, a residual moral responsibility remains, or at any rate can be cultivated by the woman if she is wise. Sisters are not in a position to give anything to their brothers, or rather brothers may not accept anything from their sisters if they observe the norms of *kanya dān* marriage, and this means that they are all the more dependent upon their sentimental regard. Premi regretted having no brothers: 'If Hemraj ever said anything to me – and I don't say that he would – but *if* he did, then where could I turn, now that my parents are elderly? A woman who has no brothers does not amount to anything.' Hemraj was in fact the mildest of men and unlikely to contest her word over anything, but the feeling of insecurity among women with no brothers was a very real one. Practical expectations of marriage, therefore, do not always tally with idealized conceptions.

How do women manage to break away from the men on whom they depend for their bread and butter? It is practically impossible for a woman to leave her husband unless she has first secured the support of her own family for her cause. The procedure for a woman who was in difficulties in her husband's household was described to me as follows:

'She must let her parents or brothers know of her condition and tell them her troubles. If they say, never mind, go back and try to put up with it – well, she must do as they say. But if they say that she has just cause for discontent and has really been ill-treated then they will not send her back, even if her father-in-law or husband came to fetch her. Then her father will take the matter to the panchayat [council] of their village[13] and they will discuss her case. If she does not like to appear in front of the panchayat herself, she can make a statement to the lady panchayat member. If the panchayat feel that she has a real grievance then they will approach the chairman of the panchayat of the husband's village and the two panchayats will meet to sort out a solution. If they jointly agree that she should return to her husband then she must comply, or they may make conditions which her husband or in-laws have to fulfil.'

(Mohan Singh (C7), chairman of the panchayat of Chaili)

Most of the cases I studied did not follow this hypothetical pattern very closely. Generally it proved difficult to get the two panchayats together, especially where the geographical distance between them was great. The preference for marrying daughters far afield has the consequence that it is hard to find intermediaries when marital disputes arise, for there will be few people who know the two families equally well and are acceptable to both sides. But if they do not often resolve marital disputes, panchayats sometimes stimulate the parties to work out solutions for themselves. Take the case of Lachman's sister (H12). This woman had a slight physical deformity and though her parents-in-law had not been troubled by this when the marriage was arranged, her husband had never taken to her. He alternately neglected and ill-treated her, and when she returned to Harbassi for the delivery of her first child she told her parents how unhappy she was. They decided that they would not send her back to her parents-in-law's house again. Her husband took the matter to the panchayat of his own village and they recommended that the girl be sent back. When the parents still refused, the panchayat of the husband's village arranged a meeting of all the parties concerned. On hearing the complaints presented by the girl's family, the panchayat agreed that the husband had been unnecessarily harsh, and the panchayat chairman promised to see to it that the girl was well treated if she was sent back. After that, Lachman said, 'it was all right because the husband had learnt his lesson'. Here the role of the panchayat seems to have been to administer a short sharp shock to the husband in a marriage dispute which might otherwise have dragged on longer, with mutual recriminations and family pride making it more and more difficult for either party to modify their position.

Another Chamar girl in Harbassi who had problems with her marriage was Vanti. She had been living with her in-laws in their village while her husband, a soldier, was stationed in some distant part of India. Vanti herself complained that her father-in-law had been pestering her with sexual attentions. The parents-in-law's complaint was that Vanti had joined with their other son's wife in quarrelling violently with the mother-in-law, as a result of which the mother-in-law had had her head split open with a rolling pin. Furthermore, they said, Vanti was no good herself since everyone knew that she had been having an affair with another man under their very noses. Vanti declared that she was not going to stay in a place where she was accused of such things and stormed home to Harbassi, bringing her three youngest children with her. After a while, her father-in-law and her husband came to Harbassi to fetch her, a visit which provoked a violent confrontation in Vanti's courtyard, which I witnessed myself. Vanti shouted that she would never go back to her husband, and brandished a stick at him. Vanti had the support of her parents, but no-one else in the village was much inclined to intervene because there was a general opinion that Vanti was no better than she ought to be and the whole affair was 'six of one and half a dozen of the other.' The in-laws then went to the local police station and told the police that Vanti had attacked her husband. As he had not actually been hurt, the police were not disposed to do anything about it, but this turn of events was enough to make Vanti and her family try to patch things up, and after a while she returned to her husband's village. I do not know whether or not the marriage prospered after this, but both parties seemed rather sobered by the whole affair.

In the minority of cases where a wife had left her husband to live with another man, this kind of confrontation was generally avoided. In two cases, the girl had eloped with her lover and the couple had simply disappeared – presumably to find work and make their lives anew in some distant town. In one rather bizarre case, the wife had formerly been married to the elder of two brothers, but the marriage had been unhappy and the husband had beaten her continually. The wife was a simple-minded girl with a rather childish nature but the mother-in-law had liked her and did not want to lose her. The household were a family of impoverished Brahmins, struggling to cultivate a small plot of land and having little cash to spare for the marriage of the younger son. The mother-in-law had liked her and did not want to lose her. The household were a family of impoverished Brahmins, struggling to cultivate a small plot of land and having little cash to spare for the marriage of the younger son. The mother-in-law, evidently a practical woman, simply suggested that the girl should live with the younger son instead, who did like her and was prepared to treat her well. Subsequently the daughter-in-law bore several children by the younger son and domestic harmony was restored.

Rattano (H17), however, had left her first husband for Chandu, a totally unrelated man who was working in the town where the couple were living at the time. Rattano left her husband and returned to her parents' home in Harbassi with her lover, after a great deal of conflict with the family of her first husband and at the cost of having to abandon the children of the first marriage to them. Her second marriage was unpopular among the other Chamars in Harbassi, not I think because of any objection to the character of her new husband nor even to any feeling that a second marriage[14] was improper, for remarriage was permitted among Chamars. The objection was to her bringing her husband home to Harbassi, since it was feared that she would now claim her tiny share of the family plot when her mother died, diminishing the amount available to her brothers. It proved difficult to assimilate a *gharjamai* (husband resident in the wife's parents' home) while the wife had a large number of brothers and first cousins already living in the village. Chandu was regarded as just another mouth to feed and another claimant to land by Rattano's caste fellows (although Rattano's mother liked him and found in him a surrogate for her younger son who had eloped with the eldest son's wife some years before).

Among the higher castes, approval of a woman's second union depends largely on whether the first was consummated or not. It will be practically impossible to find a man willing to take on a woman who has lived for any time in her husband's home, but a rejected bride may sometimes find favour with another family if they are convinced that she herself was not at fault. This was the case with Jaswinder, the daughter of Mahinder Kaur (H9). The marriage had been arranged by Mahinder Kaur's brother, who lived in Canada, with the son of an associate of his in Toronto. The wedding had taken place in Canada without the groom's family having seen the bride. After the marriage, the groom repudiated Jaswinder, saying that he had expected a more sophisticated bride and that Jaswinder was only a rough country girl. In the face of this humiliating rejection, Jaswinder could do nothing but return to her uncle's house, where she stayed for over a year and took a job in a shirt factory. During my stay in Harbassi she returned to her parents for a long visit, as they were in the process of negotiating her second marriage with another boy in District Hoshiarpur. Jaswinder's parents asserted that the first marriage had been 'nothing at all. She did not stay with her husband for even one night.'

The position of an unhappily married wife who has small children is probably the hardest of all. Unless she is exceptionally well qualified and can get paid work, there is little incentive for another man to take on the burden of feeding her children. Few fathers or brothers will wish to force a girl back to a husband who severely ill treats her, but equally they are unlikely to be overjoyed at the prospect of taking responsibility for the maintenance, education, and eventual marriage of her children.

The case of Roshani (H5) is interesting as it is the only case of a broken marriage in a wealthy landlord family. Roshani, daugher of a wealthy shopkeeper and landowner lived with her husband for about ten years but was never happy during that time. The main problem seems to have been financial worries. Her parents-in-law had some land and were small shopkeepers, but her husband apparently never did any work and made no attempt to provide for Roshani and their five children. From her description it sounds as though he suffered from some kind of mental derangement. On several occasions Roshani gave him an ultimatum, that he must find a job or otherwise attempt to provide for the family if their family were not to 'sink to the level of coolies'. This had no effect and eventually she returned to Harbassi with the children. But her parents were not at all sympathetic and told her that she must return to her husband if the family's honour was not to be entirely finished. Her brothers felt sorry for her, but generally concurred with her parents' view of the matter. (This all happened forty years ago, and as Roshani herself pointed out, parents might take a less rigid view today.) A solution appeared in the form of an offer from the governors of the private school where Roshani had studied before her marriage and where she had been a star pupil. If she swore a solemn oath not to leave the school unless she was dismissed, they said, she should have a job there because they were desperately short of suitably qualified teachers. Roshani gladly accepted and swore the oath 'on the tail of the sacred cow'. She found a room in Harbassi to rent, and went about making an independent life for herself. Her brothers did give her some assistance and made generous gifts when her children were married, but Roshani was proud of the fact that she had managed to provide for her children successfully on her own and that they were all happily married with the sons settled in excellent jobs. Indeed, Roshani herself is now a great-grandmother. Roshani never blamed her parents for effectively turning her out and time had healed any bad feeling, but she had suffered great poverty and isolation during the early years after her separation, supplementing her income by taking in raw cotton to spin at home.

The only other case of a woman who had managed to set up an

independent home for herself was that of Bindo, who acted as nurse-maid and caretaker at the school where Roshani worked. This woman came from a farming family of Jats, and when her husband ill-treated her she had turned to her parents for help. She had four small children and, like Roshani's parents, her family were unsympathetic. Being uneducated, her plight was much worse and she had just about managed to struggle along, earning a little money here and there by doing domestic chores in some women's houses. How many more women, less determined or less resourceful than Roshani or Bindo, must endure wretched marriages because they have no means of becoming economically independent!

Even if a woman manages somehow to attain some kind of economic autonomy, her moral position is very uncertain. The honour of her family depends on her behaviour, but if she cuts herself off from them she has no honour of her own. Roshani, it is true, was not considered a loose woman or despised, because almost every citizen of Harbassi had learnt to read and write at her feet and she had time to make good her claims to rectitude and respectability. Bindo had little standing in the community, though she was regarded with pity more than contempt. But neither of these women had obtained the respect they enjoyed without working very hard at it and dealing with both financial hardship and insulting gossip from a position of moral isolation.

If it is almost impossible for a woman to 'go it alone' it is not particularly easy for her to set in motion the machinery of negotiation, reconciliation, and compromise without the practical assistance of others. The position of a young woman, whether as daughter or daugher-in-law, is a weak one. She has little economic leverage and no recognized authority in the household. If other members of the husband's household are unwilling to help smooth over domestic disputes, then she must rely on her parents or brothers for help. The interesting question then becomes not why so few women manage to achieve independent lives for themselves (the reasons for this are faily obvious) but why so many families nowadays are apparently prepared to receive a married daughter back again. In view of the whole ideology of *kanya dān* – with its emphasis on the total transfer of responsibility for the girl to her husband's family – and of the financial sacrifices which the parents have undertaken in order to marry the girl, one would not expect parents to receive back a discontented bride lightly. I may be trying to generalize from insufficient data, but it does seem that a young woman who finds life with her husband intolerable will not find it impossible to transfer her economic dependence back to the natal family, in spite of the pomp and ceremony with which the husband has been invested with responsibility for her welfare. It can be argued, of course, that even if few women can become financially independent, a returning daughter's labour in the home is still an economic asset, especially if there is a shortage of adult women in the household. This is an explanation which has conventionally been put forward by anthropologists to explain the higher incidence of divorce among the low castes; where a woman makes an important economic contribution to the household, it is argued, it will be easier for her to control her own matrimonial destiny (e.g. Jammu 1974: 68; Ishwaran 1968: 71).

I find this explanation inadequate for two reasons. Firstly, it seems to me that it has to be demonstrated that in areas like Punjab and Himachal broken marriages really are more common among the low castes and labourers. High-caste people certainly talk as if this was the case, and low-caste people seem to find divorce and second marriage less shocking, but the only rural group among whom permanent separation seems very uncommon was the wealthy landowners in Punjab. (It is, of course, possible that this is a modern situation and that formerly it was true that only low castes practiced divorce.) Returning daughters are not only taken back among impoverished peasant families, where their labour might be of most economic value, but among the landless petty tenant and labourers as well as the rich peasants, where the value of their labour is less likely to exceed the cost of their maintenance.

Secondly, this explanation does not tell us why parents are apparently more willing to take daughters back now than they were a generation ago (Roshani was the only case that I came to know about of a permanently separated wife who was married more than thirty years ago). Larger amounts of money than ever before are invested in the marriage of daughters, and yet the same women are received back when the marriage proves a failure.

But perhaps it is not so much a matter of parents being willing to receive their married daughters back as of husbands being unwilling to pursue a departing wife and to try to persuade her to come back. It has always been normal for recently married daughters to visit their parents for long periods, and unhappily married women may stay on in default of any attempt on the part of husband or in-laws to fetch them back. Looking at the matter from the point of view of the husband's family, there is much less urgency for them to re-establish good relations between husband and wife, since it is so much easier for a man to find another wife. We have already seen that women can remarry with honour only on certain conditions. Either she must belong to one of the castes which have openly acknowledged the legality of divorce and remarriage (mainly scheduled castes), *or* the first marriage must be capable of being treated as invalid because of non-consummation, *or* the woman can quietly be transferred to a husband's brother. But for a man, no such conditions apply. A man whose first wife has left him may be regarded as a rather poor prospect if he is known to have been cruel to his first wife. But he will not find it impossible to get a second wife if he is well placed and his family are prosperous. (This, at least, is the case among the Jats and allied castes. I am uncertain as to how far I am entitled to generalize to other high castes from my limited data. There was only one Khatri couple among the eleven cases recorded in *Table 5*, and no Brahmans.)

This asymmetry with regard to ease of remarriage could certainly explain why broken marriages have become more common among clean castes who did not countenance divorce before (if this really has been the case), dowry being the hidden factor. There is considerable evidence that the high rates of dowry payment has been responsible for the increase of deaths among young brides in North India.

'Demands for dowry have soared in the past two decades and more and more young brides are being murdered or driven to suicide if their parents do not pay up. In Delhi alone, the police reported 200 such deaths in the past year. Unofficial figures are said to be even higher.'

Burning the wife by soaking her clothes with kerosene and then setting light to them seems to be the most popular way of getting rid of a dispensible wife, for it can easily be disguised as a mishap with a kitchen stove. We have seen that men do rely on women for the labour they perform in the home and fields and for their capacity to bear children, but a man does not depend upon a *particular* woman for these things; they can treat women as disposable in a situation where another wife (hopefully with an even bigger dowry) can be got in place of the first. Many Himachalis, particularly older people, pointed out that this kind of thing was unheard of in the days when bride-price was paid. A husband might make his wife work hard in the fields, but you did not allow the woman for whom you had paid Rs 400 to abandon you without going to considerable trouble to get her back.

If this interpretation is correct, it might explain why I did not find more cases of permanent separation in Chaili. In Chaili the increase in dowry payment is marked, but not so dramatic as in Punjab and many families never paid dowry at all before the present generation. Also where dowry is paid it consists almost entirely of household goods (very little cash or jewellery, or other items which could be converted into cash). A second dowry is less useful in such cases; even a very poor family can only use a certain number of beds or saucepans. Few men in Chaili have the kind of resources that would offset a reputation of greed or cruelty in negotiating a second marriage. In Chaili everything militates in favour of the husband actively seeking a reconciliation with a wife who is disposed to sulk at her parents' home, instead of simply cutting his losses and looking for a more tractable girl.

I am not claiming that there is any less marital stress in Chaili or even fewer ruptured (as opposed to permanently broken) marriages. Some women endured unhappy relationships for years, with their parents unwilling to have them back and their parent-in-law determined that they should not leave, and not the remotest possibility of economic independence. But in an area like Chaili it is unlikely that a woman will be left in a kind of moral limbo like Roshani or Bindo, with neither husband nor parents-in-law inclined to expend much effort to mend the relationship. The case of Prito's brother Ram Prakash is a good example. When Ram Prakash married, his wife Lachmi did not find her new home to her liking. She felt that it had not been made clear that the boy's family were very poor and that she would have to shoulder a heavy burden of agricultural and domestic work almost alone. As well as this, she and Ram Prakash did not take to each other at once. When she became pregnant, she returned to her parents' home, saying that she did not intend to come back. Her mother-in-law became desperate. There was no-one at home to help her with the farm work and looking after the younger children, and she had been looking to her son's marriage to provide her with a helper and companion in her work. There was no chance whatsoever of Ram Prakash making a second marriage. Her daughter

Prito's wedding had completely drained the family's limited funds and there were five other children yet to be married. Ram Prakash was sent to his wife's home to make a number of conciliatory visits but it was only after a full year that she was eventually persuaded to return with her baby, much to the relief of everyone in Ram Prakash's family. This indicates that in social groups where women's labour is of vital economic importance to the household we might expect *less* separation and divorce than in groups where women are a financial liability, since the husband's family will be more willing to make concessions to retain a daughter-in-law whose contribution cannot be dispensed with. The value to the household of a woman's labour is not the only factor in the economics of marriage breakdown; equally important are factors such as household composition, the direction of marriage payments, and the cost and likelihood of remarriage for both parties.

## Widowhood

When a woman's husband dies, does she gain any greater control over her own life or any independence which she did not have before? In both the areas I studied, one influential ideal is that widowhood should not alter a woman's relationship with her husband's family, although not all widows can manage (or wish) to observe it. The husband's family should, ideally, enjoy the same rights to the widow's services and loyalty as they did before, and if her husband has not already separated his share of the family land or property, then she has the same right of maintenance from the family's resources as she did before his death. The chief change should be her own behaviour and outlook, since she ought now to follow a discipline of chastity and asceticism. A widow is ritually inauspicious and she should not expect to enjoy the things of the flesh, only to devote herself to the service of her parents-in-law and children. This ideal is not too onerous for women widowed in later life. Elderly women are expected to lead a simple life; it is the turn of the younger generation to enjoy whatever fine food and good clothes the household can afford. A literate widow may find solace in the practice of taking a religious text such as the Ramayana or the Bhagvad Gita and reading a set number of pages every day. The unlettered may take a spiritual and aesthetic pleasure in regular domestic worship, which they did not have time for before. Widowhood is seldom a shock for an elderly woman, for women are generally younger than their husbands, and in some peasant families they are quite a lot younger.

So far as a young widow is concerned, there are at least three different patterns of behaviour which prevail. In high-status Punjabi families, a widow will not remarry, save possibly in the exceptional circumstances of her marriage not having been consummated. In spite of the local influence of the Arya Samaj, a Hindu reforming sect which pioneered widow remarriage and which used to have many adherents in Harbassi, there has been little change in this respect. But among scheduled castes in Punjab the situation is rather different. As one informant put it:

'When a woman's husband dies, she has a choice. She may stay with her husband's family or she may return to her parents. If she goes back to her parents they may find another husband for her. There will not be an elaborate ceremony for the second marriage. The couple will just exchange garlands and there will be no dowry. But her marriage is valid and quite acceptable. If she stays in her husband's home, though, people will think better of her and will admire her more.'

Low-caste informants did point out, though, that it would be difficult for a young widow with small children to find a second husband and so not many widows would in fact remarry.

In Chaili we find a different situation again, and a rather anomalous one. In this part of Himachal low-caste widows may remarry, just as they may in Punjab. High-caste widows are, in theory, subject to the ideal of chastity as they are in Punjab, but in practice a young widow is very likely to make a second union of some kind. In my previous fieldwork in Ghanyari I came across several cases in which a high-caste woman widowed in her twenties simply started to cohabit with her husband's younger brother, generally with the blessing of the husband's family. This kind of leviratic marriage used to be customary among Jats in the Punjab and might still be acceptable (Pettigrew 1975: 53), but it was out of the question for Brahmans or Rajputs. In the hills, however, these very castes appear to practice it sometimes informally. In other cases, a Pahari widow might simply form a union with an older man of another family, usually a widower or a middle-aged bachelor whose poverty had stood in the way of a proper marriage earlier. I knew of two such instances in the neighbourhood of Chaili. The expression used for such unions translates as 'she settled down in so-and-so's house'. This arrangement solves a widow's short-term problems and need not meet with much public disapproval, but it often causes complications when the second husband dies. The wife will have forgone any rights to inherit her first husband's land on her children's behalf by virtue of having made a second union. She is unlikely to be able to claim any share in her second husband's estate if he has children by a previous marriage as they will almost certainly obstruct this in any way they can. Even if there are no children by a previous marriage, other relatives who stand to gain by the deceased man's lack of immediate heirs will do all they can to dispute the validity of the marriage even though the couple were treated as legitimate husband and wife while the man was alive. In both the cases which came to my notice this was precisely what had happened. One woman had only managed because her son by the second marriage had purchased land for himself and could keep his mother comfortably even though denied a share in his father's land. In the other case, the woman was on bad terms with her only son (child of her first marriage), and was almost destitute, subsisting largely by begging from neighbours.

In families where woman are responsible for much of the agricultural work, widowhood in early or middle life hits a woman hard. Durgi (C2) had been widowed when her eldest child was about ten and when her husband had already separated his land and property from that of his brothers. She was now the head of a household, but without any other adult to share the domestic and agricultural work with her. Even now that the children were growing up, she found it hard to manage.

'A woman cannot plough her own land, so I always have to get someone else to do it for me, since my son can never get enough leave from his work as a bus conductor. And who is going to plough my land before they have ploughed their own? That means that my crops are always going to be behind everyone elses. All the family business falls on me. Today I had to go to buy *ghi* (clarified butter) for my daughter who will be coming here for the delivery of her baby. That means that I had to take the day off to travel to another village. Without a man to help you in this kind of work you face difficulties all the time.'

Durgi was justly proud of the fact that she had managed to feed and educate her five children, but she did not regard her independence in decision making as any kind of privilege.

## The providers: husbands and sons

So far, I have dealt scarcely at all with women's relationships with the men on whom they largely depend. Husband and sons have up to now only featured as bridegrooms and divorcees.

The quality of a woman's relationship with her husband is as difficult to gauge in India as it is anywhere else. It is the most private of private relationships. Anthropologists have frequently drawn attention to the fact that a married couple are expected to suppress any overt show of affection or sexual interest in each other (Madan 1965: 134; Hitchcock and Minturn 1963: 241; Jacobson 1977: 65). When I asked women what in their opinion made for good relations between husband and wife, most replied in terms of the husband's capacity to provide, rather than in terms of his capacity to give companionship or affectionate attention.

> 'A good husband is the one who gives you money when you need it without asking what you did with the last lot. My husband is very good to me. When he gives me money each month he trusts me to spend it as I think best. He does not look over my shoulder to see where every penny goes. If I need something, for instance, clothes for the children, he does not grumble. He just gives me whatever he can manage.' (Kamla, C1)

In other words, a good husband provides for his wife and children but is tactful enough not to remind the wife constantly of her financial dependence. Women tend to see their duty to their husbands in terms of personal service. The term *seva kerna* – to serve someone by attending to his or her needs – is often used to express this duty, as also a woman's duty to all the people of her husband and his family. Premi told me:

> 'Husbands do beat their wives; I have seen it. But then wives sometimes cause the beating themselves. You see, they nag the husband when he comes in from his work, saying that he should give them this, that or the other, or that some job needs to be done. A woman should give her husband a glass of water when he comes in and make him comfortable. Then they can talk together quietly about what needs to be done.'

Tact and restraint on the part of both husband and wife provide the foundation for a satisfying married life.

But if women do not show their appreciation of their husbands in terms of personal attributes or affective qualities, this does not mean that the husband may not be a source of great emotional support. The woman whose relationship with her husband is co-operative and harmonious will deal more confidently with her relationships with other people in her husband's home and village than one who feels that her husband belittles her or is indifferent to her needs and feelings. Women whose husbands are away serving in the army or working outside the village miss the moral support and confidence which a good relationship can give. 'Whatever he is like, it is just not the same when your husband is not at home,' one wife in Chaili told me, although in some cases it is clear that the husband's frequent and prolonged absence from home makes a bad relationship tolerable for the wife.

A woman's relationship with her son does not receive the same symbolic expression as her relationship with her daughter. There are no festivals on which married sons return to their homes or on which their mothers send them gifts or sweetmeats, for the reason that, ideally at least, the son never leaves his mother, and they are always members of the same household.

Whether or not this ideal pattern is followed, it is true that at some point in her life a woman transfers her dependence from her husband to her son or sons. This transference takes place directly if the father dies when the son is adult and can take over his father's responsibilities and property. Or it may happen gradually, as when the husband slowly withdraws from active economic participation and both husband and wife come to depend on the work or earnings of their sons. The process is interrupted in the case of a woman who is widowed while her sons are still children; in this event there is a hiatus in the process of transference during which she must either manage the family resources independently or must be maintained by some other member of her family, usually her father-in-law or her own father, until the children grow up.

All the songs which are sung at the birth of a boy celebrate the mother's pride in her child, a sentiment which is not given expression at the birth of a girl. Having less responsibility for his training, a mother can enjoy her relationship with her young son in a relatively relaxed manner, less preoccupied with the need to discipline him and train him for marriage as in the case of a daughter. Yet there are potential tensions in this relationship also, for the shift from the mother being a provider to her being a dependent does not always take place smoothly. Occasionally a son exploits his elderly mother's dependence, or a mother cannot find it in her to hand over the management of the household to her son and daughter-in-law gracefully, and tension and quarrelling result.[15] One old woman in a village near to Chaili had quarrelled with her son and daughter-in-law to the extent that they had decided that she should no longer live with them. They had assigned her separate quarters in the house and she cooked for herself. There was nothing she could do, she said, since her daughter also sided with the son, and of the rest of the family no-one took her part. For all I know, she had made the lives of the others miserable and they were getting their revenge now that she was old and helpless. But clearly there are latent tensions behind the idealized and sentimental picture of the son as his mother's pride and joy which must be recognized just as the acknowledged tensions inherent in, say, the mother-in-law/daughter-in-law relationship.

In another case, that of Kamla's husband's aunt, the quarrel was between an elderly woman and the son of her husband's other wife. She had had no sons of her own and had been quite satisfied when her husband decided to marry again, for she thought that if sons were born to her co-wife they would regard her as their mother also and would care for her when she grew old. But after the death of both the co-wife and the husband her step-son inherited the land of her dead husband and denied her any rights in it. She challenged this in a court case, living meanwhile on the proceeds of the sale of the house her husband had owned. She divided her time between her daughter's house (she was on good terms with her daughter), and various other relatives who were prepared to offer hospitality. This case illustrates two points. Firstly, that all the potential tensions between a woman and her real son are likely to be multiplied in her relationship with a step-son. Secondly, the ideal that one receives from a son and gives to a daughter breaks down in the face of unusual circumstances or extreme poverty. I came across several cases in Himachal Pradesh where an elderly woman depended upon a married daughter, either because she had no living son or because the son would or could not support her. In Punjab this seems rare, although I did find some cases among low-caste landless labourers. Sita (H15) for instance, had had to maintain her widowed mother for several years. Her mother was left destitute after the death of her father, a landless labourer. Sita had spent much of her early married life moving back and forth between her husband's and her mother's homes. After her mother also died she was left to care for her two small brothers whom she took to live with her in Harbassi. She and her husband had borne the expense of the elder boy's marriage and would probably provide for the younger boy in the same way, although they were extremely poor themselves. In this family, one finds a reversal not only of the concept that one does not receive from daughters but also of the idea that brothers give to their sisters.

Although it is generally accepted that a son ought to support his parents when they are old, this does not mean that there need be no dispute as to how much support is due or how a son should balance his obligations to his parents with those to other kin – his wife or sisters, for instances. This is more likely to become a problem when a couple have several sons, for there is no conventionally acepted way of dividing the responsibility for elderly parents among sons who may have different incomes, live in different places and enjoy different degrees of confidence or intimacy with their parents. A woman will expect her sons' help, not just to help maintain herself but also to help pay for the education and marriages of any younger children. At the point where sons are beginning to move out of their immediate authority, parents may find it difficult to communicate to them precisely what their expectations are, because these expectations can no longer be expressed as orders. When Prito (C9) was married, for instance, her mother and father were clearly relying on receiving a good deal of help from other kin since their resources were very limited. Prito's two brothers were in urban employment in Punjab, and Prito's mother Shakuntala was eagerly expecting their arrival to know how much they would be able to contribute to their sister's wedding expenses. The elder son was a long time in arriving and Shakuntala was sick with anxiety at the thought that he might be intending to lie low until a few days before the wedding and thus shirk his contribution. There were some tense days, during which Prito's father sent telegrams to all the places where he thought his son might be, relieved by the boy's eventual appearance and his delivery to his mother of a sum greater than she had hoped for.

It seems common for a woman who has several sons to favour one of them above the others, consciously or unconsciously setting up a kind of competition between them for her affection or approval. The favourite may be the best endowed and most prosperous son, or it may be the most unambitious. Devraj (C10), for instance, was the eldest of four sons, but the least educated. The others had all succeeded in getting some education and had become army officers. They had married educated girls from prosperous families and lived very well indeed, returning to the village only occasionally. Their mother had consistently favoured Devraj however, maybe on account of some personal quality of his, maybe because she felt less intimidated by his illiterate wife than by the sophisticated and articulate girls her other sons had married. Or perhaps she had in mind that the more wealthy sons were made to compete with their stay-at-home brother, and more they would try to win their mother's approval with gifts and contributions to the household expenses. These kind of tensions seem much less common (or at least much less obtrusive) among the rich landlord and professional families in Punjab, where in all probability the parents will have an independent income of their own in the form of pensions or farm proceeds, and will be less directly dependent on their sons for economic support.

We must distinguish between the satisfaction which a woman derives from bearing children and seeing them grow up and the satisfaction she derives from the quality of her relationships with them. Bearing children gives a woman full adult status which marriage alone does not confer. To be childless is a source of despair and often sours a woman's relationships with others. Having children is regarded as a painful and hazardous business but it constitutes more than anything else the justification of her womanhood. But while her children are little, a peasant woman whose time is fully accounted for with agricultural and domestic work does not look on them as companions or intimates as the British middle-class woman is encouraged to do. If they provide her with emotional support and understanding this will be much later when their indisputable adulthood entitles them to an intimacy which the respect and constraint due to elders inhibited when they were younger.

## Conclusion

No member of any household is regarded as making decisions as an autonomous individual, even though it is recognized that some have greater authority in the family than other, so it is always hard to isolate the influence of any one person or category of people. But the economic and moral dependence of women upon men means that women are in a particularly weak position to exercise control over their own marital affairs. They may participate in the arrangement and undoing of the marriages of others in the family once they are of adult status, but they can seldom act unilaterally on their own behalf. It is not surprising then that they tend to regard themselves as very much passive victims of fate. It is according to one's *kismat* that one gets a good and considerate husband or a callous and greedy one, and according to God's will that one's husband lives to a ripe old age or is cut off in his youth. Fate provides a harsh, tyrannical mother-in-law or a kind and understanding one. Young girls tend to think of themselves as burdens on their parents (even when they patently contribute a good deal to the household in terms of earnings and work) since their marriages usually exhaust their household's entire savings. This means that they are diffident about asserting their own wishes in any matter in which they are not directly consulted.

I have argued that the shift from bride-price to dowry, and from modest dowries to enormous ones, tends to reinforce all those tendencies in the economic and normative structure of the household which underlie women's dependence on others. If there is any expansion in women's higher education and technical training in rural areas, whatever economic independence this may bring will be swallowed up by the moral dependence consequent upon the expansion of the dowry system. Any legislation enacted to promote women's legal independence will be ineffective until the legislation which has already been passed limiting dowry expenditure is actually enforced.

Notwithstanding, the women in the villages I studied often showed great courage and determination is standing up for themselves in difficult circumstances. One has to respect women like Roshani, Durgi, and Rattano for their resourcefulness and refusal to be defeated by hard work, public disapproval, and moral isolation. They have found ways of balancing their own needs with those of others in the family in a moral environment which does not acknowledge either the need or the capacity for women to act independently.

## Notes

1   So whilst it is disastrous to have too many daughters (because of the

expense involved when they are married) it is inconvenient to have none at all (because, after the Brahman, a daughter is the most fitting recipient for gifts made to earn religious merit).

2  The word commonly used is *pardesin*, i.e. a foreigner or outsider. In one song the bride addresses her sisters and friends:

> Console my mother after I am gone, my dear friends,
> And cheer her heart for me.
> Today, my dear friends,
> I have become a *pardesin* in my parents' house.

3  See Remy, 1973. Boserup also suggests that 'In regions where women do most of the agricultural work it is the bridegroom who must pay bridewealth . . . but where women are less actively engaged in agriculture, marriage payments come usually from the bride's family' (Boserup 1970: 48).

4  Anthropologists usually refer to the payment made to the bride's family at marriage as bridewealth, presumably because the term bride-price suggests that a sale has taken place. This, however, is precisely how it is seen in India. The term most commonly used is *mul* (i.e. price or payment). I see no reason to be more mealy mouthed than my informants.

5  Whereas a Jat family holding five acres or more might have paid about Rs 500 to marry a daughter in the 1920s (see Darling 1928: 59) a similar family nowadays would consider themselves fortunate if they managed to spend less than Rs 4000.

6  Darling comments on the relationship between creditworthiness of the peasantry and the tendency to inflation of marriage expenses (Darling 1928: 58). Parry makes the same connection in respect of Himachal Pradesh, noting that marriage expenses (in this case, bride-price) rose most rapidly in the period immediately after British rule had been established. This was because under the British it became possible to alienate or mortgage land in order to raise cash for marriage payments, which had not been possible with the land system operating in pre-British times (Parry 1979: 245).

7  There is, for instance, exchange marriage or *vatto* where a brother and sister are married to a sister and a brother. Also in some marriages there is a small dowry given as a matter of form, but a bride-price is also paid which exceeds the dowry in value. These forms are still found in Himachal though many regard them as disreputable and rather old-fashioned.

8  This view is supported by evidence from some parts of India that educated brides, capable of earning a substantial income after marriage, can make a good match with a dowry smaller than that which would be given for a bride who could not earn her own living (Van der Veen 1971: 40).

9  This term is applied to various kinds of grouping within the local caste group. In general we can say that it denotes a named group who are held to be descended from a common ancestor or deity. Therefore they are like kin to each other and cannot marry, though there need be no other kind of connection amongst them.

10 Even in urban families, though, the role of women seems to be important. Jeffery's excellent account of how matches are made among *pirzada* Muslims in Delhi shows that even in a group where the women observe strict purdah while the men work in an occupation which brings them into contact with a wide range of people, it is still the older married women who play the most important part in proposing suitable matches (Jeffery 1979: 28ff).

11 Perhaps through her brother's wife. The sister-in-law often acts as a channel of communication between a girl and her parents where intimate matters are concerned (see Das 1976: 6).

12 None of the cases discussed here ended in a legal divorce. Divorce procedures in India are slow, expensive, and tedious and there is little incentive for either party to sue for a divorce in the courts in the majority of cases, especially since according to customary practice a man need not divorce his first wife before marrying a second.

13 A panchayat is an elected village council, one of whose function is to arbitrate disputes among local people.

14 I use the term 'second marriage' but just as formal divorce is uncommon, second unions are seldom formalized with any special ceremony. At the most, some simplified form of the wedding ritual is used. People judge second unions more on the basis of whether or not the wife was justified in leaving the first husband than on the presence or absence of the proper rituals.

15 Pocock notes that some sons do quarrel with their mothers but suffer from a kind of trauma afterwards which they do not experience after rows with their fathers, perhaps because they feel they have violated what ought to be a purely tender and affectionate relationship (Pocock 1972: 96). Ross gives an account of a similar pattern of relationships among urban Hindus (Ross 1961: 146-9).

# 7 Neighbours and kin: women's relations with other women

The modern feminist movement has stimulated an interest in the relationships that women have with each other, both in western societies and in others. If women have been regarded as characteristically lacking solidarity with members of their own sex, is this because of the influence of an essentially male view of women (women as male property, women as adjuncts to men, repositories of male honour)? Or does their subordinate position really leave no room for the flowering of sincere and satisfying relationships among women themselves?

Women can hardly be more isolated from each other than are housewives in capitalist societies, it would appear (see Oakley 1974: 8). In many non-capitalist or transitional societies female roles and activities are highly segregated from those of men, and women co-operate with each other in various day-to-day or long-term activities. This does not necessarily lead to any kind of political solidarity among women in their separate female world (see Caplan and Bujra 1978: 15). Yet research by feminist anthropologists has frequently revealed that informal (and hence usually unrecognized) networks and relationships among women may have political and economic significance overlooked by traditional (male oriented) ethnographers (e.g. Maher 1976, and many of the contributions to Rosaldo and Lamphere 1974).

So far as Indian women are concerned, there are two quite conflicting views of women's subjective experience of their social roles and of their relations with each other. According to writers like Jacobson, a woman's role subjects her to many trying and painful situations — separation from her own parents at marriage, conflict with the mother-in-law or other members of her husband's household. Yet Indian women do not experience doubt in themselves as women and few would 'trade places with anyone else', largely because they have been firmly socialized into these roles and learn to find satisfaction in them which increases with age and authority in the household (Jacobson 1977: 107). Sarah Hobson, on the other hand, paints a picture of south Indian women who find their roles unsatisfying and full of tensions. Women united in the same household co-operate under conditions which make it difficult for them to obtain genuine love and support from each other; even less are they likely to find warmth or understanding from their menfolk (Hobson 1978).

As observers, it is when we try to make judgements about the quality of women's lives and relationships that we are most likely to be influenced by subjective factors. We will be affected by orientations to our roles as women on our own society which we have taken with us to the field. We may also be influenced by the attitudes of the women with whom we form the closest relationships in the field. But this is an important area of research; the scope for satisfying relationships which female roles offer to women is one of the things which will decide their investment in these roles and determine whether they are likely to wish to defend or change these roles in the future. So I offer this chapter somewhat tentatively, as an essay on the quality of women's lives, bearing in mind that the women I studied were as much divided among themselves by class and caste as they ever were united by their sex.

## Relationships among women

Relationships among women themselves are given little specific recognition in North Indian culture and when they are, they are usually seen in terms of stereotyped cultural expectations. A girl's relation with her mother is seen as one of intimacy and affection whose interruption at the time of marriage will be a source of grief to both. The relationship with the mother-in-law is seen as one of probable conflict. Punjabi women often say that your own mother is your mother 'in sin' (*pāp ki mā*) whereas the mother-in-law is your mother 'in righteousness' (*dharm ki mā*), which is an idea contained in the very term mother-*in-law*. What they are saying is something like what the anthropologist would express by saying that one's own mother is given by nature but one's relationship with one's mother-in-law is constructed by culture.[1] One must attempt to regard one's husband's mother in the same way as one regards one's own mother, but it is recognized that this is not always easy (it does not 'come naturally'). Other relations between women are also stereotyped in terms of the contrast between the warmth and intimacy enjoyed with the women of one's own *peke* and the tension and antagonism likely to develop among women in their *saure*. Wedding songs depict the bride's sisters and girl friends as parting sorrowfully at the time of marriage, while in her *saure*, her husband's sisters lord it over her and tell tales of her to their mother.

I think that anthropologists have been over-reliant on their informants' own stereotyped accounts of relations within the household and village. An enumeration of cultural expectations and roles prescribed for woman's relationships with the various members of the household does not provide a full or reliable map of women's social experience. What such an account does provide is a guide to the structural strains in the household and local community which are the potential source of fission and conflict. They may or may not develop into actual quarrelling, and there may be other unrecognized sources of tension to which such accounts do not alert us. If we take the case of the relationship between a wife and her husband's sister, we see that the expectation of conflict and sour relations refers to a lack of community or interest between the two women. The wife expects her husband's economic and moral support, but the sister also cultivates her brother's continued interest and affection after marriage. Yet this potential conflict does not generally ripen into actual quarrelling. The husband's sister is destined to be married elsewhere and is not likely to spend many years under the same roof as her brother's wife. Provided that she is happily settled in her *saure*, her demands on her brother are not likely to be excessive. Most of the women I knew had cordial though not particularly intimate relationships with their husband's sisters and if there were serious tensions, these lasted for only a short period.

After marriage, a woman's most significant relations are with her mother-in-law and her husband's brothers' wives – a group of women who, if they do not actually share a house, will usually live close to each other and must co-operate in family activities. In terms of kinship vocabulary women married to a group of brothers are identified with each other. They may address each other as 'sisters', they will call each other's relatives by terms appropriate to relationships in one's *peke*, and they will not veil themselves from each other's brothers or fathers (see Vatuk 1969: 260). As we have seen in the previous chapter, they may well be actually related to each other as consanguines. In theory, relations among this group of women are ordered by seniority. They must all defer to their mother-in-law, and the *jethāni* (husband's elder brother's wife) is owed respect by her *durrāni* (husband's younger brother's wife). But in actual fact, if the age differences among the sisters-in-law are not very great, this pattern will be modified by many other factors, e.g. the kinds of relations which they husbands enjoy with each other, whether the mother-in-law favours one at the expense of the others, whether or not the women are already related to one another. Being married to the co-parcenors in the same estate, there is potentially a profound conflict of interest among them. If one of the women fails to bear children, the children of the others will profit by her infertility. If the mother-in-law favours one of them and makes over a good deal of her jewellery to her, then there is less available for the others and their daughters. At the same time, the woman's sisters-in-law are generally her closest neighbours and she will wish to be on good terms with them so that she may look to them for help in everyday matters. Sometimes the relationships among a group of sisters-in-law form stable alliances, sometimes there are shifting patterns of friendship and co-operation.

Let us take the example of Premi (H12) and her sisters-in-law. Satya, the wife of Bishan Das (H14) is related by blood to Premi, although she is a good deal older than Premi and they were not brought up in the same village. They did not have a particularly close relationship before their marriage, though the fact of being related predisposed them to friendship. But a complicating factor has been that their mother-in-law lives with Satya and the matter cannot help being influenced by her attitude, which is to favour Bishan Das and Lachman (H13) at the expense of Premi's husband Hemraj, whom she looks upon as something of a failure compared with her other sons. This attitude rather soured the relationship between Premi and Satya. Satya is mildly critical of Premi behind her back, but does not quarrel with her. Premi's relationship with Lachman's wife, Bhagvati, however, can only be described as stormy. When Premi

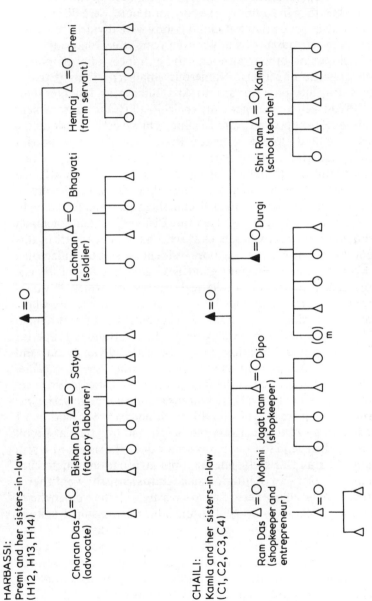

*Figure 1* Relations between sisters-in-law in two families.

was married all the brothers were living together, although the household was partitioned soon after. Premi and Bhagvati never got on well while they lived under one roof and both were disgruntled over the way in which the household goods were divided, although the issues are very obscure by now, seven years later. Bhagvati is still Premi's closest neighbour although the entrances of their houses face in opposite directions. Numerous small irritations (Premi's chickens stray into Bhagvati's courtyard, Bhagvati's daughter slaps one of Premi's children) aggravate their hostility and cause violent quarrels to flare up from time to time. On several occasions the women have used physical violence. Premi hinted tht she thought Bhagvati had tried to use sorcery to harm her children. In fact Premi's relations with both Bhagvati and Satya had been affected for several years by the fact that while they had no difficulty in producing male offspring, it took Premi nine years (and four daughters) to produce a healthy son. Hemraj, Bishan Das, and Lachman have an elder brother, Charan Das, who has not featured in this account because he has for long been resident outside the village in a city in Uttar Pradesh. He made good as an advocate at an early age and invested his savings in an electrical goods store, which now does very well. This brother arranged his own marriage in the city where he was settled with a girl whom, he claimed, was of a Brahman family. Whether or not this was the case, she is certainly of superior social standing and education compared with Satya, Premi, and Bhagvati. She seldom visits the village, but when she first came, Satya was most impressed by the fact that this sophisticated creature actually touched her feet. ('I said that she should not do this; she was my *jethāni* and it was I who should touch her feet. She said that I might be her *durrāni*, but I was the oldest and my marriage took place before hers, and so I was really senior of all the sisters-in-law.') No doubt Charan Das's wife felt she could afford to show deference to a junior sister-in-law of inferior social status since she would never have to live in the village herself or co-operate with the women there. The brothers themselves enjoyed an amicable relationship in spite of the tensions between their wives. Lachman and Bishan Das had always felt rather sorry for Hemraj as he was the poorest and least educated, but they also relied upon him to keep a protective eye upon their wives and their mother while they were away at work, and had given him considerable financial help on occasion.

Another example of the complex relationships among sisters-in-law can be taken from the family of Shri Ram (C1) and his brothers. The eldest brother, Ram Das (C4), was much richer than the others, and as well as the shop he kept in the village, he had a flourishing transport business. He and his wife lived in a house which the other sisters-in-law regarded as pretentious, being newly built in the flat-roofed plains style, rather than to the traditional Pahari design. Ram Das's wife was much older than her sisters-in-law and kept rather aloof from them, even though all four were related to each other as consanguines. Kamla complained that her sisters-in-law Durgi and Dipo, who were her cousins (but real sisters to each other) were in league with each other against her. At the time when the household had been partitioned they had, she said, combined to cheat her and her husband of some of the land they were entitled to. She agreed with them both, however that Ram Das and Mohini, the eldest couple had done best out of the partition and were probably not entitled to their present prosperity. Kamla felt sorry for Durgi, who had suffered from poverty and overwork since her husband died, and she sometimes helped her by making small loans from her house-keeping money, although this almost always led to quarrels when she asked for the money back. It was Kamla who had arranged for Durgi to do some domestic work for me when I first arrived in Chaili and I think that she derived a curious double satisfaction from this; she could feel both a righteous satisfaction that she had really helped to alleviate her *jethani*'s financial distress and a mean satisfaction in seeing Durgi perform menial work for another woman. Dipo (C3) did not get on particularly well with anyone except Durgi, although I think that a long and debilitating illness from which she was just recovering had made her irritable. The four sisters-in-law's houses were very close together and all had to cross each other's courtyards to reach their fields and cattle sheds. In her weakened condition this general lack of privacy and the constant intrusions of the other women's small children caused her temper to flare up frequently and violently.

These examples should demonstrate the complexity and frequent ambivalence of relations among sisters-in-law. But how far are these relations independent of the pattern of relationships among their respective husbands? It is almost a cliché among social anthropologists that the partition of a joint household will usually be attributed to the inability of the womenfolk to get along together (Mandelbaum 1972: 91-2; Ishwaran 1968: 69). Some feminist anthropologists have been critical of a tendency to accept uncritically the accounts of male informants who exaggerate the extent of women's quarrels and project the tensions in their own relationships onto their wives (Caplan 1973). Sometimes personal incompatibilities between women do make it impossible for them to live together and these tensions have nothing to do with the relations among the brothers to whom they are married. But in other cases, women's quarrels have everything to do with matters like the division of property, and in their hostilities to each other they are expressing solidarity with the interests of their husbands (see Madan 1965: 171). For their husbands it may be harder to express these conflicts openly; brothers do quarrel but it is less acceptable for them to indulge in public slanging matches than it would be for their wives. We can see in the detailed examples I gave above that in both Kamla's and Premi's families personal antipathies interact with tensions over property and differential economic status to produce a particular pattern of relationships among the women.

It seems to me that women's quarrels are neither more or less trivial than those which erupt from time to time among men. The difference is that they erupt more easily (because of the small irritations involved in sharing kitchens and courtyards) and are also made up more quickly (because one cannot afford to sulk too long if one is looking to other women for practical help). Therefore these quarrels may appear to both male villagers and to outsiders as less rational and more spontaneous than men's quarrels, which are almost always over property and often lead to litigation. I would disagree with Hitchcock and Minturn (Hitchcock and Minturn 1963: 262) and their informants, who regard men's quarrels as less frequent but more serious. Women's quarrels occur more frequently not because they are more petty but because they have chronic causes which women are not in a position to resolve on their own.[2]

A woman's relationship with her own sisters is often one of supportive affection, but because it has no recognized structural significance it has been neglected by anthropologists in their accounts of family relationships. Sisters are depicted in popular culture as parting sorrowfully at marriage but my data show that sisters often continue to have important contacts with each other after marriage, circumstances permitting. Premi had a younger sister Jyoti, married but as yet childless, of whom she was very fond. Jyoti visited Premi in Harbassi several times a year, always bringing some little gift for the children. Santosh was on particularly good terms with a sister married to a government official in Simla, and she and her children had often spent their holidays in Simla. Among the poorer families, the visit of a sister is often a welcome relief from routine. Women would make a fuss of a neighbour's visiting sister, especially if she were newly married or particularly amusing or good looking. She was a guest whose company they could enjoy without any of the potential tensions already described in the relations of women with their husband's kin.[3]

Whereas in high-caste families women's parents will not accept a daughter's hospitality for fear of violating the principle that one does not receive where one has given a daughter in marriage, there is no such prohibition on a woman receiving hospitality in a sister's home, provided the sister's husband is agreeable. As we have seen, a woman will often take the responsibility for arranging her younger sister's marriage, or the marriage of one of her sister's children. The relationship between sisters is not marked by the formal and ritual celebration which attends the relationship between brother and sister, but it may still be a source of important emotional and practical support.

**Relationships outside the family**

So far we have been discussing relationships between women who are related to kin or affines. Is there such a thing as friendship between village women who are not kin? Friendship is distinguished from kinship among both men and women although there are separate terms for a man's male friend (*dost, mittar*) and a woman's female friend (*saheli*). In practice, though, the concept of friendship among men is more distinctly recognized than the idea of friendship among women. The term *saheli* is not used much among rural women except to express the relationship among unmarried girls of the same village. Among men we find a fairly free use of the term *dost* to express a relationship formed with e.g. an associate at work, a classmate at school or college. One of the reasons for this difference is that men are more mobile. They are more likely to leave the village to study or work and hence to meet and make friends with people totally unrelated to them. Even men who are normally resident in the village have greater freedom to move about in public with the opportunity to form friendships with people outside the immediate circle of neighbours and kin. Women are less likely to form friendships not already subsumed under some other category, such as kin or neighbour.

Kinship terms are used widely outside the family by members of both sexes as a matter of etiquette, even with people whose relationship to the speaker is only slight. So where women are concerned it is difficult to identify a category of 'friends' within the wide range of people who will be addressed as though they were kin. There are at least three modes of fictive kinship noted by anthropologists: (a) 'village' kinship, (b) courtesy kinship, and (c) ritual kinship.

Village kinship is the extension of kin terms or (for in-marrying women) affinal terms to all members of the same village, even to people of different caste. The actual terms used often refer to a fictive genealogical plan of the relationships between families in the village (Mayer 1960: 145; Freed 1963: 91-95; Sharma 1978a: 224) which is modified somewhat with respect to the relative status of speakers (Ullrich 1975; Freed 1953: 101). Thus a married woman will refer to senior men in her husband's village as though they were her husband's uncles or older brothers, and will behave towards them much as she would to her husband's real uncles and older brothers (i.e. she will veil her face from them). In this sense almost all the women in a village will be fictive sisters or sisters-in-law to each other, daughters, aunts or daughters-in-law, even where no known relationship can be traced between their families.

Courtesy kinship is the extension of kinship terms as a matter of politeness to any person whom one meets in the course of everyday activities. In her own *peke* or in her husband's village, a woman will use terms appropriate to the village kinship system. But elsewhere (for instance, if she goes to live in a town or if she lives in a village where neither she nor her husband is a native) a woman has a good deal of choice as to how she addresses other women. Vatuk notes a tendency to prefer an appellation which makes the women 'sisters', provided they are of the same generation, since the relationship between real sisters is regarded as warmer and more relaxed than that of sisters-in-law (Vatuk 1969: 266). Vatuk has also noted that in towns the systems of fictive kinship which develop among close neighbours are 'oriented around women and the type of role women prefer'. This may lead to inconsistency so far as relationships among the men and among the women's children are concerned which are less evident in the more formalized systems of 'village kinship', was commoner in smaller settlements. With a population of six thousand or more, the system of fictive genealogical connection cannot so easily be sustained. No-one can keep track of the generations, no-one will even know (and hence be able to place) all the other inhabitants, and there will be too many immigrant families to be incorporated easily. In Harbassi women such as Balvinder Saini's mother would address the other Saini women in accordance with a system of village kinship, i.e. she would refer to women married in Saini families as sisters-in-law if they were of her own generation. But so far as non-Saini women were concerned she would use any convenient terminology, usually that of sisterhood. Similarly Roshani, a daughter of the village but separated from her husband, addressed most Khatri women married in the village as *bhabi* (brother's wife) but she would call her Brahman friends Santosh and Kaushalya her sisters, although if a complete system of village kinship had operated they also would be called *bhabi* or by some other affinal term. Where women had a very close relationship, friendship would often be commuted into a genuine affinal relationship through one of the women arranging marriages between her own kin and those of her friend.

So far as I myself was concerned, there was enormous inconsistency in my relations with others. Some women in Harbassi preferred to assimilate me as an affine. Thus Roshani openly referred to me as her 'daughter-in-law'. To Santosh's children I was *bhabi* (brother's wife) as they had known my husband before they got to know me, but my husband and I also addressed Santosh herself as *bhabi*, thus confusing generations as well as the affinal/kinship dimension. On the other hand, Balvinder Saini's sister addressed me as *didi* (elder sister) and to Premi I was *bahinji* (sister) and my husband was *jiyaji* (sister's husband).

In Chaili the terminology which I used and which others used towards me was more consistent and favoured viewing me as an in-marrying woman. The men would refer to my husband as their brother and to me as *bhabi* or *parjai* (brother's wife) while the women would normally address me as *bahinji*, which means sister but which is used as a term of address nowadays for a brother's wife also. They would never refer to my husband as *jiyaji* (sister's husband) as many of my friends in Harbassi would. There were two reasons for this difference. I think. Firstly, Chaili is a smaller settlement that Harbassi and in small settlements it is easier to maintain consistently the fiction that all the men are agnatically related.

Second, although my husband was not personally known to more than one or two individuals in Chaili before we arrived to do field research there, he was known to belong to a local family and many of his aunts and sisters-in-law had been born in the hamlets around Chaili. It was therefore simpler to assimilate me as a woman married into the district. The only exceptions to this usage were a few families who did not belong to the neighbourhood (e.g. the forest guard, the social worker) and who generally used our personal names or titles.

The third type of fictive kinship, ritual kinship, is deliberately adopted by two individuals who want their relationship to be recognized as having more to it than the ordinary extension of kinship terms as a matter of courtesy. There are various ways of contracting such a relationship. One may become ritual brother or sister to someone initiated into a cult or sect at the same time as oneself (Mayer 1960: 139). In Himachal the married woman appointed to remove the wrist decorations of a new bride when she is received into her husband's home becomes ritual sister to the bride. In Punjab a girl can adopt a ritual 'brother' by tying an auspicious thread on his wrist at the brother-sister festival of Rakhi. Or the individuals concerned simply agree that from now on they will regard each other as brothers or sisters, and thereafter they make the appropriate ritual gifts to each other at festivals and family occasions. This is one way in which a woman can form an acceptable relationship with a man who is not her kin, but in my experience it is not very common and usually takes place where a woman has no real brothers or male cousins and the man has no real sisters. Ritual kinship involves much the same obligations as real kinship, that is, ritual sisters or ritual brothers will be expected to make gifts on all the occasions when real brothers or sisters make gifts, although the value of the gifts need not be so great. Many close friendships among women really fall between the categories of courtesy kinship and ritual kinship. Two women who live close together will start out by calling each other 'sister' as a matter of etiquette, but as their friendship develops it approaches ritual sisterhood since each feels obliged to make appropriate gifts at weddings and other family celebrations, even though there is no formal enactment of the transition of their affections as there would be in ritual kinship. Ritual kinship itself is not undertaken lightly. Most people have difficulty enough discharging all their obligations to their real kin and will not formalize a friendship beyond a certain point unless they have no siblings or children of their own.

Women who wish to express feelings of friendship have few idioms other than that of kinship available to them, but the vocabulary of kinship in North India is rich enough in possibilities. The difference between the system I have outlined above is mainly one of focus. The village kinship system is focussed on relations among men; it supposes real or fictitious kinship between all men born in the same village and women's relationships are structured accordingly. The system of courtesy kinship among neighbours may be focussed upon men or upon women, but more usually upon women since, as Vatuk points out, among a group of unrelated neighbours it is the women who are likely to interact more (their husbands will probably work in different occupations or at different places). The women therefore, are more likely to set the pace for relationships between their families (Vatuk 1969: 268). Ritual kinship is focussed on the choice of individuals although obviously other members of those individuals' families will be affected (e.g. a woman's children will call her ritual brother *mamaji* – mother's brother).

There are two points which we need to note about the structuring of friendships among local women. Firstly, the more urbanized or complex a community, the more choice individual women have about how they address each other – they can express the friendships which develop among them in the terms which they prefer. On the other hand, they are still constrained to express their relationships with each other primarily in terms of kinship. Men also use fictive kinship to express friendship or regard, but they have other options as well. Even men of the same village are more likely to use each other's personal names than are women. There are more titles, occupational terms, and nicknames available to men which they can use to strike the particular note they desire in their dealings with one another.

It is possible to become quite intimate with a woman without learning her personal name. The names of senior women were particularly hard to discover since there is a general taboo on hailing any senior person by name. But even if he is not addressed by it, the name of any man who is head of a household will be known to all, for it will serve as a tag for the whole family (who will then be referred to as 'so-and-so's wife', 'so-and-so's daugher', etc.). Very few women's names were used in this way, however influential or respected their owners.[3] The individuality of women is suppressed far more than the individuality of men so far as the local community is concerned. A woman's social personality is communicated through her position in the systems of kinship (real and fictive) rather than through her name. This being so, it is possible to see why friendship among women receives less recognition than friendship among men even though it undoubtedly exists. There is no room for the concept in the local vocabulary since women are primarily wives, mothers, daughters-in-law, sisters-in-law etc. from the point of view of the local community i.e. they are adjuncts or dependents of men. If they form independent relations among themselves, these must be assimilated to fictive kin relations of some appropriate type.

### Women as neighbours

Women do not control substantial resources in the household and are therefore not in a position to provide much in the way of financial support to a friend or neighbour in need – or not without the knowledge and consent of others in their households. Women do loan sums of money among themselves but friendships among women are as often cemented by small acts of co-operation and mutual aid. In Harbassi, Roshani used to call upon Santosh every morning to see if there was anything she wanted from the *bazar*. Santosh observed a degree of purdah while Roshani did not, so Roshani's aid in shopping was of real service to Santosh. Kamla (C1) used to supply a Rajput woman who was her friend with ghi when her buffalo produced excess milk. My own friend, the overseer's wife in Chaili, used to supply me with free firewood through her husband's contacts with the forestry department. Friends and neighbours will be called upon for special help when there is a wedding or birth ceremony, or any other occasion when the family is expected to entertain large numbers of people. When Jivan Kaur (H10) sponsored an *Akhand pāth* (reading of the Sikh scriptures in their entirety), she borrowed utensils from her neighbours to cook food for her many guests. She asked her neighbour Santosh to allow the guests to park their bicycles in Santosh's courtyard since there was not enough room in her own. When Durgi's daughter bore a son, Durgi relied heavily on her friends and neighbours to help her cook food and entertain her daughter's in-laws when they came to see the new baby. Women friends, kin, or neighbours characteristically co-operate in domestic and ritual matters. Agricultural work tends to be organized very much on a household basis. Men do sometimes lend agricultural implements and a widow like Durgi may be obliged to ask a male neighbour to plough for her, but families do not ordinarily exchange agricultural labour as a form of mutual help.

With so much informal co-operation at the level of the village or neighbourhood, there is hardly any need for formal associations among women, and where social workers have tried to set up special *mahila mandals* these have met with varied success. The *mahila mandal* (ladies' circle) is conceived by the political authorities as a grass roots movement among women, organized in the first place by the social workers who are responsible for rural development programmes among women, but eventually run by women themselves. They are intended to provide a means of furthering schemes for growing vegetables, raising poultry, disseminating knowledge of better nutrition and family planning, etc. I formed the impression that *mahila mandals* were successful where they provided some activity through which women could earn money, or at any rate save money in some very tangible way. One *mahila mandal* not far from Chaili flourished when the women started to produce and market their own soap and laundry blue through a modest co-operative. In another, they had formed a consumer's co-operative to buy in bulk items such as cloth, children's school books, toilet soap and other items which tend to be expensive in isolated villages. In Harbassi there was no *mahila mandal*, and as far as I know there were none that were operative in the hamlets nearby. In Chaili the social worker, Savitri, had tried to get a *mahila mandal* started. She proposed that Sarla (C5) should be the first president. Sarla agreed, but did nothing for several months on the grounds that the recent death of her husband had made it difficult for her to undertake much social activity. Savitri visited her several times and made suggestions as to how she could get the group started. For instance, she could hold a *kirtan* (a religious meeting at which women sing devotional songs) and I accompanied her when she went to visit some of the women who had initially expressed an interest. But Sarla always gave some reason why the *kirtan* would have to wait until next month and I could see that she was reluctant to make the first move. Savitri saw this as just another example of the suspicious and unreliable nature of uneducated village women. From the point of view of the women, however, I think there was more to their unwillingness than this.

Some of the women were critical of the social worker behind her back. 'She sits on a chair and tells us that we should grow more vegetables and rear poultry; but she is a college-educated woman. When did she ever dig a field or clean a chicken house?' Or as Sarla said, 'Who wants to know about chickens, nasty dirty things? Our family are Brahmans and we have never eaten eggs or chicken's meat'. Savitri was not as out of touch with the village women's attitudes as these comments might indicate, but her brief was to organize something which the women themselves were not convinced that they wanted. They saw the networks of kinship and neighbourly co-operation which they already had at their disposal as adequate for their practical and social needs. As well as this there was, I think, a real dislike among women of taking any role of leadership or authority over other women beyond the roles already written into the kinship structure of the household. A middle-aged woman might be prepared to order the activities of her daughters or daughters-in-law, but she would shy away from any role of formal authority over her neighbours and status equals. When I asked Durgi why women did not like to stand for the panchayat elections, she did not answer (as I had thought she might) in terms of women's dislike of being seen in public, or their shyness in taking public roles, but in terms of their relations with each other.

> 'If I were elected as a panchayat member, then I might have to judge a dispute among my own neighbours. If I gave judgement against a woman, do you think that she would help me when I needed help? I would have to make an enemy of one woman or the other. No-one likes to be in that position.'

A position of overt power over one's neighbours is incompatible with the friendly and informal reciprocity which women like to feel they can expect from neighbours. In Harbassi, the one woman member of the municipal council was the wife of a confectioner and ice-cream seller, himself a member of the council. She was not disliked by the other women, but led a rather self-sufficient life in a house set in the fields at a little distance from the main settlement. Most of the women who do stand for election to village panchayats or town councils seem to be the wives of men who have already been elected (or who expect to be elected), and their political role is to strengthen their husbands' positions rather than to wield an independent power among the women of the neighbourhood. This should not be taken as any slight upon the political sophistication of north Indian village women. It is really an indication that they do not regard the public arena of formal political roles as appropriate or useful for themselves.[4]

Anyone who has observed a village wedding or feast will know that women have extremely effective modes of informal organization. When Jivan Kaur's nephew got married, all the relatives and neighbours gathered in her brother's house, and I travelled with Jivan Kaur and her nieces from Harbassi. Jivan Kaur's brother's wife, Manjit, had already hired a village woman, a poor widow, to spend the whole day cooking for the guests. The rest of the labour needed to prepare food for the feast would be provided by Manjit's immediate neighbours and relatives. The women assembled at her house were not a group who normally co-operated with one another, coming as they did from different villages. But with the minimum of directives the work somehow got done; I found myself with a knife in my hand and a pile of cauliflowers to cut, and everyone around me was working in a quietly co-ordinated fashion.

## Summary

Through the dominant use of kinship terms, women's relationships among themselves are defined as belonging to the private sphere of the domestic and familial. Women seem to prefer the private modality of these roles and resist attempts to transform women's forms of co-operation or leadership into systems of public roles. This means that men can either ignore (or pretend to ignore) women's relations among themselves and can afford to be dismissive of women's conflicts or alliances as being too trivial for their serious attention. Yet it is the local team of friends, neighbours, and female kin who assist a woman (not without conflict at times) in fulfilling her obligations as a wife. It is they who provide domestic help at weddings and other rituals, and who stand in for her as cook and child minder if she is ill, confined, or obliged to be away from home. Therefore a woman's capacity to maintain good relations with the local women have important consequences for all the members of her household, even though they do not recognize it.

**Notes**

1   See Das (1976) for a fuller discussion of Punjabi kinship as 'a dialectic between the rules deriving from nature and the rules derived from culture'.

2   Hitchcock and Minturn note that men seldom champion women's quarrels with each other. But this is not evidence of the triviality of such quarrels so much as of the conditions which make it difficult for women to resolve them. By standing aloof from such quarrels men can avoid confronting underlying tensions which they would prefer to ignore as long as possible (particularly the potential competition among brothers), but they ensure that the women play out these tensions on their behalf. Mohan Singh (C7) told me that he would be ashamed if a woman brought a case against another woman in the panchayat of which he was chairman. In a respectable village, he said, it ought not be necessary for women to air their differences in public and he would encourage women to accept the arbitration of a kinsman or neighbour rather than use the panchayat. I found similar attitudes among panchayat members in some of the villages near Harbassi. This seems to me to be an abdication on the part of men of their real power to help women solve real disputes, and so it is no wonder that women's conflicts are more persistent.

3   Ullrich points out that it is quite possible for high-caste women to be ignorant of the names of low-caste neighbours whom they see frequently; here status distance reinforces the tendency to identify women by reference to their husbands or fathers. (Ullrich 1975: 61)

4   This does not mean that women never exercise informal leadership among their neighbours. Kamli (H16), recalling her childhood, described her mother thus:

> 'She was a strong and sensible woman. All the Chamar women in that village looked up to her. If a pedlar came by, the others would look to her to bargain with him and to see that he gave them fair measure. If there was a quarrel she would often help to settle it and would bring people to their senses.'

# 8 Discussion and conclusions

After all this ethnography we should step back and consider whether what we have learnt about women's position in production does help us to characterize their general position in Indian society. And what of the differences and similarities which I have noted between the two areas which I studied? Are these of relevance in our attempt to theorize about women's roles, or must they be treated as so many cultural and geographical accidents?

Women in Himachal and Punjab certainly see themselves as divided by enormous differences. From my own point of view it felt very different to be living among Himachali women after six months spent in Punjab. Punjabi women 'come across' as more open and assertive in their personal manners than Himachali women, yet they also appear more housebound and more restricted in their movements and public activities. The contrast between the restrained public demeanor of Punjabi women and their spontaneity in the private company of other women is striking. Himachali women seemed to me more reserved at all times though less obliged to refer their behaviour and movements to men (if only because so many of their menfolk were absent from the village for so much of the time).

Yet I concluded that whilst these differences were experienced as very important, when it came to analysis they were less significant than they seemed. The similarities in the underlying structure of the female situation turned out to be much greater than I had expected. In reality the chances for economic independence and the control over their own activities which this might bring are as limited for Himachali women as for Punjabi women, even though the former are more actively involved in agricultural production. I found, for instance, that it was not automatically the case that women who perform such agricultural work have any greater say in agricultural decision making than women who perform little agricultural work or none at all. Or if they do have greater say, it is as likely to be due to the negative fact of their husbands' absence as migrant labourers as to the positive fact of their own productive activity. In other areas of social life, women's capacity to influence decisions and exert control was just as likely to depend on factors unrelated to the kind or amount of productive work which they do. One particular sphere which I examined in some detail (in Chapter 6) was that of match making; here the power which women wielded and their importance in determining household policy depended on factors quite other than their capacity to work or generate income. Their control in this field had much more to do with their structural position as links between households in a system which favours marriage outside the circle of immediate kin and neighbours but within the caste group. If some women (e.g. low-caste women and some of the poorer high-caste women in Himachal Pradesh) seem to have greater freedom to leave their husbands or to make second marriages with men of their own choice, this is not primarily because they are economically more independent of men than other women. It is probably more closely related to factors such as the organization of property, and patterns of marriage payment, especially the distribution of the *kanya dān* type of marriage with its associated ideology. In theory we might certainly expect to find that women who work for wages (and even women who work as family labourers) have a greater say in household matters than women who perform domestic work only, and this is an assumption that has often been made both by anthropologists and others. But the female labourer usually earns wages which are too small and sporadic to lend her any special leverage in household politics, and the work of female family labourers does not give women any particular control over the products of their labour.

As we have seen, there are variations in the internal structure of the household and its political machinery which are related to the kind of work which its members do and especially to the sexual division of labour. But these are not as conspicuous as the broad similarities in role patterns and the organization of authority. A wife is a wife, in whatever kind of work she spends her time, and a daughter-in-law a daughter-in-law. The subordination of female to male and junior to senior pervades family life in both areas and in all classes, whatever modifications we find in particular groups. I have not dealt with women's participation in collective political processes in the village, largely because it was difficult to make any worthwhile observations in the short time available in each area. But here also, what I was able to observe confirms the impression that there was much overall likeness between the two areas, at the village level at least. In both places, women's participation in community affairs is severely limited by general standards of female behaviour in public which stress women's invisibility and passivity and which circumscribe their movements, especially their contacts with men. Their political effectiveness, whatever their role in production, depends on their domestic power and their contacts with other women; the direct routes to political influence are blocked and for the most part they have to exploit the opportunities offered by their situation within the household.[1]

This review shows that considered as a determinant of women's social power, their participation in agricultural work is only one variable among many. It cannot (on its own) explain differences in marriage practices, dowry payments, and divorce arrangements, as has often been assumed by anthropologists and others.

There is a fund of common norms of and images which all the women I studied recognized as bearing on their lives, a warp of common values regarding women's special role which underlies all the differences due to class and regional culture. There are general similarities in the rules which govern women's public mobility, the organization of marriage, kinship terminology and the domestic role system. There is likely to be even greater cultural convergence in future as the geographical isolation of hill areas is broken down by modern communications. Many Paharis living near the borders of Punjab listen to Jullundur Radio rather than Simla Radio – as much a matter of taste as of better reception. Many Paharis will have worked in Punjab or lived there for periods of time and there is a greater wish to conform to universal rather than regional models of proper Hindu behaviour, even if there is not always total unanimity as to what these models ought to consist of. The dominant images of female behaviour which are carried in popular culture – the dutiful wife, the revered and indulgent mother, the modest and submissive bride – remain as strong and attractive as ever and are now disseminated by a variety of powerful media (the press, cinema, popular religious literature, and mythology). It is possible that further ironing out of regional differences will occur.

So do we simply have a case of 'Ideology Rules O.K.'? Perhaps the traditional functionalist approaches which I criticized in the first chapter are valid after all? After all, why trouble to scrutinize the precise tasks which women perform or the exact degree of their control over production processes if we can explain everything that is important about female roles by appealing to the force of ideals of proper female conduct (which do not vary much for women of different groups)?

I hope it will be clear that I do not think that this is the way out. If there is any explanatory 'key' to women's position in both Punjab and Himachal it is more likely to be women's dependence upon men than their submission to men. Women depend on men because men may own land and hold tenancies and women (on the whole) cannot. The etiquette of public invisibility, the avoidance of male affines, the subordination of women within the household, the tendency to educate women to lower standards than men – all these practices elaborate secondary sources of dependence upon men (moral, practical, and ritual) which feed and reinforce their primary economic dependence. Variations in the pressure and force of these practices can now be seen as responses to differences in the economic sources of women's dependence upon men rather than as 'just' regional and cultural differences. The ideology of dependence is required by the material structure of production.

But this does not tell us why the economic dependence of women is required in the first place. This is a much harder problem to answer, but I think that the ethnography I have presented here does suggest some answers. The most important factors here are the allocation of property (especially land) and the allocation of the right to work, i.e. to command wages. I shall deal with these separately.

## Women and property

The main kind of property which it is relevant to consider in a book about rural women is land, or rights in land. These rights are transmitted through a thoroughly male inheritance system. Familial values are not merely congruent wth this male property system, they are actually geared to maintaining its maleness. Sons must be produced at all costs. In spite of a general rise in age at marriage in the last fifty years, marriage still takes place at a relatively early age in rural families (few of the women in the sample households were married at later than twenty years old). Couples therefore have many years in which to try to produce a male heir. Those who do not produce sons at first will go to great lengths, both magical and medical, to ensure that sons are conceived. As is well known, sons are given a religious and cultural value that is not given to daughters; the birth of a son is marked with much more elaborate ceremony than that of a daughter, and women who cannot produce sons are regarded with pity. Any women of child-bearing age who has not already borne sons will constantly be reminded by others that she has not yet done her duty by her husband and his family and this pressure is kept up until she either produces a male heir or resigns herself to failure. A man who fails to produce sons by his first wife may by custom marry again. Even the Hindu Code Bill, which prohibits polygamy among Hindus, has not been effective in this respect, so forceful is the imperative for male heirs. Adoption (usually of a brother's son) is another solution, exemplified in the case of Jivan Kaur (H10). Lastly, in the past female infanticide was not unknown among the propertied class in Punjab and some other parts of North-West India, and even now it is likely that male children are given preferential treatment when resources like food or medical treatment are limited (the demographic imbalance of the sexes in most states in India can scarcely be explained otherwise).

In short, while female children remain (legally) the residual heirs of male property, people see to it that there are male heirs to inherit as far as it is within their power.

Another point is that for reasons which I have already made clear (see p.48). I do not think that it is useful to regard dowry as it is practised in North-West India as a form of inheritance, although this might be a useful way of analysing dowry in other societies. Or, if we do wish to consider dowry as a form of inheritance, then we might just as well regard it as inheritance on the part of the son-in-law as on the part of the daughter. Dowry gifts go *with* the daughter *to* the son-in-law (or his parents) rather than to the daughter herself. Also dowries in North-West India consist of particular types of property, and the chief difference between the kinds of property transferred at marriage and those transferred to sons at a man's death is that the former does not usually include wealth-generating forms of property. As far as I know, land is never gifted as dowry. I would therefore disagree with Goody in regarding dowry as a means by which daughters inherit in Eurasian societies, at least in so far as India is concerned.

If we want to understand the system of property and inheritance which obtains in northern India today it is necessary to look at practice rather than at legal codes alone. The statutes which allow for equal participation in inheritance on the part of daughters are not a dead letter by any means, but they are appealed to in certain circumstances – in cases of disputes among siblings or where land ceiling legislation makes it expedient for large estates to be broken up 'on paper' among male and female heirs. Ordinarily daughters waive the rights which the law gives them and would be considered selfish sisters if they did not do so (see p.57).

In addition to inheritance practices we need to look at the pattern of effective control, since it is clear that many women who do inherit land or who have land registered in their names have only minimal control over the land they officially own. This happens because norms governing women's movements in public inhibit them from taking an active part in the management and administration of estates and in all the legal business attendant upon landholding. Usually a man – the husband or the brother in most cases – will act on the woman's behalf.

So what we actually find is a system of inheritance only slightly modified by modern legislation, in which daughters are certainly preferred to a man's more distant collateral heirs, but in which they do not actually inherit very often. Everything in the system of property which I have described tends to establish the primary control of income generating property in the hands of men. Women may have a good deal to say in the way in which land is administered and farmed and they may also have effective control of other forms of property (domestic goods, furniture, clothing, and jewellery), especially as they reach positions of seniority in the household. But they have little direct control over wealth-generating forms of property.

Even those forms of property which do not of themselves generate new wealth (household equipment, agricultural implements) are passed on from father to son, with daughters entering only in the absence of sons. For many men, this is the only kind of property which they are likely to inherit since their fathers have no land to leave them. But even among labourers, once the tiniest plot of land is acquired, the property rules which I have just outlined assert themselves.

All this means that, *pace* Goody and *pace* the Indian legislators who have attempted to shift things in favour of female inheritance, the system is still firmly male. Diverging devolution remains a possibility within this system only as a last resort, and therefore does not seem to me to be a very useful term with which to characterize the system as a whole. Now it is possible to see such practices as purdah, avoidance of male affines, women's public invisibility, etc. not so much as antidotes to misalliance (though they certainly do perform this function) so much as a system of practices which reinforce the male control of productive resources. Specifically they protect this system against modern attempts to modify it through legislation in favour of women. The ideology of the good sister ensures that women do not claim land which their brothers might inherit, and the ideology of the deferential and dependent wife ensures that a woman will find it difficult to control land registered in her name independently of the assistance of her husband or some other male relative (see p.104). The norms governing female roles by no means exclude women from an active role in agricultural and other productive work but they limit the ways in which women can actually use whatever economic power they may derive from their role in production, whether collectively (in the community) or as individuals (in the household).

These ideological constraints sustain the 'maleness' of the property system in a very direct way. We are not strictly obliged to appeal to the need for women to marry status equals in a class society (as Goody does) in order to explain purdah and associated practices, when a more direct connection between property and gender roles can be traced. However, this does not mean that these less direct paths of causation are irrelevant for all purposes. Had I been writing a book about the class structure of North Indian villages rather than one which is focussed upon gender roles, I would have had to make the connection between property and purdah via the problem of status group endogamy and the dominant classes' need to prevent dispersal of the productive resources they control. Those writers who have seen purdah in relation to social differentiation are not incorrect in their views, only in their tendency to stress the dimension of 'status' or 'prestige'. The surveillance of women and the restriction of their movements and autonomy, especially as they affect the possibility of women marrying outside their own group has an important function in relation to the organization of property if we consider that even if daughters rarely gain direct control of their fathers' estates, a son-in-law may well gain access to the household's productive resources in the absence of sons.

The subordination of women within the household also plays an important role in respect of class, which is not diminished by the fact that some assertive and strong-minded women exercise far more control within the household than the ideologies of the submissive daughter-in-law and the deferential wife allow to be recognized. I noted earlier that in rural households at all socio-economic levels it is quite usual to find a number of different class interests represented through the diverse activities and sources of livelihood of their members (see p.00). The solid structure of the household authority system, with its emphasis on the subordination of women and junior members (see p.81). The solid structure of the household authority members' interests, may well explain why divergent interests do not tear such households apart.

Purdah, then, has a double ideological function. It favours the consolidation of property-owning groups (and the emulation of these groups' values and culture by others). It also favours the concentration of the direct control of property in the hands of the male members of the group. I have stressed the latter aspect in this book, but the former is not necessarily less important.

By why should property be concentrated in the hands of men and not of women? Why should the distinction between the sexes constitute the watershed for the definition of economic rights and duties in the household? It is not possible to suggest more than a few rather crude answers to this question here.

Any system of property and inheritance organizes both the relations of people with each other and the relationship between people and resources. A system of inheritance which limits transmission in any way limits the fragmentation of estates which can occur when large number of children are produced. The integrity (or relative integrity) of estates in a class society ensures that some members of the property-owning group maintain its position from generation to generation. Those who do not inherit may be provided for in ways which do not threaten the integrity of the landed estate, as when consumer durables are gifted as dowry to ensure the good marriages of non-inheriting daughters. Or non-inheriting children may not be provided for at all; all but the youngest, all but the eldest, or all but the elected heir among couple's children may be left to fend for themselves or assigned inferior positions within the dominant class (there are useful discussions of these issues in Goody, Thirsk, and Thompson 1976).

In the case of North-West India it is daughters who are excluded, and they are 'exported' to become wives in different, and often distant, households; the farther away they are married, the less of a threat they represent to the income and property of the natal group. Some household income is diverted in the form of dowry and other prestations to ensure that they marry status equals (or even superiors) and that having been married, they stay married and do not return (although as we have seen in Chapter 6, this arrangement is likely to backfire and indirectly make marriage breakdown more likely for some groups when dowry gifts become too lavish).

Within the propertied classes, the exclusion of daughters and the partition of the land among sons maintains a constant balance between people and land, or at least it does so in periods of demographic stability. In the past fifty years the population in India has increased enormously and the fragmentation of holdings among some peasant groups is a serious problem. In fertile areas like Punjab, the profitability of modern agriculture and the presence of accessible markets for agricultural produce has meant that those who already have land are even more likely to resist measures which encourage the further fragmentation of estates. In both the areas studied, men who already have land usually feel that they would like to have more of it, and those who have no land wish to become land-owners (rather than diverting resources into other kinds of property). Under these circumstances we should not expect measures designed to divide holdings further by admitting daughters as heirs to find much favour in practice. Both men and women rationalize the unwillingness of daughters to exercise their new rights to inherit in quite other terms (in terms of the mutual duties of brothers and sisters) but other rhetorics are available and are occasionally used with the same effect.

The exclusion of women from the inheritance of land can be seen as one of the various possible ways of controlling the relationship between people and resources in an agrarian society, although it is far easier to show why a 'male' property system stays 'male' than why it is 'male' rather than 'female' in the first place.

Much more work needs to be done on the relationship between property organization and female gender roles, especially practices like purdah and seclusion. Whilst Goody's contrast between the African and Eurasian systems remains useful, comparisons within the Eurasian group need to be made if we want to understand why and how the experiences of women in these societies differs. On recently re-reading Campbell's material on Greek peasants I was struck by many similarities to my own north Indian material, especially by his accounts of ideas of female honour and the status of brides (Campbell 1964).

On the other hand, it may be possible that there are systems in which women have been even more thoroughly excluded from the control of property than in India (pre-revolutionary China comes to mind as a possible example). Also, as yet there has been no analytical comparison between North and South India in respect of the relationship of women's roles to property organization. The tendency on the part of many anthropologists to stress the cultural distinctiveness of Indian society (either explicitly or implicitly) has inhibited such constructive comparisons between India and other peasant societies, but there are signs that in the field of gender relations at least this isolationism is beginning to break down.

## Capitalism, the cash economy, and women

India is no longer a peasant society, however, it is a peasant society in the process of transforming itself into a dominantly capitalist society. Most sociologists have emphasized that capitalism requires the legal 'freedom' of labour; workers must not be bound to a particular employer, nor are employers committed to employ particular workers, but each sell or buy labour on an open market. This was not the case in feudal Europe, nor was it the case in the various pre-capitalist agrarian systems of India, where various forms of tied labour obtained (and still persist in many rural areas). Yet an important characteristic of industrial capitalism which has often been ignored is the differential distribution of another kind of 'invisible property'. In western capitalist societies a powerful minority is able to live on dividends and rents, but so far as the majority is concerned, the chief good to be distributed is the right to work. In fact, the right to work in general is not explicitly accorded to anyone (in spite of being enshrined in the United Nations Universal Declaration of Human Rights), although Trade Unionists have sometimes asserted that it should be. Yet clearly some workers have a status which is superior to others in this respect. Some, for instance, enjoy greater security of tenure, even in periods of unemployment, and if they do lose their jobs they are offered more substantial redundancy payments or better retraining opportunities. The right to work is explicitly denied to some (children) but there may be other groups for whom it is very limited or offered only conditionally. These may include blacks, immigrants, the elderly or disabled, and (the largest group) women.

These groups often constitute a reserve of labour which can be drawn into production during times of boom or emergency (wartime) and excluded or relegated to marginal positions in the economy in times of recession. The historically prior domestic orientation of women made it easier to exclude them or offer them only marginal and insecure forms of employment. Indeed the domestic orientation of women has been accentuated since the industrial revolution with the development of the full time 'housewife' role and the ideology of home-based consumerism. Should we expect the progress of capitalist production in India to have very different results so far as women are concerned?

On the whole there seems reason to suppose that it will not. Existing modes of agrarian production and property already emphasize women's role as dependents of men. In some senses, peasant and labouring women were already a kind of rural reserve force, being drawn into or excluded from agricultural production as the need arose – honour (women are disgraced if they work in the fields) or necessity (women have to work in the fields because no-one can afford to hire other labour) being appealed to, as the case might be.

On the whole the male head of the household retains some control over the labour of its female members. As we have seen, a girl can only train for paid work if her father wishes it and is prepared to pay for her education, and it will be difficult for a wife to work after her marriage without the goodwill of her husband and his parents. Women who do take paid employment cannot always find suitable work in the same place as their husbands, and Indian courts are now being asked to determine whether a wife has an independent right to decide where she should work, and, if necessary, maintain a separate establishment from that of her husband – independent, that is, of her husband's consent. On the whole there has been a tendency to deny that right as an automatic entitlement (see Editorial Report 'Married or Bonded' in *Manushi*, Issue 1: 405).

Male control of female labour power continues, although this control must be attenuated when the women work for others. Therefore if women are entering the industrial and bureaucratic work force, it is not on the same terms as men and it is under conditions which encourage their continued subordination to men in the household. So things seem set fair for a reproduction of the western pattern of female dependence upon male wages, albeit for somewhat different historical reasons.

However, this is only a very general truth and it is important not to lose sight of the different ways in which these broad trends affect particular areas. Obviously there are considerable differences in the ways in which capitalist production and the cash economy have affected the two areas studied here.

Punjab is relatively urbanized and industrialized compared to Himachal Pradesh. There is a good deal of industry in its cities (light engineering, textiles) and considerable scope for employment in the public services (irrigation, schools, etc.). Many men can get paid work near to their own villages, even within commuting distance, and can retain an active interest in their land. But at the moment there are few opportunities for urban employment for women in Punjab, nor even of rural employment; farming among the larger landowners becomes organized on a capitalist basis, women continue to constitute a fund of seasonal labour, becoming ever more marginal as agricultural work becomes more mechanized. It is not so much that capitalist development has taken away women's traditional work and given it to men – women in Punjab never did have much chance to earn an independent income. It is rather that capitalist agriculture and industry have offered women nothing very specific as yet and so they remain as dependent on men as they ever were.

Himachal Pradesh differs in two important respects from Punjab. Firstly, men have to travel much further to find waged work and communications are poorer, so they really have to choose between being full-time wage earners or full-time peasant farmers or tenants.

There is no way in which they can participate in wage labour whilst retaining an active involvement in the day-to-day demands of a farm. Even more agricultural work devolves upon women (as family labourers) in addition to the extra domestic work which they must undertake when men are not at home to help in fetching water, going to the *bazar* etc.

Secondly, land in the foothills is not productive enough to make it worthwhile investing large sums of cash earned in employment in its improved exploitation. Some workers do invest in buying more land, but this extra land must be farmed by traditional methods. Again, it is the migrant's wife who will do the extra work, with perhaps very occasional hired help, unless land is rented out to share croppers. The peasant households whose men go to the cities to work can only achieve the standard of living they enjoy (which is not always very high) because they depend on the double sources of agricultural production and waged work. The land is an important souce of security against old age or unemployment and will not lightly be abandoned, but there is increasing specialization within the household. Working on the land becomes the concern of the women, and earning wages becomes the business of men. This specialization in agriculture does not bring women any particular rewards however, other than more work, and it certainly does not bring them an income of their own or any other kind of wealth which they could use on their own account. It does mean that their daily lives are relatively unsupervised by men and they have somewhat more freedom of movement than most Punjabi women, but these are not necessarily seen as valuable assets. As one migrant's wife complained, 'It is all very well for people like my husband. We women stay at home and do back-breaking work even if we are feeling ill or if we are pregnant. There is no sick leave for us. But we do not have any money of our own and when the men come home we have to cast our eyes down and bow our heads [i.e. act submissively] before them'.

In neither area does the development of a cash economy and capitalist production mitigate the dependence of women on men. If anything it increases it by adding to their old dependence on men as property holders a new dependence on men as wage earners. In spite of this, women in Punjab probably feel that they have had a better deal than Himachali women since these developments have at least brought many of them increased leisure and comfort. The main thing which they have brought for Himachali women is an increased work load.

I am not sure whether it would be better to end this book with a rousing call for the provision of more opportunities for rural women to gain access to independent sources of income, or with a rousing call to the defence of my original thesis that women's role in production does indeed explain much else about their social roles that has previously been explained in purely functionalist terms or in terms of the distinctive cultural features of the sub-continent.

I am aware that my arguments need theoretical refinement; I have certainly over-simplified some local and class differences in order to accommodate the wide range of data which I was able to gather. I only hope that in doing this I have not done too much violence to the complexity of the social structure which I have studied.

But I have satisfied myself that the kinds of concerns which feminist anthropologists have demonstrated in studies of peasant and industrializing societies are as valid in South Asia as anywhere else. Women's role in production does provide a useful starting point for an analysis of their general position provided always that we interpret this phrase 'role in production' in a structural sense (and not just as meaning the amount of work which women do) and provided that women's role in reproduction is considered also.

So far as the question of providing economic opportunities for women is concerned, the problem is a difficult one. I think that it is one which will only be tackled properly when rural women demand it themselves. A little well-meaning intervention from rural development experts, a few schemes to stimulate local crafts among village women – these are not going to change the structure of production although they will undoubtedly be worthwhile for the women who benefit from them directly. Most of the women I knew did not experience their position *as women* as being oppressive, though they might express a sense of impotence as landless labourers, of insecurity as over-worked peasants on tiny holdings or frustration as housewives making do on a husband's low salary in the face of rapid inflation. The female life cycle holds promise of greater power and prestige in the household with age; a woman knows that as she gets older and her sons bring brides into the household, her position there will be more privileged. Therefore, she is likely to accept the constraints and disabilities imposed on a young wife. The segregation of women means that they are less likely to compare themselves with men, but more likely to see their prestige and standing as derivative of that of their menfolk. Also, the ethic of the female as the repository of family honour does not conflict with an ideology of individual achievement and self-fulfillment as it does in the West. Women tend to see their position as dependants as problematic only when the machinery of dependence breaks down – when the husband fails to provide, when he is sick or dies and the wife is left with no provider.

When I was doing the fieldwork on which this book is based, a question which I often used to ask my friends and informants was 'In your next life, would you prefer to be reborn as a man or as a woman?' I will conclude by presenting some of the responses I got to this question, all of which are representative in different ways of women's attitude to themselves and their position in society.

*Urban housewife, married to a government employee (Punjab):*
'I would rather be a woman anytime. Men have to go out to work, travel on buses and run about, and when they get home they are too tired to even enjoy their food. I would rather be a woman at home and enjoy what I have. Even if you are not very rich you can meet your neighbours in the afternoon when you have done your work, put on a nice sari and go to the cinema or just sit and talk together.'

*Landless labourer (Punjab):*
'It is much better to be a man. A man can be ritually pure and clean. A woman . . . well, you know what I mean, she menstruates every month and can never be as pure as a man. And then you have to clean the babies when they shit, collect cowdung and all that kind of work, you know.'

*School teacher (Punjab):*
'I have never thought about it. I do not think it makes very much difference. A man or a woman can be equally happy if the family has plenty of money and there is enough to eat so that they do not have to worry all the time about how they are going to pay for things.'

*Peasant farmer, a widow (Himachal):*
'A man's life is better on the whole. Of course, if her husband is alive and if he is not stingy, then a woman's life is all right. But even then

you have to ask for money. The husband will say 'why did you spend so much, do you need money again already? If a woman earns money herself, then it is different. But how many women earn money like that?'

# Glossary

*Note:*
I have not adhered to any particular system of transliteration, nor have I used diacritical marks except to indicate long vowels in some unfamiliar and polysyllabic words where some guide to pronunciation might be helpful. Some Indian words (such as purdah) have been omitted from the glossary because they have been virtually assimilated to the English language, and have been treated as such in the text.

| | |
|---|---|
| *bazar* | shopping area or retail market |
| *bhabi* | brother's wife |
| *birāderi* | the local caste community or related group of families living in the same village |
| *cho* | a shallow water course in the submontane areas of the Punjab plains which floods in the monsoon season |
| *dāj* | dowry |
| *dihāre* | day labouring |
| *durrāni* | husband's younger brother's wife |
| *ghar* | house, household, home |
| *ghar da kam* | housework |
| *ghar jamai* | a man who lives in his wife's parents' home (the term *gharjamwantru* is used in Pahari areas) |

| | |
|---|---|
| *ghi* | clarified butter |
| *izzat* | honour |
| *jajmāni* | the *jajmāni* system (as it has been termed by anthropologists) was a system of relationships – usually hereditary – between landowning families and specialist artisans or labourers. The latter provided services in return for customary payments in kind. The system is largely defunct nowadays, at least in its traditional form |
| *jethāni* | husband's elder brother's wife |
| *kanya dān* | the gift of a virgin daughter in marriage; according to Sanskritic tradition, the noblest form of marriage. In this kind of marriage a dowry is customary but no payment is received from the groom's family |
| *khad* | stony watercourse in the Sivalik hills, often situated in a deep ravine |
| *khet* | field |
| *kheta da kam* | farm work |
| *lāvā* | the central rite of the Hindu wedding ceremony in which the bride and groom walk round the sacred fire |
| *mahila mandal* | 'ladies circle' – the government encourages the establishment of such circles to disseminate ideas about nutrition, child care, etc. |
| *mul* | price – in the context of marriage, the term is used to denote bride price paid by the groom's father to the bride's family |
| *pahari* | of the hills, hill person (from *pahar*, meaning hill) |
| *peke* | a married woman's parents' home, or by extension their village |
| *pind* | village |
| *qasbah* | a large village or a small country town which serves as a market centre |

| | |
|---|---|
| *saheli* | female friend |
| *saure* | one's in-laws' home or village |
| *vatto, vatta satta* | exchange marriage in which a family takes a bride from the household in which they have married their daughter |

# References

Aaby, P. (1977) Engels and Women. *Critique of Anthropology* **3** (9 and 10): 25-53.

Arens, J. and van Beurden, J. (1977) *Jhagrapur; poor peasants and women in a village in Bangladesh.* Birmingham: Third World Publications.

Bailey, F.D. (1963) *Politics and Social Change: Orissa in 1959.* Berkeley and Los Angeles: University of California Press.

Beechey, V. (1978) Women and Production; a critical analysis of some sociological theories of women's work. In A. Kuhn and Ann-Marie Wolpe (eds) *Feminism and Materialism.* London: Routledge and Kegan Paul.

Berreman, G. (1963) *Hindus of the Himalayas.* Berkeley and Los Angeles: University of California Press.

Beteille, A. (1971) *Caste, Class and Power. Changing Patterns of Stratification in a Tanjore Village.* Berkeley and Los Angeles: University of California Press.

Bhasin, K. and Malik, B. (1975) The Status of Women in Changing Rural Society. *Indian Farming*, Vol. XXVC(8): 48-52.

Bland, L. Brunsdon, C. Hobson, D. Winship, J. (1978) Women 'inside' and 'outside' the relations of production. In *Women Take Issue. Aspects of Women's Subordination.* Women's Studies Group, Centre for Contemporary Cultural Studies. London: Hutchinson.

Boserup, E. (1970) *Women's Role in Economic Development.* London: Allen and Unwin.

Bossen, L. (1975) Women in Modernizing Societies. *American Ethnologist* **2**(4): 587-600.

Bott, E. (1957) *Family and Social Network.* London: Tavistock Publications.

Breslow-Rubin, L. (1976) *Worlds of Pain.* New York: Basic Books.

Brown, J. (1970) Economic Organization and the Position of Women among the Iroquois. *Ethnohistory* **17**: 151-67.

Bujra, J. (1978) Introductory: female solidarity and the sexual division of labour. In Caplan and Bujra (1978).

Campbell, J.K. (1964) *Honour, Family and Patronage*. Oxford: Oxford University Press.

Caplan, P. (1973) *Ethnographic review of Gaon: Conflict and Cohesion in an Indian Village*. London: Women's Anthropology Workshop. (cyclostyled report).

——(1978) Women's Organizations in Madras City, India. In Caplan and Bujra (1978).

Caplan, P. and Bujra, J. (1978) *Women United, Women Divided*. London: Tavistock Publications.

Chatterjee, M. (1977) Conjugal Roles and Social Networks in an Indian Urban Sweeper Locality. *Journal of Marriage and the Family* **39** (1): 193-202.

Coulson, M., Magas, B., Wainwright, H. (1975) The Housewife and her labour under Capitalism – a critique. *New Left Review* **89**.

Darling, M.L. (1928) *The Punjab Peasant in Prosperity and Debt*. London: Oxford University Press.

——(1930) *Rusticus Loquitur*. London: Oxford University Press.

Das, V. (1973) The Structure of Marriage Preferences; an account from Pakistani fiction. *Man* **8**(1): 30-45.

——(1976)a Masks and Faces; an essay in Punjab Kinship. *Contributions to Indian Sociology* (n.s.) **10**(1): 1-30.

——(1976)b Indian Women; work power and status. In B.R. Nanda (1976).

Desai, I.P. (1964) *Some Aspects of Family in Mahuva*. London: Asia Publishing House.

De Souza, A. (ed) (1975) *Women in Contemporary India*. Delhi: Manohar Book Service.

Dube, S.C. (1975) *Indian Village*. London: Routledge and Kegan Paul.

Dumont, L. (1970) *Homo Hierarchicus*. London: Weidenfeld and Nicolson.

Eglar, Z. (1960) *A Punjabi Village in Pakistan*. New York: University of Columbia Press.

Engels, F. (1972) *The Origin of the Family, Private Property and the State*. London: Lawrence & Wishart.

Epstein, T.S. (1973) *South India, Yesterday, Today and Tomorrow*. London: Macmillan.

Frankel, F. (1971) *India's Green Revolution; economic gains and political costs*. New Jersey: Princeton University Press.

Freed, S. (1953) Fictive Kinship in a North Indian Village. *Ethnology* **2**: 86-103.

Friedl, E. (1967) The Position of Women; appearance and reality *Anthropological Quarterly* **40**(3): 97-108.

Gadgil, D.R. (1965) *Women in the Working Force in India*. London: Asia Publishing House (for University of Delhi).

Goldstein, R. (1972) *Indian Women in Transition: a Bangalore case study*. Metuchen, New Jersey: Scarecrow Press.

Goody, J. (1976) *Production and Reproduction: a comparative study of the domestic domain*. Cambridge: Cambridge University Press.

Goody, J. and Tambiah, S. (1973) *Bridewealth and Dowry*. Cambridge: Cambridge University Press.

Goody, J. Thirsk, J. Thompson, E.P. (eds) (1976) *Family and Inheritance*. Cambridge: Cambridge University Press.

Gore, M.S. (1968) *Urbanization and Family Change*. Combay: Popular Prakashan.

Hershman, P. (1977) Virgin and Mother. In I. Lewis (ed) *Symbols and Sentiment*. London: Academic Press.

Hitchcock, J. and Minturn, L. (1963) The Rajputs of Khalapur, India. In B. Whiting (ed.) *Six Cultures*. New York: John Wiley and Sons.

Hitchcock, J. (1959) The Idea of the Martial Rajput. In M. Singer (ed.) *Traditional India; Structure and Change*. Philadelphia, American Folklore Society, Bibliographical Series, Vol. 10.

Hobson, H. (1978) *Family Web*. London: John Murray.

Hunt, P. (1980) *Gender and Class Consciousness*. London; Macmillan.

Hoshiarpur District Gazetteer 1883-4. Lahore: Punjab Government.

Indian Council of Social Science Research (1977) *Programme of Women's Studies*. New Delhi: ICSSR.

Ishwaran, K. (1968) *Shivapur: a South Indian Village*. London: Routledge and Kegan Paul.

Jacobson, J. (1970) *Hidden Faces: Hindu and Muslim Purdah in a Central Indian Village*. Ph.D. dissertation for the University of Columbia.

——(1977) The Women of North and Central India; Goddesses and Wives. In D. Jacobson and S. Wadley, *Women in India. Two Perspectives*. Columbia: South Asia Books.

Jammu, P.S. (1974) *Changing Social Structure in Rural Punjab*. New Delhi: Sterling.

Jeffery, P. (1978) *Frogs in a Well*. London: Zed Press.

Kapur, P. (1970) *Marriage and the Working Woman in India* (abridged edition). New Delhi: Vikas Publications.

Kessinger, T. (1974) *Vilayatpur 1848-1968. Social and Economic Change in a North Indian Village*. Berkeley and Los Angeles: University of California Press.

King, U. (1975) Women and Religion; the status and image of women in major religious traditions. In A. de Souza (1975).

Khare, R.S. (1976) *The Hindu Hearth and Home*. New Delhi: Vikas Publishing House.

Kuhn, A. (1978) Structures of Patriarchy and Capital in the Family. In A. Kuhn and Ann-Marie Wolpe (eds) *Feminism and Materialism*. London: Routledge and Kegan Paul.

Lewis, O. (1958) *Village Life in Northern India*. New York: Random House.

Luschinsky, M.S. (1963) The impact of some recent Indian Government legislation on the women of an Indian village. *Asian Survey* 3(12): 573-83.

McCrindle, J. and Rowbotham, S. (1979) *Dutiful Daughters*. Harmondsworth: Penguin Books.

Madan, T.N. (1965) *Family and Kinship. A study of the Pandits of Rural Kashmir*. Bombay: Asia Publishing House.

Magas, B., Coulson, M. and Wainwright, H. (1975) The Housewife and her Labour under Capitalism. *New Left Review* **89**: 59-71.

Maher, V. (1974) *Women and Property in Morocco*. Cambridge: Cambridge University Press.

Maher, V. (1976) Kin, Clients and Accomplices; relations among women in Morocco. In S. Allen and D. Barker (eds) *Sexual Divisions and Society; Process and Change*. London: Tavistock Publications.

Mandelbaum, D. (1972) *Society in India*. Berkeley and Los Angeles: University of California Press.

Mayer, A. (1960) *Caste and Kinship in Central India*. London: Routledge and Kegan Paul.

Mazumdar, V. (1975a) Status of Women in India. *Demography* **IV**(2).

——(1975b) Women in Agriculture. *Indian Farming* **XXV**(8).

Mehta, R. (1976) From Purdah to Modernity. In B.R. Nanda (1976).

Meillasoux, C. (1964) Are there castes in India? *Economy and Society* **2**: 89-111.

Mitchell, J. (1971) *Women's Estate*. Harmondsworth: Penguin Books.

Nanda, B.R. (ed.) (1976) *Indian women: from purdah to modernity*. New Delhi: Vikas Publishing House.

Nath, K. (1965) Women in the New Village. *Economic Weekly* **17**: 813-16 (May 15).

Oakley, A. (1974) *The Sociology of Housework*. London: Martin Robertson.

——(1976) *Housewife*. Harmondsworth: Penguin Books.

Papanek, H. (1973) Purdah: Separate Worlds and Symbolic Shelter. *Comparative Studies in Society and History* **15**(3): 289-325.

Parmar, S. (1975) The Saga of Women in the Hills. *Indian Farming* **XXV**(8).

Parry, J. (1979) *Caste and Kinship in Kangra*. London: Routledge and Kegan Paul.

Pettigrew, J. (1975) *Robber Noblemen. A study of the political system of the Sikh Jats*. London: Routledge and Kegan Paul.

Pocock, D. (1972) *Kanbi and Patidar: a study of the Patidar community in Gujerab*. Oxford: Clarendon Press.

Rao, M.S.A. (1968) Occupational Mobility and Joint Household Organization. *Contributions to Indian Sociology* (n.s. 11).

Remy, D. (1973) Towards an Economic Anthropology for Women. London: Women's Anthropology Workshop (cyclostyled report).

Rogers, S. (1975) Female Forms of Power and the Myth of Male Dominance: a model of male/female interaction in peasant society. *American Ethnologist* **12**(4): 727-56.

Rosaldo, M.Z. and Lamphere, L. (eds) (1974) *Women, Culture and Society*. Stanford: Stanford University Press.

Ross. A. (1961) *The Hindu Family in its Urban Setting*. Toronto: University of Toronto Press.

Rowbotham, S. (1973) *Women's Consciousness, Man's World*. Harmondsworth: Penguin Books.

Sanday, P. (1974) Female Status in the Public Domain. In Rosaldo and Lamphere (1974).

Sandhu, H.K. (1976) Technological Development versus Economic Contribution of Women in Rural Punjab. *Social Change* **6**(3 and 4): 13-21.

Seccombe, W. (1974) The Housewife and her Labour under Capitalism. *New Left Review* **83**: 3-24.

Seymour, S. (1975) Some Determinants of Sex Roles in a Changing Indian Town. *American Ethnologist* **12**(4): 757-69.

Shah, A.M. (1973) *The Household Dimension of the Family in India*. New Delhi: Orient Longman.

Sharma, U.M. (1977) Migration from an Indian Village: an anthropological approach. *Sociologia Ruralis* **XVII**(4): 282-304.

——(1978a) Women and their Affines; the veil as a symbol of separation. *Man* (n.s.) **13**(2): 218-33.

——(1978b) Segregation and its consequences. In Caplan and Bujra (1978).

——(forthcoming) Purdah and Public Space. In A. de Souza *Women in Contemporary India* (new edition) Delhi: Manohar Book Service.

Sridharan, S. (1973) In Chhatera – Maya, Bhim Kaur and Chalthi. *Indian Farming Today*. **XXV**(8): 43-46.

Stokes, E. (1978) *The Peasant and the Raj: studies in agrarian society and peasant rebellion in colonial India*. Cambridge: Cambridge University Press.

Thomas, P. (1964) *Indian Women through the Ages*. London: Asia Publishing House.

Ullrich, H. (1975) Etiquette among Women in Karnataka; forms of address in the village and the family. In A. de Souza (1975).

Van der Veen (1972) *I give thee my Daughter*. Assen: Van Gorcum.

Vatuk, S. (1969) Reference, Address and Fictive Kinship in urban North India. *Ethnology* **8**: 255-272.

Vreede de Stuers, C. (1968) *Parda; a study of Muslim Women's Life in Northern India*. New York: Humanities Press.

Wadley, S. (1977) Women and the Hindu Tradition. In D. Jacobson and S. Wadley *Women in India. Two Perspectives*. Columbia: South Asia Books.

# Subject Index

Acts of Parliament, 25, 28, 47, 53, 56, 199
adoption, 199
affines, 6-7, 135-6, 187
age and marriage, 147
agriculture: and caste, 26-7, 33, 119-20, 123; in Chaili, 16, 31-33, 92, 101-104, 121, 196, 205-207; changes in, 26-28, 196, 205-207; decision making in, 101-103; in Harbassi, 25-26, 92, 102-104, 117-23, 196, 205-207; incomes from, 103-105; types of, 13-14; and women, 29, 90, 92-6, 102, 116-32 *passim*, 168, 196, 205-207; work in, 90-97, 100, 110, 113-32 *passim*, 168, 212; *see also* 'Green Revolution'; land; share cropping
*Akhand path* (scripture reading), 190
anthropology, 2-3
*Apni jegeh* (one's own place), 45
artisan castes, 30; *see also* low caste

*bahinji* (sister), 187
*bahu* (daughter-in-law), 4; *see also* daughter-in-law
Bangladesh, 17n
*bazar* 22, 29, 31, 41-4, 93, 96, 107, 211
behaviour, women's, 41; *see also* mobility; subordination; taboo; women

*bhabi* (brother's wife), 211
*birādari* (caste community), 153-54, 211
Brahman caste, 31, 84, 187; and agriculture, 119-20; households, 60-61, 71-74; marriage in, 139-40, 145, 167, 182; *see also* caste; high caste
bride-price, 137-42, 164-65, 174-75n; *see also* dowry; marriage
brothers: as co-owners of land, 77; friends as, 40; ritual, 188; roles of, 56-7, 135, 156-7, 161, 172, 179, 201; *see also* male; sisters; sons
brother-in-law, 187
budgeting *see* income

capitalism, 204-210; *see also* industry
cash *see* income
cash economy, 33, 204-8; *see also* industry
caste: and agriculture, 26-7, 119-20; and broken marriage, 156, 161, 163-64; interdictions, 24; and marriage, 139-40, 145, 153-54, 167, 182; and occupations, 81-82; of research households, 21, 60-74; scheduled, 21, 84, 125; *see also* Brahman; Chamar; high-caste; Jat; Julaha; Khatri; Kumhar; low-caste; Rajput; scheduled caste; Sunira
cattle, care of, 127-28, 131, 133n
Census, 31

# Name Index